Symptoms of the Planetary Condition

Symptoms of the Planetary Condition: A Critical Vocabulary

edited by
Mercedes Bunz, Birgit Mara Kaiser
and Kathrin Thiele

μ meson press

**Bibliographical Information of the
German National Library**
The German National Library lists this publication in the
Deutsche Nationalbibliografie (German National Biblio-
graphy); detailed bibliographic information is available
online at http://dnb.d-nb.de

Published in 2017 by meson press, Lüneburg
www.meson.press

ISBN (Print): 978-3-95796-085-6
ISBN (PDF):   978-3-95796-086-3
ISBN (EPUB): 978-3-95796-087-0
DOI: 10.14619/018

Design concept: Torsten Köchlin, Silke Krieg
Proof-reading: Jacob Watson
Editorial assistance: Frederik Rettberg

The print edition of this book is printed by Lightning Source,
Milton Keynes, United Kingdom

The digital edition of this publication can be downloaded
freely at: www.meson.press

Contents

Introduction

Symptoms of the Planetary Condition

*Rather than going for the new object of study,
the new product to consume, one should work
on new ways of seeing, of being, or of living the
world. Perhaps it is time to look at the nature
of our own understanding of what you just
called "productive resistance" and to assess
how – in our very "resistance" – we may have
been working in complicity with what we set out
to criticize.*

– Trinh T. Minh-ha, D-Passage, 122

In 2015, the *Los Angeles Review of Books* launched a series entitled
"No Crisis" to examine the state of critique in the humanities
understood as both a university institution and a theoretical field.
In view of what was at the same time acknowledged and refuted
as a crisis of the humanities, the series wanted to show how
criticism is "actually written in the present," a decade and a half
into the 21st century. In her contribution, Johanna Drucker notes
that an important move for contemporary criticism would be to
leave behind the principle of "'critique' and negation, a stance of
moral superiority and outsider position" (Drucker 2015). Instead
of maintaining negation, opposition (and judgment, we might
add) as the traditional attributes of critique, a crucial step would
be to recognize the complicity of oneself, of one's criticism, of
any critical practice, with-in the conditions or phenomena that

are under critical consideration. These are not exactly Drucker's words. The way she puts it is:

> Oppositional tactics are always reactive. We have to realize that negative notions, like the bankrupt ideas of critique, don't offer a way forward. They keep us at a superior distance from reality. We need to formulate a modernism of engagement founded in a recognition of complicity – ours and its – with the machinations and values according to which we live. (Drucker 2015)[1]

The project of this vocabulary starts from a similar hunch: namely that negativity and judgment, the modes in which critique and critical analyses were practiced and thought since Kant, have run their course. Seeking to maintain an outsider's stance vis-à-vis the phenomena or situations that are critically examined, reaching for an Olympian objectivity, disinterest: these, the instruments of Enlightened critique, are exhausted. They have, as Drucker suggests, not only run their course because they are in a Nietzschean sense "reactive" – that is, because they are unable to bring forth real **transformation** and newness. They have also run their course because this 21st century is slowly realizing a transition in daily experiences (technological, biomedical, ecological) from a Newtonian to a quantum universe. Due to this transition, **entanglements** at a fundamental level must be taken into account or, in other words, the complicity and co-emergence of any knowledge or assessment with what is known and with whoever knows, its always **perspectival,** situated and implicated nature. Complicity and entanglement at such a fundamental level preclude the neat distinctions between subject and object, knower and known that practices of critique traditionally rely on. Rather, these distinctions themselves emerge in relational fields of **power**, and in that sense are deeply entangled and complicit.

1 Drucker is revisiting T. J. Clark's *Farewell to an Idea: Episodes from a History of Modernism* (1999), as each contributor was asked to engage with a favorite critic.

Unlike Drucker, however, we do not want to conclude from this description of matters today that critique is bankrupt. While the compilation of terms in this book starts from the assumption that negativity, judgment and opposition as *modes* of critique have indeed "run out of steam" (Latour 2004), we insist that critique as an attitude and a manner of enquiry has not. It remains a crucial aspect of the work done in the humanities and the arts, inside and outside academic institutions, and it is worth striving to keep critique as such a crucial attitude, an important angle from which to pose questions and contest political quietism. Furthermore, different from the "No Crisis" project, but also in difference to recent re-turns to critique such as Rita Felski's *The Limits of Critique* (2015), this project understands critique as a much broader practice than merely a textual one. Even though critique is resolutely affirmed here as a practice of reading, such reading is not undertaken mainly or exclusively in the realms of literary, textual or even cultural criticism. Situations, constellations, power relations and technological connected-ness also have to be read. Nor are we interested primarily in a new, however radical or "post-critical" (Felski) hermeneutics or criticism. If we speak of critique, we do not mean primarily the activity of professional critics, although that activity may be part of it. Rather, our project affirms critique as a praxis of intellectual and **worldly** intervention, as an attitude that not only comes to bear on the writing (and critical reading) of texts, but also affects the material, habitual, everyday and minute dimensions of living. For the process of outlining such an embodied mode of critique, which has immediate implications for political, ethical as well as media-material thought-practice, the humanities are of crucial relevance. The strength of the humanities lies precisely in the methodological, onto-epistemological questioning of how to proceed, in view of what and in the interest of whom – therefore moving critique not only from matters of fact to matters of con-cern (Latour 2004), but taking it a step further to interested and situated matters of care (Puig de la Bellacasa 2011). Accordingly, the humanities are understood and exercised here as worldly practices themselves.

The overall aim of this vocabulary is to begin reexamining critical practice under the conditions of the 21st century, which means first of all to assert critique as a crucial tool of intellectual and practical intervention. At the same time, it also means to acknowledge that contemporary realities are **immanent**, **terran** and co-dependent in multiple ways; ways that even the enumeration of the attributes of these co-dependences – economic, ecological, symbolic, socio-political, intra-species, historical, **technological**, **affective**, to name but a few – do not exhaust.

To begin with, it means to acknowledge that there is no outside from which to gauge things, which has two implications for critical practice. On the one hand, as poststructuralism and deconstruction have brought to the fore for quite a while already, and science and technology studies, quantum theory and their recent humanities receptions demonstrate today, there is no categorical separability in critical endeavors. Rather, as Karen Barad argues in *Meeting the Universe Halfway* (2007) with recourse to Niels Bohr's analysis of "measurement interactions," any measurement has an effect on what is being measured. The insistence on indeterminacy or "the indeterminable discontinuity" which quantum theory shows "undermines the classical belief in an inherent subject-object distinction" (Barad 2007, 127). Barad explains this as follows:

> Making the ontological nature of this indeterminacy explicit entails a rejection of the *classical metaphysical assumption that there are determinate objects with determinate properties and corresponding determinate concepts with determinate meanings independent of the necessary conditions needed to resolve the inherent indeterminacies.* (127)

With this in mind, an outside stance from which to assess and judge things becomes an illusion – and with it the "superior distance" which Drucker rightly rejects. The calm distancing that enables judgment, achieved by way of setting apart, dissecting and reflecting is no longer tenable (Haraway 1997). Such an approach presumes molar units (Deleuze/Guattari 2000), which – after Bohr, but also after Simondon's idea of individuation (Simondon 2007) or Margulis's concept of symbiogenesis (Margulis 1998) (and we could name others, too) – we are coming to understand as molecular processes. The traditional practice of critique ignores this **processual** entanglement of what is known with the one who does the knowing, so that "reflection" as its central image is best to be traded for new images of critical practice. The entries that make up this volume hope to work towards such new images.

On the other hand, in terms of political imaginaries, to acknowledge that there is no outside from which to gauge things means that any *terra incognita* was only ever a powerful (in both senses of "effective" and "dominant") narrative to imagine "progress" or "redemption." Yet, specifically today, it is evident that there is no untouched corner of the planet that could entice us to believe in better versions of ourselves, to be achieved in a New World. The **spectre** of a *terra incognita*, haunting the phantasmatic machineries of escape, adventure, social experimentation and political progress, has always been in denial of the fact that it was only *incognita* to those who recently arrived at its shores in pursuit of power, money or a better life for themselves. The geographical, political and industrial exhaustion of the earth – of its spatial expansion, as well as its natural resources – has also slowly exhausted the political purchase of the phantasm of an *incognita* or a new start (Glissant 1997, Wynter 1995). The classical understanding of critique as laying bare the presumed boundaries of a status-quo in order to establish a "better" political project, an "elsewhere" in linear spacetime, is thus also no longer plausible. The past centuries have witnessed the downsides or downfalls of earlier "better" projects that promised social emancipation (from humanism, real existing socialism to bourgeois nationalism/colonialism), but did so only for certain groups. Social and philosophical critique was, however, often articulated in the name of these projects. Given these histories of our co-dependent, entangled world(ing)s, social and philosophical critique done "in the name of" this or that "better" political project or social experiment has lost traction. The power of utopias as achievable solutions is dwindling, as historical **experience** has shown that they tend to rely on sameness and exclusion at the expense of difference. And yet, **utopia** as a name for the possibility of difference *and* deferral, as a horizon of social justice, remains a powerful force for critical thinking and practice. Thus, the question that our project also aims to address is how to practice critique with no concrete "better" and "final" solution in view.

The contributors to this book hold that giving up on critique as intervention – that is, on questions motivated by the ambition of furthering social and ecological justice – is not an option. The world today has indeed become (or has always been, but today comes to be more and more understood as) a *terra critica*: a planet in critical economic, ecological, symbolic, socio-political, intra-species condition, demanding an un/relearning of dominant habits and practices (Guattari 2008, Stengers 2015) *and/as* a re**vision** of the modi and methods of critical intervention. In respect to what Spivak calls planetary conditions (Spivak 2003), established knowledge-regimes need to be unworked so that we can learn to know, feel and live otherwise. Thus, it is time for an earthly form of critique. Yet again, precisely with that goal in mind, the question remains: What would critique under such conditions be like? What are the symptoms of our planetary condition, which are starting to become visible, but are not yet fully readable? And how are we to intervene in effective ways in conditions commonly indicated with descriptors such as finance capitalism, the anthropocene and neoliberalism?

The present book will, of course, not deliver definitive answers to those questions. How could it? Un/relearning social, affective and corporeal habits as well as daily practices cannot simply be done by means of a book. It requires more than that. Still, we hope for this project to be a starting point. It stays with the above mentioned questions – weighs them, turns them over, **translates** them into a set of terms which are tentatively explored here as one way of figuring critical practice otherwise. Evidently, the terms in this vocabulary are not new; many of them have a long philosophical, critical tradition and are in frequent use. Their assemblage does not strive for a complete or exhaustive survey of relevant terms. Others could be added, for sure. Neither do the individual entries aim to provide encyclopedic, neutral definitions of each term. The ambition here is not to offer a dictionary, or to arrive at a new, neat definition of critique. Instead, the book sees itself as a rhizomatic and **speculative** toolbox that offers multiple entries and routes into the question of critique. Its aim is to inspire potential additions to the assemblage of terms offered here and different practices of critique and critical intervention for future use.

The present assemblage of terms emerged out of the past four years of work done by *Terra Critica*, an interdisciplinary network for the critical humanities (www.terracritica.net). The network was founded in 2012, and the terms that appear in this vocabulary surfaced as crucial tools-to-think-with. Each contributor to the vocabulary participated in one or more of the network's workshops, and the entries have grown out of the pool of perspectives, reference points and terminologies that appeared and reappeared in these meetings. Each entry offers a personal take on the term. This means that collectively, these terms have been significant in *Terra Critica's* work, yet individually, each of them carries the mark of its author. Had a term been explored by someone else, its presentation would have been somewhat different, perhaps distinctly different. It is precisely this open and in/determinate toolbox characteristic that we **affirm** as a most fruitful presentation of critical **work**.

In that sense, this book does not represent the network *Terra Critica*. Rather, it is a **stutter**: every entry makes a new attempt to articulate what might be the sense of critique today, without arriving at a clear silhouette or conclusive statement. The book can be used as a rhizomatic map, to be entered at any point, where each entry gives evidence of its author's distinct style of writing and conceptual registers. Composed as an open assemblage, the terms can nevertheless call forth various constellations. They can be read with and through each other and as such, like a watermark, hope to bring forth the sets of problems that we are concerned with: How to practice a kind of critique that helps to dis/entangle our contemporary planetary conditions? How to read the symptoms of those conditions, and which symptoms to begin with? And how to develop the conceptual and terminological tools needed in order to approach them in meaningful ways? This book is a step to develop those tools, offering various potential itineraries, some of which we suggest in the diagrams at the end of the book. The diagrams propose constellations of terms that speak to each other in prominent ways and that – taken as a interference pattern (a *diffraction*) – highlight, according to our reading, particularly relevant aspects of the question of critique today. And we invite readings to be added.

We have stressed the necessity to re-evaluate critical practice *today*, in the early decades of the 21st century, partly from a sense of acute crisis (which has been tied to critique and the humanities at least since Husserl (1936) and Kosellek (1959)) to which we feel we must respond. Yet, our concern comes also from the insight that any "today" requires re-evaluation and work: in the spirit of here and now "think we must," as Virginia Woolf (1966, 62) stresses in *Three Guineas*, written on the verge of World War II. And, as Jacques Derrida demonstrates in *The Other Heading* (1990), *today* is always anew "this time that is ours" (79) – the "now" that urges us to **regard** what "*is taking place now*" (30). Such a task, then, falls upon every era, on every "today," as Walter Benjamin also notes in "On the Concept of History": "In every era the attempt must be made anew to wrest tradition away from a conformism that is about to overpower it." (Benjamin 2006, 391) At the same time, every era needs to find its own, specific responses – it is *our* today for which critique needs to be sharpened. There is a tradition to draw on, but no models to follow. At present, critique is perhaps in particular need of being reconsidered as an attitude, in view of the neoliberal-capitalist machineries that ingest all critique and celebrate difference as lifestyle. This underlines the continuing validity of Derrida's question: "Is it not necessary to have the courage and lucidity for a *new* critique of the *new* effects of **capital** (within unprecedented techno-social structures)?" (Derrida 1992, 57).

In their engagements with the legacies of critique and the demands made on it in the present, i.e. "today," the contributions to this vocabulary therefore affirm two things at once: critical practice is vital for any pursuit of social and ecological justice, yet it also needs to be wrested from its tradition as judgment, which threatens to stifle it and is no longer pertinent to the planetary conditions we live in today. In view of these conditions, our conceptions of critique need to be adjusted, revised, reexamined. Only then does critique become a critical ontology of ourselves *today*, in Foucault's terms:

> The critical ontology of ourselves must be considered not, certainly, as a theory, a doctrine, nor even as a permanent body of knowledge that is accumulating; it must be conceived as an attitude, an ethos, a philosophical life in which the critique of what we are is at one and the same time the historical analysis of the limits imposed on us and an experiment with the possibility of going beyond them …. (Foucault 1997, 319)

We hope that this book will be used – critically, that is affirmatively and **creatively** – as such an experiment. That it will help wrest terms away from their present (socio-ethico-political) overdeterminations to put them to new uses, so that we can start to invent new ways of speaking and new ways of living with-in always (re-)productive power relations. That it will remind us that critique means to dare to take **risks** and to exploit the leeway for negotiations that power permits: to push power a little.

References

Barad, Karen. 2007. *Meeting the Universe Halfway: Quantum Physics and the Entanglement of Matter and Meaning.* Durham: Duke University Press.

Benjamin, Walter. 2006. "On the Concept of History." In *Selected Writings.* Vol. 4, *1938–1940*, edited by Howard Eiland and Michael W. Jennings, 389–400. Cambridge, MA: Harvard University Press.

Deleuze, Gilles and Félix Guattari. (1980) 2000. *A Thousand Plateaus: Capitalism and Schizophrenia.* Minneapolis: University of Minnesota Press.

Derrida, Jacques. 1992. *The Other Heading: Reflections of Today's Europe.* Bloomington: Indiana University Press.

Drucker, Johanna. 2015, May 3. "Recognizing Complicity." *LA Review of Books.* Accessed February 29, 2016. https://lareviewofbooks.org/article/recognizing-complicity.

Felski, Rita. 2015. *The Limits of Critique.* Chicago: University of Chicago Press.

Foucault, Michel. (1984) 1997. "What is Enlightenment?" In *Michel Foucault: Ethics, Subjectivity and Truth*, edited by Paul Rabinow, 303–319. New York: The New Press.

Guattari, Félix. (1989) 2008. *The Three Ecologies.* London: Continuum.

Glissant, Édouard. 1997. *Poetics of Relation.* Ann Arbor: University of Michigan Press.

Haraway, Donna. 1997. *Modest_Witness@Second_Millennium.FemaleMan_Meets_OncoMouse: Feminism and Technoscience.* New York: Routledge.

Haraway, Donna. 2010. "Staying with the Trouble: Xenoecologies of Home for Companions in the Contested Zones." *Cultural Anthropology.* Accessed April 3, 2016. http://www.culanth.org/fieldsights/289-staying-with-the-trouble-xenoecologies-of-home-for-companions-in-the-contested-zones.

Husserl, Edmund. (1936) 1970. *The Crisis of European Sciences and Transcendental Phenomenology: An Introduction to Phenomenological Philosophy.* Chicago: Northwestern University Press.

Koselleck, Reinhart. (1959) 1998. *Critique and Crises: Enlightenment and the Pathogenesis of Modern Society.* Camebridge, MA: MIT Press.

Latour, Bruno. 2004. "Why Has Critique Run Out of Steam? From Matters of Fact to Matters of Concern." *Critical Inquiry* (Special Issue on the Future of Critique) 30 (2): 225–248.

Margulis, Lynn. 1998. *Symbiotic Planet: A New Look at Evolution.* Amherst: Basic Books.

Minh-ha, Trinh T. 2013. *D-Passage: The Digital Way.* Durham: Duke University Press.

Puig de la Bellacasa, Maria. 2011. "Matters of Care in Technoscience: Assembling Neglected Things." *Social Studies of Science* 41 (1): 85–106.

Simondon, Gilbert. (1989) 2007. *L'individuation psychique et collective.* Paris: Aubier.

Stengers, Isabelle. 2015. *In Catastrophic Times: Resisting the Coming Barbarism*. London: Open Humanities Press; Lüneburg: meson press.

Spivak, Gayatri Chakravorty. 2003. *Death of a Discipline*. New York: Columbia University Press.

Woolf, Virginia. (1938) 1966. *Three Guineas*. Orlando: Harcourt.

Wynter, Sylvia. 1995. "1492: A New World View." In *Race, Discourse, and the Origin of the Americas*, edited by Vera Lawrence Hyatt and Rex Nettleford, 5–57. Washington, DC: Smithsonian Institution Press.

Affect

Bettina Papenburg

Affect – a palpable intensity, the atmosphere in a room – is transmitted below the threshold of conscious perception, manifesting as bodily tension and relaxation. Affect is involuntary, non-conscious, contagious, and to a certain degree automatic. Thus affect is at odds with the conception of the rational subject, a clearly bounded entity, the self-contained individual that is markedly differentiated from others, which for centuries has been assumed to be the sole agent capable of critical thinking. Rather, the very workings of affect hint at connectedness, at interaction, at interdependency. Or, as philosopher Teresa Brennan puts it in her reflections on the transmission of affect: "The origin of transmitted affects is *social* in that these affects do not only arise within a particular person but also come from without. They come via an *interaction* with other people and an environment. But they have a *physiological impact*." (Brennan 2004, 3, emphases mine) As Brennan aptly notes, affect flows and circulates between people, effectively mediating between our shared biological dispositions and culturally shaped meanings. Affect takes hold of the person in the interaction with other people in a shared space, most palpably perhaps in the synchronization of kinetic movements of bodies collectively attuned to vibrations or frequencies. Affect is in essence communal, yet tangible for each of us as energy that enhances or diminishes our capacity to act.

The "affective turn" evolving since the early twenty-first century in fields as broad as philosophy, media studies, cultural studies, and gender studies signals an intense scholarly engagement with affect. The label announces and propels a thorough investigation of the complex feedback loops connecting people and environments, which bring forth specific moods facilitating a thought **process** and enabling meaningful social actions and political activism. Scholars working in this vein challenge the tradition that links the production of knowledge to rational thinking alone, to value-free neutrality and to disembodied objectivity, a tradition that hinges on the exclusion of affect.

Affect, however, is not solely positive and certainly not always politically subversive – indeed there is a growing body of scholarship in feminist and queer theory that engages the "negative affects" such as pain, hate, fear, disgust, anger, depression, and failure. Ever so often affects are mobilized for uncritical ends – when, for instance, television commercials entice viewers to attach specific positive feelings to consumer goods, or when video games require immediate sensorimotor responses from players. Affects are even employed for achieving destructive purposes – as in "scarless torture," a practice used in the "war on terror" in detention camps like Guantanamo Bay, which, without leaving visible traces on the victims' bodies, severely diminishes the victims' capacity to act. In the German context, the affective mobilizing of the masses creating a group mob as in, for instance, Hitler's speech at the Nuremberg Rally, or most recently by the Pegida movement, an anti-immigration movement gathering forces stretching from the far right to the center of German society. In light of these examples, the question that arises is then: how can affect work as a critical political force?

In an essay entitled "The Autonomy of Affect," published in *Parables for the Virtual. Movement, Affect, Sensation* (2002), philosopher Brian Massumi develops an elaborate theory of sensation that adequately accounts for the sensing and feeling body. However, one of the drawbacks for a more encompassing understanding

of affect's critical potential is that Massumi, following the line of
Baruch de Spinoza, Gilbert Simondon, and Gilles Deleuze, insists
on sharply differentiating between affect and emotion. Massumi
sees emotion as contained by the subject and affect as existing
in excess of the subject. He stresses the "irreducibly bodily and
autonomic nature of affect" while asserting that an "emotion is a
subjective content, the sociolinguistic fixing of the quality of an
experience which is from that point onward defined as personal"
(Massumi 2002, 21, bold added). While affect is a force or intensity
flowing through subjects, an emotion becomes a property of the
subject. Yet, as Massumi admits, affect and emotion are closely
related: while emotion contains affect, emotion does not exhaust
affect.

Different from yet closely related to thinkers following Deleuze's
line of thought, literary scholar and queer activist Ann Cvetkovich
employs the terms "*affect, emotion,* and *feeling* … more like key-
words, points of departure for discussion rather than definition"
(2012, 5, emphases in original). Cvetkovich uses "affect in a generic
sense, … as a category that encompasses affect, emotion, and
feeling, and that includes impulses, desires, and feelings that get
historically constructed in a range of ways (whether as distinct
specific [sic!] emotions or as a generic category often contrasted
with reason)" (2012, 4, brackets in original). Rather than pursuing
the task of definition, Cvetkovich is interested in the question of
how affect works politically. The political project Public Feelings
that she herself pursues together with fellow thinkers and
activists, testifies to affect's critical and **transformative** potential
and, indeed, its political force.

Public Feelings, a "cell" of a larger project entitled Feminism
Unfinished launched by academics and activists at the University
of Texas in 2001, with various spin-offs across the US, hinges on
participants professing, sharing, and publically declaring their
feelings, including negative feelings, such as feeling depressed.
In the context of this collective endeavor, it became apparent
that depression, generally understood as a medical condition, is

not an individual malaise, but more accurately that it might be a **symptom** for larger social and political structural inadequacies, and that there could be alternative cures than simply treating it in a medical sense. Depression – which Cvetkovich envisions as "a form of being stuck" (2012, 26), a (conceptual) blockage, an impasse – is widespread among academics, and, as the group Public Feelings asserts, must be grasped as an effect of the political conditions, including the working conditions in academia, the marginalization of the humanities, doubts about the social relevance of one's work, and – in the case of the US – the stifling consequences of the fact of being citizens of a nation at war.

In her personal politics and practices, Cvetkovich found remedy to depression in a combination of various forms of mental, emotional, and bodily movement – her antidote to inertia –, enabling flexibility and creativity, in a turn to the embodied senses, specifically to the haptic and the tactile, and in new ways of relating to temporality to challenge ideas of progress by emphasizing retrograde and lateral moves. In terms of academic research and writing practices, she suggests "alternatives to critique and new ways to describe feelings" (2012, 24). Her book *Depression: A Public Feeling* offers an example for what she proposes, since it combines classical methods, such as conceptual work, close reading, and narrative analysis, with the genre of the "critical memoir" (a term proposed by Jill Dolan), to the effect that portions of Cvetkovich's book take the form of a depression diary.

On the one hand, the political employment of affect, the sharing of feelings that is, in the Public Feelings project is a very interesting and inspiring example for how processes of political transformation can be initiated on a micropolitical, affective plane, and for how negatively coded emotions traditionally linked to the medicalization of depression can be effectively recoined. It seems very promising, as this brings such feelings into position for launching a critique of social institutions and for mobilizing them against the more subtle social pressures. However, the turn to spirituality, handiwork, and do-it-yourself work, which is the cure that Cvetkovich ultimately proposes on the other hand, is not utterly convincing.

Literary scholar Lauren Berlant, a member of the Public Feelings project and co-founder of Feel Tank Chicago – a related project "organized around the thought that public spheres are affect worlds at least as much as they are effects of rationality, rationalization, and institutions"[1] –, advocates a more persuasive, more intellectually-attuned stance. In a reflection on her intervention at a conference on political feeling (2007), hosted by Public Feelings, Berlant lays out her thoughts on acting professional in the academy: "It's our job to show up and think, to show up and think with others, to collaborate using what we know and what we don't know to push concepts beyond where they were when we entered the room" (2009, 133). Here Berlant responds to some academics who proudly consider themselves amateurs and situate themselves as politically progressive as a consequence. These scholars dismiss professionalism on the grounds of the understanding that acting professional equates with acting bureaucratic, elitist, inauthentic, authoritarian, and mediocre. Taking issue with this way of self-positioning, Berlant argues for accepting and confronting "the complexities of ambition and the desire for distinction and the role of discipline and normative skill-building in teaching" (2009, 133). According to Berlant, academics should face – and not evade – these desires and aim to foster an attitude that values merit and rigor. Berlant's reflection about the **responses** to her credo and the aftereffects of her intervention is a perfect example for how addressing head-on the anxieties that come with academic **work** can facilitate a collective thought process about the working conditions in academia, the question how to situate oneself vis-à-vis those very conditions,

1   Wikipedia entry on Feel Tank Chicago, January 29, 2015: https://en.wikipedia. org/wiki/Feel_Tank_Chicago.

24   and the reinvention of engaged academic work reaching out to groups of workers in other fields.

References

"Anxiety, Urgency, Outrage, Hope: A Conference on Political Feeling." Conference held at the University of Chicago, October 19–20, 2007.

Berlant, Lauren. 2009. "Affect Is the New Trauma." *The Minnesota Review* 71–72 (Winter–Spring): 131–136.

Brennan, Teresa. 2004. *The Transmission of Affect*. Ithaca, NY: Cornell University Press.

Cvetkovich, Ann. 2012. *Depression: A Public Feeling*. Durham: Duke University Press.

Massumi, Brian. 2002. "The Autonomy of Affect." In *Parables for the Virtual: Affect, Movement, Sensation*, 23–42. Durham: Duke University Press.

Affirmation

Kathrin Thiele

Affirmation is not the opposite of negation. If merely seen as
the opposite of negation, that is as the negation of negation,
affirmation is not taken seriously in respect to what it has the
potential for. As a critical tool, affirmation offers a different
register for thought and practice "before" or "in advance of"
the opposition of our habit of saying "yes" and "no."[1] The "no"
that instigates the statement "affirmation is *not* the opposite
of negation," is thus not to be read as a contradiction in terms.
Rather, it is what Gilles Deleuze and Félix Guattari describe in
What is Philosophy? as a pedagogy keeping "an essential relationship *with* the No that *concerns* it" (1994, 218). If we speak of
affirmation as a critical tool, it is this emphasis on concern and
relationality as giving direction to the whole undertaking that
makes all the difference.

In the history of continental philosophy, Baruch de Spinoza's and
Friedrich Nietzsche's legacies figure prominently for this kind of
different register of thought and practice. And, if one continues
to follow the Deleuzian (and Guattarian) line, it can also be read

---

1   I use "before" as an alternative to "beyond" (the German (immanent) *dies-
    seits*, instead of (transcendent) *jenseits*). "In advance of" is the formulation
    Rodolphe Gasché finds for this different register of thought in his *Geo-
    philosophy: On Gilles Deleuze and Félix Guattari's What is Philosophy?* (2014,
    102).

in certain strands of the pragmatist tradition (linked to William James's and Alfred Whitehead's "radical empiricism," and thereby also keeping Henri Bergson in the loop) where an affirmative "believing in this world" (Deleuze and Guattari 1994, 75) is what concerns "mature" philosophizing. Currently, an emphasis on "affirmation" as a critical tool can be found most explicitly in feminist traditions, where a "we are in *this* mess all together" (Braidotti 2013, 141) or an endurance "to stay with the trouble" (Haraway 2013, 137) provocatively reinstigate affirmation as critical engagement. Instead of limiting the practice of critique and the development of critical knowledges to a merely reflexive move – distancing and dissecting, whereby the critical position claims superiority – feminist thinking "at its best" (and certainly in all its plurality) "is about generation of new thought, new concepts, as much as if not more than it is about the critique of existing knowledges" (Grosz 2011, 77). Affirmative critique, there-fore, is for sure about diagnosing precisely "what is," with an eye schooled in detecting inequalities, asymmetries, and the never innocent differentiations we live in. And yet, it also always needs to do the **work** of envisioning **transformation** and change. The **risks** that such an affirmative critical approach implies are man-ifold, but they cannot be avoided. Otherwise we would succumb to those "beautiful souls" – "cultivat[ing] goodness in solitary isolation from the actual social world" (Baille in Hegel 2014) – for which Georg W. F. Hegel already felt so much contempt.

In a bit more detail then, what does affirmation as a register of thought *do* in the practice of critique? Why emphasize "affirmative critique," why turn away from critique as negation? The following aims to explicate this specific potential in keeping with a femi-nist Deleuzian approach that has already given guidance here: Affirmation both adds to thought a *concern* from which it emerges and *with* which it stays related, and it initiates a *belief*. A worldly belief, one that "becomes belief in the world, as it is" (Deleuze 2000, 172); a belief for the "here and now," radically immanent, **terran**, and earthly. Only thus does affirmative critique initiate transformation in the here and now, without the messianic promise or need for a "beyond" – another world supposedly escaping "this mess" we are in "all together."

Spinoza's entire philosophizing already expresses such an affirmative approach *in* and *of* this world, and in this sense it can be read as a critical, interventionist practice. His ontology as ethics departs from the vertical Cartesian categorical separation of transcendence (perfection) and worldliness (imperfection). For him every-thing, every mode, *is* nothing but the expression of substance itself, i.e. the "all there is." With this, Spinoza elaborates a horizontal or at least flattened ontology, according to which there is no given (moral) hierarchy between "what is" and "what should be." This utter affirmation of "what is" leads to his famous monist formula that "no one has so far determined what [a] body can do" (Spinoza 2000, 167 [EIIIP2]) as well as to his harsh judgment in *A Political Treatise* ([1677] 1951), where he shares his great discontent that "[the philosophers] conceive of men, not as they are, but as they themselves would like them to be" (Spinoza 1951, 287). Differing from idealist traditions in philosophy, Spinoza suggests in his work a radically **immanent** onto-ethology of which Deleuze once said: "There is only Spinoza who has managed to pull off an ontology" (Deleuze 2007).

After having grounded affirmation as critical tool in such onto-ethological manner with Spinoza, Nietzsche's philosophy can specify affirmation further, as a task – as an issue of "will" or "power." His affirmation thereby links life and thought. But it also becomes the "heaviest weight" of all, as he writes in *The Gay Science* ([1882] 2006). For, affirmation is to will "[t]he life as you now live it and have lived it … to live once again and innumerable times again" (Nietzsche 2006, 194); or as Deleuze's even more imperative interpretation of the "eternal return of the same" is phrased: "[W]hatever you will, will it in such a way that you also will its eternal return" (Deleuze 1983, 68). The critical task is such enduring (indifferent) affirmation which, however, in its doing has the potential to release a difference, or better still, it cannot but be released *in difference*. The formula of "difference and repetition" (Deleuze 1994) is therefore the modus of affirmative critical praxis. Nietzsche's *amor fati* as affirmation, in which even nihilism is affirmed and can no longer escape the (radically indifferent) affirmation, allows things to return "in difference." It instigates the *transvaluation* that critical endeavors aim for – in philosophy, but also in politics, and therefore in life and thought.

If today's "world, as it is" is one in which systemic destruction, exploitation, and ecological catastrophes are our everyday news, the question of critique as affirmation poses itself in all its urgency, but also in all its difficulty. What to do in the face of the violent realities shaping our today? How to approach them so as to avoid the return of the same – once again hatred and violence, further exclusion and destruction – instead another opening becomes imaginable? How to address the current fortressing of categories, borders, and boundaries in a non-negative manner, yet without losing the radical critical edge of saying "no" in such a way that this "no" keeps us concerned and related to what we refuse? These are urgent questions of the affirmative critical endeavors that no longer have the luxury of withdrawing from "what is happening to us" (Nancy 2014; Wynter 2015). There is no outside to this world – as there is no outside of power (Foucault) and no outside of text (Derrida). To instigate a *concern for*, a *relationality with* the situation we are always already participating in and **entangled** with, and thereby to instigate a *belief* "in this world, as it is" – this is the critical mantra of affirmation through which life and thought (thought as life and *a life* as thought) become so intertwined that a different attitude as *ethos* (Foucault 1997) and maybe even a different "humanness as praxis" (Wynter 2015) can be enabled. It means believing in this possibility without making a program of it. Attitude and *ethos* as praxis imply, or even better, they live from ontological in/determinacy: The condition that things are bound to be determined, yet never once and for all and always anew at every turn of the world's differential becoming (Barad 2007). What affirmation as critique

and critique as affirmation suggest is to endure the turns things
take, without ever letting go of the (critical) potential of "what our
bodies can do" (radical immanence). It means continuing the work
of critique "in-differently," because other realities and relations
are always already with-in that which actually *is*.

References

Barad, Karen. 2007. *Meeting the Universe Halfway: Quantum Physics and the Entan-glement of Matter and Meaning*. Durham: Duke University Press.

Braidotti, Rosi. 2013. *The Posthuman*. Cambridge: Polity Press.

Deleuze, Gilles. 2007. "On Spinoza." Lectures by Gilles Deleuze. Accessed April 3, 2016. http://deleuzelectures.blogspot.co.uk/2007/02/on-spinoza.html.

Deleuze, Gilles. 2000. *Cinema 2: The Time-Image*. Translated by Hugh Tomlinson and Robert Galeta. London: The Athlone Press.

Deleuze, Gilles. 1994. *Difference & Repetition*. Translated by Paul Patton. New York: Columbia University Press.

Deleuze, Gilles. 1983. *Nietzsche and Philosophy*. Translated by Hugh Tomlinson. New York: Columbia University Press.

Deleuze, Gilles and Félix Guattari. 1994. *What is Philosophy?* Translated by Hugh Tomlinson and Graham Burchell. New York: Columbia University Press.

Foucault, Michel. 1997. "What is Enlightenment?" In *Ethics: Subjectivity and Truth: Essential Works of Foucault 1954–1984*. Vol. 2, edited by Paul Rabinow, 303–319. New York: The New Press.

Gasché, Rodolphe. 2014. *Geophilosophy: On Gilles Deleuze and Félix Guattari's What is Philosophy?* Evanston: Northwestern University Press.

Grosz, Elizabeth. 2011. "The Future of Feminist Theory: Dreams of New Knowledges." In *Becoming Undone: Darwinian Reflections on Life, Politics, and Art*. 74–87. Durham: Duke University Press.

Haraway, Donna. 2013. "Sowing Worlds: A Seedbag of Terra Forming with Earth Others." In *Beyond the Cyborg: Adventures with Donna Haraway*, edited by Margret Grebowicz and Helen Merrick, 137–146. New York: Columbia University Press.

Hegel, G. W. F. (1807) 2014. *Phenomenology of Mind*. With translator's comments by John Baille. Accessed April 7, 2016. https://ebooks.adelaide.edu.au/h/hegel/phenomenology_of_mind/part7.html.

Nietzsche, Friedrich. (1882) 2006. *The Gay Science*. Cambridge: Cambridge University Press.

Spinoza, Baruch de. (1677) 1951. *A Political Treatise*. New York: Dover Publications.

Spinoza, Baruch de. (1677) 2000. *Ethics*. Oxford: Oxford University Press.

Wynter, Sylvia, and Katherine McKittrick. 2015. "Unparalleled Catastrophe of Our Species? Or, to Give Humanness a Different Future: Conversations". In *On Being Human as Praxis*, edited by Katherine McKittrick, 9–89. Durham: Duke University Press.

Capital

Mercedes Bunz

Capital is a term whose meaning one cannot catch. Several words and **worlds** unfold it in inconsistent directions. One thing, however, is certain: It is currently the term ruling the present discourse, rather lonesomely, ever since economy has taken over the place once reserved for politics, which it had stolen before from religion. That there is a link between politics and religion was noticed by Walter Benjamin, who wrote "one can behold in capitalism a religion" warning that its universalism affects the position of critique: "We cannot draw close the net in which we stand" (1921, 259). Today, capitalism's universalism seems to be stronger than ever, leaving no outside to flee to. Capital has successfully infected areas formerly addressed as autonomous, such as education and the idea of the university, but also science, culture, or art. In other words, it has successfully positioned itself as the sovereign ruler of our contemporary discourse. What else can we do but to stare at capital's powerful ruling insignia – "measurement" and "efficiency" – as if we were conservative Catholics enveloped by an unfurling enlightenment? Where is our imagination? It is needed in a time in which one cannot see an end to capitalism, although it had a beginning: Following Marx, theorists from Rosa Luxemburg (1913) to David Harvey (2014) have treated capital as a historical phenomenon starting when stable property was converted into fluid wealth invested to bring gain.

Unfortunately, it seems to have become more fluid and more universal ever since. The hope of facing capital as a historical phenomenon with an end in sight seems to be gone. But never mind. The present is a formidable place to escape our gloomy future.

Theorists have taken up the challenge of a sovereign capitalism with new answers, for example, to question the role of human agency (Parisi 2004; Noys 2011; Zizek 2014). Furthermore, historical reasons (the end of actually existing socialism) as well as contemporary reasons (that the actual crisis of existing capitalism has no crucial effect on capital) gave rise to discontent regarding once powerful political ideas like communism and communization (Noys 2011). The fact that capitalism is continuously appropriating alternative approaches has lead to a call for a radical non-relation: "The new mantra is: *we have no demands*. We don't want political representation. We don't want collective bargaining. We don't want a seat at the table" (Galloway 2011, 244). An elegant suicidal gesture that needs to be thought through further.

The effect of having no demand is withdrawing. To withdraw, however, also means that the "we" is not turning somewhere else affirmatively. As such, withdrawing replaces opposition with a non-relation, which causes the dispersion of one's own collective force. In being withdrawn, there will be no "we" anymore. Our highly individualized time (which with hindsight could be called "the era of the individual") seems anyway to have a weakening effect on critique. Withdrawing from a collective force means to leave a tool of critique even further behind. For when we **work** together to become someone else (a force we can call upon each time we turn up music and dance, or write texts, build organizations or houses or computer programs, are with friends, live a relationship, or simply: speak) we question the capitalist idea that a collective is nothing more than the sum of individual, exchangeable people. Using a collective force means unlocking capitals of critique that do not reply to capitalism.

Capitalism, however, has replied – and successfully appropriated
its other. The environmental protests of the 1970s and 1980s,
which accused companies of exploiting Planet Earth in addition to
workers, have been turned into the concept of the organic super-
market and the fair-trade brand to allow a healthy consumption
for the better-off. Although capitalism presents itself with a
friendly face – as if it could be a dialectical unity of itself and of its
other – it is not. Starbucks might sell fair-trade coffee and "Ethos"
water with the claim of "helping children to get clean water," but
its water, to illustrate the general problem with one example,
is continuously involved in scandals: Despite an exceptional
drought in California, Starbucks has used a water supplier located
in drought territory; the bottles did not contain recycled **plastic**;
and only five cents of the retail price ($1.95) is given to the charity.
A bit of googling quickly shows that the water's social wrapping is
primarily a commercial for a for-profit organization.

Here, it becomes apparent that capital – always full of contradictions – managed to assimilate the position of its opponents
while still operating capitalistically. This trick has created a
paradox reality, which weakens capital's political opponents as
much as it challenges the concept of political thinking. For what
becomes of resistance when resistance just gets appropriated
by capitalism? An urgent question. Although one could also ask
a very different and in no sense a less urgent one: Might it be the
case that to render resistance as "useless" means playing into
the hands of capital? Irritated by this, one must move. "Think we
must!" (Woolf 2006, 62). In order to enter this problem from a
different perspective that makes resistance distinguishable and
allows one to be anti-capitalistic, one could face contemporary
capitalism informed by Karen Barad's method of diffraction, for
example. So what is her take on diffraction?

As a conceptual approach, diffraction avoids focusing on
essential otherness and oppositions to involve reading insights
through one another, a process Barad (2007) has turned into an
inspiring method. In the humanities so far mostly recognized as

a reading method (for example Kaiser 2014, Tuin 2011), Barad also indicates that one could understand diffraction patterns in a far broader sense as "the fundamental constituents that make up the world" (2007, 72). Applying the method of diffraction when exploring the problem of contemporary capitalism resonates in so far as one faces two moments, which at first sight seem to be indistinguishable: like Starbucks pretending to be a charity, the physical phenomenon of diffraction is based on the inter-ference of waves being interwoven with each other. However, although the different elements are intra-acting, not everything has become just the same. Here, Barad demands attention to the details: "fine-grained details matter" (90). Turning to these details shows that five cents of the water bottle are devoted to social engagement, while the rest is following capitalistic inter-ests of making the most profit. The look of resistance has been appropriated, but this should not be mixed up with resistance itself. When studying the material closely, differences emerge, because "details of diffraction patterns depend on the details of the apparatus" (91).

In other words, the political meaning of resistance always evolves from and with a concrete set-up. With this, it becomes the task of critique to turn to the fine details. It is the fine details that give a glimpse of today's paradoxical reality, which finds capitalism assimilating the position of its opponents, interweaving formerly antagonistic positions that no longer seem to be oppositional. But only at first sight does this appear to produce the problem Benjamin described when saying "one can not draw close the net in which we stand" (1921, 259). A dialectical tension is still there: withstanding capitalism is not capitalism, although it cannot be rigidly coupled anymore to something (there is no political essence, even not an anti-capitalistic one). In the post-dialectical setting of today, oppositional relations are given, but they don't operate anymore in an antagonistic mode. Instead, they function as the flipside of each other: "/" instead of "vs." Which (flip-)side someone or something is on depends on the details: on the apparatus used, the setting, the waves.

In fact, the force of capital itself has a flipside, since there is a small but crucial difference between capital and capitalistic interests. While "capitalist" and "capitalism" describe the exploiting principle of making profit, an inconsistent term like "capital" is not necessarily capitalistic – which is why we could, for example, take part in a seminar about the "Capital(s) of Critique."[1] Capital is, however, necessarily imaginative and surprising – a productive force that is always creating new space. Being new, it is open to be used in order to make the evidence of a different world appear. Or as Benjamin would say: "Someone is sure to be found who needs this force without making profit from it" (1931, 541).

References

Barad, Karen. 2007. *Meeting the Universe Halfway: Quantum Physics and the Entanglement of Matter and Meaning*. Durham: Duke University Press.

Benjamin, Walter. (1921) 1996. "Capitalism as Religion," translated by Rodney Livingstone. In *Selected Writings*. Vol. 1, *1913–1926*, edited by Marcus Bullock and Michael W. Jennings, 288–291. Cambridge, MA: Harvard University Press.

Benjamin, Walter. (1931) 1999. "The Destructive Character," translated by Edmund Jephcott. In *Selected Writings*. Vol. 2, pt. 2, *1931–1934*, edited by Michael W. Jennings, Howard Eiland, Gary Smith, 541–542. Cambridge, MA: Harvard University Press.

Galloway, Alexander. 2011. "Black Box, Black Bloc." In *Communization and Its Discontents: Contestation, Critique, and Contemporary Struggles*, edited by Benjamin Noys, 238–249. New York: Minor Compositions.

Harvey, David. 2014. *Seventeen Contradictions and the End of Capitalism*. Oxford: Oxford University Press.

Kaiser, Birgit Mara. 2014. "Worlding CompLit: Diffractive Reading with Barad, Glissant and Nancy." *Parallax* 20 (3): 274–287.

Luxemburg, Rosa. (1913) 2003. *The Accumulation of Capital*. Translated by Agnes Schwarzschild. London: Routledge.

1   The seminar took place at the annual meeting of the American Comparative Literature Organization 2014 at NYU and was chaired by Kathrin Thiele and Birgit Mara Kaiser. For Marx and Engels, capital is first of all a force of transformation, and as such it can unify contradictory aspects. This is why the bourgeoisie has had "a most revolutionary part" (Marx and Engels 1848, 15), while not being a revolutionary class.

36   Marx, Karl, and Friedrich Engels. (1848) 2010. "Manifesto of the Communist Party." Marxists Internet Archive. Accessed April 18, 2016. http://marxists.org/.

Noys, Benjamin, ed. 2011. *Communization and its Discontents: Contestation, Critique, and Contemporary Struggles*. New York: Minor Compositions.

Parisi, Luciana. 2004. "Luciana Parisi Interview," edited by Matthew Fuller. Accessed April 18, 2016. http://www.spc.org/fuller/interviews/luciana-parisi-interview/

Van der Tuin, Iris. 2011. "'A Different Starting Point, a Different Metaphysics': Reading Bergson and Barad Diffractively." *Hypatia* 26 (1): 22–42.

Woolf, Virginia. 2006. *Three Guineas*. Boston: Houghton Mifflin Harcourt.

Zizek, Slavoj. 2014. *Trouble in Paradise: From the End of History to the End of Capitalism*. London: Allen Lane.

Creation

Kiene Brillenburg Wurth

Creation is **speculation**. To *speculate* is to consider, to think through, and to guess. The uncertainty, the openness inherent in the verb *speculate* indicates our direction to think through creation. The oldest frame for conceptualizing creation is *creatio ex nihilo*, the speculation about absolute beginnings that bring in the new: to generate something new out of nothing. For a long time – we tend to say until the Romantic era – *creatio ex nihilo* was an activity preserved for the gods. It was an activity beyond existing knowledge, beyond existing rules: an act of freedom. What was created was truly new, that is to say, distinct from god, and it was good, as it emanated from an overflow of gratuitousness (Blowers 2012, 168–169). We can see in this early conception of creation the kernel of modern conceptions of human *creativity*: the ability to operate beyond established criteria and rules of the game, to produce new modes of thinking, feeling, experiencing, sensing, or knowing. The overflow of gratuitousness of a creative god already announces, we might say, the Kantian purposefulness without a purpose that was to be the blueprint for Romantic creativity. To create out of freedom something that need not serve a purpose outside of itself – that modern notion of art as autonomous holds within itself a religious idea of creation. Wordsworth's "overflow of powerful feeling" signals this embedded presence of creation.

Modern philosophers like Alfred Whitehead (1925, 1926, 1929) and Gilles Deleuze (1988), as well as process- and relational theologists (such as Catherine Keller in *The Face of the Deep*, 2003) have a problem with *creatio ex nihilo* because it starts from the model of an origin that annuls all difference and halts all movement. Everything begins and ends with this origin that typically generates the new as order out of chaos, form out of monstrous formlessness. We do not want this origin, not only because it is violently charged but also because the dichotomy between order and chaos does not do justice to creation as *constant **process***. Keller and others (Bauman 2009; Justaert 2012) have therefore started to rethink origin as *beginning*: the logic of an opening that, as Edward Said already observed in *Beginnings*, "encourages nonlinear development, a logic giving rise to the sort of multileveled coherence of dispersion" (Said 1985, 372f.). If we reconceive of creation as a process that is always already scattered, and as such always happening anew, the archaic notion of *creatio continua* we find in Maximus and Hildegard von Bingen (Keller 2003) gains new significance. *Creatio continua* holds that creation did not happen once and for all by an all-powerful divinity but is an ongoing presence: the cut that creation marks is the onset of a process.

Sigmund Freud invokes this process in *Jenseits des Lustprinzips* (1920) where he thinks the creative **entanglement** of life and death in terms of molecular diffusion: the pressure of matter to return to its original, inanimate state. Elaborating on Arthur Schopenhauer and contemporary speculative biology, Freud suggests that matter may have once been shocked out of inanimation, and then inadvertently became ever more complex to preserve itself. Evolving life is, as it were, a constant attempt to ward off the shock of animation of which it is the effect. What drives such matter is a compulsion to return: Life is just a detour to death, and as such not "its own" but an ongoing effect of a primary trauma. Creation here no longer emanates from a single principle (God) but is present as an irreducible trace in every being as becoming – or rather, a becoming that veils a desired unbecoming. The shock of animation is not an identifiable single moment: It is, comparable to Derrida's concept *différance*, a movement that may signal beginnings (and deferrals) but no origins. Freud's speculation very sharply shows us *creatio continua* as processual de-creation. Towards the end of the twentieth century, Jean-François Lyotard (1997) would adopt this Freudian logic of accidental, ongoing creation in his aesthetics of the sublime: the instance of the "now here happening," an instant that overwhelms through its incalculable occurrence. The sublime is invasive as it makes the soul or *anima*, as Lyotard calls it, aware of its own dependability on an "outside." The soul is not itself, but an other that propels its animation or creation: "Existing is to be awoken from the nothingness of disaffection by something sensible over there." (Lyotard 1997, 243) In the feeling of the sublime, the soul senses its vulnerability, its contingency on a violence that poses itself as "external" but is at the same time always already internal in its constitutive force. The experience of the sublime could thus be seen as an experience of one's own creativity.

To regard creation as continuous, and happening in every moment, is not only to allow for change but also to acknowledge *potentiality* as an ontological force – in everyone and everything. Creation in this perspective is *distributed* and *as such* can be thought of as a "first" principle. This is a way of thinking about creation that can in part be traced to Henri Bergson's notions of virtuality and of duration as differentiation (Bergson 1911, 1946). Duration is the space that opens up becoming. As Elizabeth Grosz explains the double movement of duration:

> Duration is that which undoes as well as what makes: to the extent that duration entails an open future, it involves the fracturing and opening up of the past and the present to what is virtual in them, to what in them differs from the actual, to what in them can bring forth the new. This unbecoming is the very motor of becoming. (Grosz 2005, 4–5)

Difference propels becoming as a continuous multiplicity. Continuous multiplicity is what constitutes the virtual: a dynamic estuary of the actual that can only be gauged through intuition. In intuition, we appreciate and tap into the flux that perception casts as static material. Though never opposed to the intellect, intuition requires a different kind of thinking that is creative to the extent that it combines concentration with distraction: it is fluid.

A wonderful example of such a fluid, creative thinking is offered in the picture book – the search book – *The Yellow Balloon* by Charlotte Dematons (2004). This book offers a series of landscapes that include different time scales simultaneously – eighteenth-century air balloons alongside twenty-first century planes, medieval German farmhouses next to twentieth-century Dutch houseboats – as if they were cities in which such time scales have been spatially deposited. It is clear for us to see that *The Yellow Balloon* is in fact not just about looking for a yellow balloon drifting through different landscapes with their multiple time scales. Rather, it is about the exploration of the conceptual space of storytelling: there are no plots or margins, no words or storylines, just fragments of events that give the impetus to multiple narratives. An endless number of narratives could be created. Yet, *The Yellow Balloon* is not about distraction and multiplicity alone: It shows us the double movement of intuition. On the one hand, there is the purposive- or directedness of searching for the tiny yellow balloon on each page. On the other, and at the same time, there is the purposelessness of the virtual – the dynamic estuary of virtual stories that is real, though not yet actualized, on every page.

The felt and fruitful tension between such a limiting and limitless thinking epitomizes creation as a constant becoming and differing – in being, but also in art. In twentieth-century psychology, these contrasting but interrelated attitudes of thinking have come to be known as convergent and divergent thinking: thinking in a specific, perhaps pre-determined direction, and thinking that is freer in that it does not start from a set goal. Convergent thinking means finding the "right" answer, based on skills and knowledge, while divergent thinking means finding as many (unapparent) answers to a problem as possible, based on analogical patterns. Divergent thinking is what Gilles Deleuze and Félix Guattari preached when, in *What is Philosophy?* (1994), they posited philosophy (and science) as an inventive discipline, opening up new fields with the creation of new concepts. Divergent thinking is the production of novelty and the production of novelty that is useful and valuable nowadays makes up "creativity." While philosophy and critical theory after Deleuze have spent a lot of time thinking through difference, repetition, virtuality, and creation as becoming, the concept of creativity has not been thought through as rigorously. We need to turn to psychology and cognitive theory to make the transition from creation to creativity, from ontology to epistemology and aesthetics. If creation is differing, how can we critically conceive of creativity as an ability to generate novelty? If we start from the concept of creation as sketched out here, we would want to move beyond the idea of a creative author (whether artist or common individual) paralleling the idea of a creative god. We would have to invoke our knowledge of inter/intratextuality, actor-network theory, and new materialism to rethink creativity as productive potentiality: a potential in *things*, generating ever new forms, images, and ideas in the collision with other things. However, creat*ivity* requires an entirely new entry in this book of critical concepts. Alfred North Whitehead, thanks to whom the term "creativity" became current in the twentieth century, would be the logical starting point for such an entry.

We have moved from theology to philosophy to a little psychology, from being to thinking, to unravel creation as a critical concept. This entry has only done a little justice to this concept (for instance, it did not even begin to invoke philosophers like Baruch de Spinoza and Gottfried Wilhelm Leibniz) because, as we have seen, creation is bound up with the most pressing questions in Western philosophy: questions about origins and beginnings, about the future, perception, experience, experimentation, the infinite, the soul, time, language, and difference. At the same time, it is difficult to carve out the concept of creation in itself because we still lack a specific critical theory of creation and creativity. Such a critical theory is especially urgent today now that creation and creativity has been appropriated all around us, from innovation sciences to organizational psychology, without a proper conceptual regime.

References

Bauman, Whitney. 2009. *Theology, Creation, and Environmental Ehtics: From Creatio ex Nihilo to Terra Nullius*. London: Routledge.

Bergson, Henri. (1911) 2007. *Creative Evolution*. Translated by Arthur Mitchell. Houndmills: Palgrave MacMillan.

Bergson, Henri. 1946. *The Creative Mind: An Introduction to Metaphysics*. Translated by Mabelle L. Andison. New York: Philosophical Library.

Blowers, Paul. 2012. *Drama of the Divine Economy: Creator and Creation in Early Christian Theology and Poetry*. Oxford: Oxford University Press.

Deleuze, Gilles, and Félix Guattari. 1988. *A Thousand Plateaus*. Translated by Brian Massumi. Minneapolis: University of Minnesota Press.

Deleuze, Gilles, and Félix Guattari. 1994. *What is Philosophy?* Translated by Hugh Tomlinson and Graham Burchell. New York: University of Columbia Press.

Dematons, Charlotte. 2004. *The Yellow Balloon*. Honesdale: Front Street; Rotterdam: Lemniscaat. Some pages can be seen at: www.lemniscaat.nl

Freud, Sigmund. (1920) 1967. *Beyond the Pleasure Principle*. Translated and edited by James Strachey. New York: WW Norton.

Grosz, Elizabeth. 2005. "Bergson, Deleuze, and the Becoming of Unbecoming." *Parallax* 11 (2): 4–13.

Justaert, Kristien. 2012. *Theology after Deleuze*. New York: Continuum.

Keller, Catherine. 2003. *The Face of the Deep: A Theology of Becoming*. London: Routledge.

Lyotard, Jean-François. 1997. *Postmodern Fables*. Translated by Georges van de Abbeele. Minneapolis: University of Minnesota Press.

Said, Edward. (1975) 1985. *Beginnings: Intention and Method*. New York: University of Columbia Press.

Whitehead, Alfred North. 1925. *Science and the Modern World*. New York: Macmillan Company.

Whitehead, Alfred North. 1926. *Religion in the Making*. New York: Macmillan Company.

Whitehead, Alfred North. 1929. *Process and Reality: An Essay in Cosmology*. New York: Macmillan Company.

Entanglement

Kathrin Thiele

It seems all too easy to speak in terms of entanglement today: Everything is connected with everything – economically, ecologically, politically. Who would not know that? The discourse that everything depends on something else is omnipresent; and also that really changing anything is impossible, because everything is always entangled with everything else. Neoliberalism is the short term for this discourse (Butler and Athanasiou 2013; Brown 2015; Harvey 2007), and its current grip must also be seen from within this framework. Its (sad) ideology of self-sufficient individuals can only ever be so effective under conditions in which no-thing, not even the cosmological nothing as quantum field theory shows (Barad 2012), is categorically separable from every-thing (else). So, one thing that I want to claim here, somewhat "in general," is that today's realities make aware – everywhere and to everybody (though *precisely not* in the same way to and for every-body [Ferreira da Silva 2009; Wynter 1994]) – that in this globalized and interconnected **world** one major critical symptom of the planetary condition is the very state of being entangled: often painfully entangled, implicated, caught up, and complicit.

From this beginning the problem of making entanglement an **affirmative** critical tool is obvious: criticality must be at **work** in order to twist entanglement away from the above characterization – another **vision** of and **regard** for entanglement is needed. Karen Barad's use of diffraction – a term that Donna Haraway introduced into critical discourses as "a metaphor for another kind of *critical consciousness*" (Haraway 1997, 273) – might be inspirational here. In Barad's quantized version (which in no way implies a removal from "reality"), diffraction is the phenomenon of entanglement *par excellence*. In *Meeting the Universe Halfway*, she spells out that "[i]n fact, diffraction not only brings the reality of entanglement to light, it is itself an entangled phenomenon" (Barad 2007, 73). And in her central chapter on "Quantum Entanglements: Experimental Metaphysics and the Nature of Nature," which discusses the quantum mechanical and mathematical details of the two-slit diffraction experiment and its lively discursive history in twentieth-century quantum physics and beyond, Barad specifies further:

> Importantly, I suggest that Bohr's notion of a phenomenon be understood ontologically... phenomena do not merely mark the epistemological inseparability of "observer" and "observed"; rather, *phenomena are the ontological insepa-rability of intra-acting "agencies."* That is, *phenomena are ontological entanglements.* (333)

Speaking of the ontological inseparability of intra-acting "agencies" emphasizes the necessity to no longer envision entanglement(s) as based on pre-existing relata. Rather, "relata-within-phenomena emerge through intra-action" (334); or, as Vicki Kirby argues in her *Quantum Anthropology*: "Entanglement suggests that the very ontology of entities emerges *through* relationality: the entities do not pre-exist their involvement" (Kirby 2011, 76).

Compared to the neoliberal diagnosis, the approach to entanglement as *relational ontology* introduces then a significant difference. With Gregory Bateson one can say it introduces "a difference which makes a difference" (Bateson 1972, 453). Entanglement here is precisely not a descriptive matter of fact (the neoliberal "everything is entangled"), which relies on the claim that its measurement is not (part) of the same entangled constellation it seeks to understand; or, put differently, that "we" could simply be taken out of the equation when measuring (this assumption also underlies the classical image of critique in which the subject of critique is clearly delimited from its object). To the contrary, as soon as entanglement(s) are engaged in the quantized sense outlined above, they matter. They are *constructive* matters of concern. "Phenomena are the basis of a new ontology" (Barad 2007, 333), and entanglements, therefore, imply the real possibility for the **transformation** of how things *are*.

Yet, this claim for transformation, a new ontology, should not mislead us, and neither should the understanding of entanglement as foundational relationality. We might easily believe that these hopeful sounding attributes in themselves necessitate a "better" toward which "we" are heading; as if a progressive direction could still guide us here. Nothing would be a greater misunderstanding of the quantum critical registers, which show that temporalities are anything but linear and in which (ontological) indeterminacy rules. A strong claim for this can once again be found in Barad's discussion of "nature's queer performativity" (Barad 2012) in which she stresses the *onto*-epistemological dimension of indeterminacy (Bohr) over uncertainty (Heisenberg). While the latter zooms in on the epistemological dimension only and ultimately maintains a humanist (and therefore progessivist) linearity, the entanglement of ontology and epistemology shakes up such an understanding. The radical *onto*-epistemological dimension of indeterminacy can no longer offer a progessivist **temporality** on which an understanding of indeterminacy as (epistemological) uncertainty would still stand.

To recapitulate then, instead of taking entanglement as a mere "given" to which there is no alternative (neoliberalism) or proposing it as the "better solution" (progressivism), working with entanglement as an affirmative critical tool entails something else. It means attending to the constructive and/as relational ontology in a diffractive sense and/as utter indeterminacy. It means attending to the phenomenon as a question to *arrive*. Here, I refer to Jacques Derrida, whose radical thought of "undecidability" and "hauntology" (instead of onto-theology) lives of the same warped (or queer) temporality: "Turned toward the future, going toward it, [the question] also comes from it, it preceeds *from* [*provient de*] the future. It must therefore exceed any presence as presence itself." (Derrida 1994, xix)

If entangledness as undecidability and indeterminacy is the (onto-/hauntological) state of every-thing; if there is, therefore, no non-related (outside) position from which an authoritative or prescriptive critical judgment and evaluation can be issued, what follows for how we can take measure of the world – this **capital** of critique that we cannot afford to loose, although we realize how entangled, implicated, or complicit we *are*? What definitely follows is that **responsibility** for how things take shape with-in their entangledness will in no way shrink, but instead is growing. If entanglement is not seen as a mere descriptive denominator of how things appear today (matter of fact) but is rather taken seriously as the entangling situation itself in which *how* something is accounted becomes just as important as *what* is accounted for (matter of concern), then one can once more agree with Barad's statement: "Accountability cannot be reduced to identifying individual causal factors and assigning blame for this or that cause…. Taking account entails being accountable, for all ac/countings are from within, not without" (Barad 2012, 46–47).

We have moved from a matter-of-fact-engagement with entan-glement to one that still acknowledges its systemic – and therefore intra-active – nature, yet approaches it as a matter of concern, a mattering matter in need of attunement and care (Chow 2012; Latour 2004; Puig de la Bellacasa 2011). Entan-glement in this **perspective** – as hauntology – entails that there is no simple opposite to entangledness, but only the in(de)finite re-arrangement of every-thing in its differential becoming. Every cut, split or categorical delimitation, in as much as every turning away in indifference or as refusal, does not escape the condition of entanglement or relationality. Instead, it is but one form of (non-)relating to the issues at stake. In this matter lie both the painful or **terrifying** aspect of entanglement and its ethico-political potential. As Sarah Nuttall announces in her study on post-apartheid South Africa:

> Entanglement is a condition of being twisted together or entwined, involved with; it speaks of an intimacy gained, even if it was resisted, or ignored or uninvited. It is a term which may gesture towards a relationship or set of social relationships that is complicated, ensnaring, in a tangle, but which also implies a human foldedness. (2009, 1)

The ethico-political potential lies in the ways we fold, or better yet, in the ways we become fold, i.e., the ways we practice (our) foldedness. Nuttall continues: "A focus on entanglement in part speaks to the need for a **utopian** horizon, while always being profoundly mindful of what is actually going on." (11, emphasis added) And Barad spells this out as follows: "An ethics of entanglement entails possibilities and obligations for reworking the material effects of the past and the future" (Barad 2012, 47). Final redemption is never the goal of such an ethics. Rather, in a most affirmative sense it calls for the persistent work of opening up, in as much as it demands the "wit(h)nessing" (Ettinger 2006) of the very specific entanglements we are inhabiting: They are never innocent, always with-in asymmetrical **power** relations and always having certain lives more precariously affected than others.

References

Barad, Karen. 2012. "Nature's Queer Performativity." *Women, Gender & Research* (1–2): 25–53.

Barad, Karen. 2007. *Meeting the Universe Halfway: Quantum Physics and the Entanglement of Matter and Meaning.* Durham: Duke University.

Bateson, Gregory. 1972. *Steps to an Ecology of Mind.* New York: Ballantine Books.

Brown, Wendy. 2015. *Undoing the Demos: Neoliberalism's Stealth Revolution.* New York: Zone Books.

48   Butler, Judith, and Athena Athanasiou. 2013. *Dispossession: The Performative in the Political*. Cambridge: Polity Press.

Chow, Rey. 2012. *Entanglements, or Transmedia Thinking about Capture*. Durham: Duke University Press.

Derrida, Jacques. 1994. *Specters of Marx: The State of the Debt, the Work of Mourning, & the New International*, translated by Peggy Kamuf. London: Routledge.

Ettinger, Bracha. 2006. *The Matrixial Borderspace*. Minneapolis: University of Minnesota Press.

Ferreira da Silva, Denise. 2009. "No-Bodies: Law, Raciality and Violence." *Griffith Law Review* 18 (2): 212–236.

Haraway, Donna. 1997. *Modest_Witness@Second_Millennium.FemaleMan©_Meets_ Onco Mouse™*. London: Routledge.

Harvey, David. 2007. *A Brief History of Neoliberalism*. Oxford: Oxford University Press.

Kirby, Vicki. 2011. *Quantum Anthropology: Life at Large*. Durham: Duke University Press.

Latour, Bruno. 2004. "Why Has Critique Run Out of Steam? From Matters of Fact to Matters of Concern." *Critical Inquiry* 30: 225–248.

Nutall, Sarah. 2009. *Entanglement: Literary and Cultural Reflections on Post-Apartheid*. Johannisburg: Wits University Press.

Puig de la Bellacasa, Maria. 2010. "Matters of Care in Technoscience: Assembling Neglected Things." *Social Studies of Science* 41 (1): 85–106.

Wynter, Sylvia. 1994. "'No Humans Involved': And Open Letter To My Colleagues." *Forum N. H. I.: Knowledge for the 21st Century* 1 (1): 42–73.

Experience

Annemie Halsema

In standard philosophical encyclopedias you will not find an entry on "experience." That does not imply that the notion is not referred to, but that it is too encompassing and disputed to dedicate one single entry to it. Also in critical studies, such as feminist theory, it is a contested notion (Scott 1991). Should it then be part of a vocabulary that aims at bringing together notions around critique in the twenty-first century? Is experience not contaminated by **power** structures and practices, as critical philosophers from Karl Marx until Michel Foucault have argued, and as Joan Scott contends for feminist thinking? Should the immediateness and the first person **perspective** that experience implies not be criticized and embedded within a discourse that analyzes the practices that constitute something like it? Are we capable of interpreting experience, of philosophically analyzing it, as phenomenology is supposed to do? Or should we be suspicious of the immediate knowledge it presumes to offer? And last but not least, does experience not centralize the philosophies of the subject too much, instead of thinking ahead of them? This entry will therefore first show why experience is disputed, only to argue subsequently that despite this critique, it still is a notion that deserves to remain central in critical thinking.

In the philosophical tradition, experience mainly plays a role in epistemology, and was contested already long before critical philosophers doubted it. In fact, it is a crucial notion in the distinction between appearance and reality that is discussed from Antiquity onwards; it plays an important role in the idealism-realism discussion in the seventeenth and eighteenth centuries; and in the rationalism-empiricism debate in epistemology; it is presumed to be *the* central concept in twentieth-century phenomenology but has already been contested by the discipline's founding father Edmund Husserl.

The notion of experience as human experience, often related to the sensations, starts playing an important role in modern philosophy, that is, from the seventeenth century onwards. In ancient Greek philosophy, contemplation of ideas was central in acquiring knowledge – be it more importantly so in Plato than in Aristotle – and human experience was not the main source of reaching true knowledge about reality. But when in modern philosophy the subject becomes the origin and foundation of knowledge, the notion of experience also gains influence. Yet, not without being questioned from the start.

One of the problems the notion of experience faces is that it can be deluded or misled and does not lead to true knowledge. René Descartes's famous problem is that one's experiences can be deceived in dreaming or by an evil demon. His doubt experiment in the *Meditations* aims at reaching the foundation of all knowledge and thus at absolutely certain knowledge. He contends that because I cannot exclude that I am dreaming, my present belief in my sensations is not sufficiently justified. While dreaming doubts the sensual perceptions, the possibility of an evil demon even calls into question the seemingly evident mathematical truths.

Another important step in thinking about experience is taken by Immanuel Kant in the *Critique of Pure Reason*. While we may experience the outer world as existing independent of us, Kant contends that human experience, that is to say, sensory perceptions, are constructed by the human mind as a

combination of sensory matter that we receive and *a priori* forms
supplied by our cognitive faculties (Rohlf 2014). Kant makes the
famous distinction between analytical judgments *a priori*, synthetic judgments *a posteriori* and synthetic judgments *a priori*.
While the analytical judgments do not pertain to experience, the
synthetic do. The synthetic judgments *a posteriori* are based on
experience in the sense that we need perceptual information
in order to judge whether they are valid. These judgments are
experiential (for instance, "this paper is white"; because paper
can have several colors, I need to check on the basis of sense
perception whether this paper indeed is white). The synthetic
judgments *a priori* combine experiential knowledge with the *a
priori* character of knowledge, that is, its universality and necessity. In other words, they are based upon experience but are not
confined to experiential knowledge. This is the kind of knowledge
to be found in mathematics, natural science and metaphysics.

Kant in his analysis of synthetic *a priori* judgments bridges
the gap between empiricism and rationalism by arguing that
there are two components of knowledge: there is something
that is known, the contents given to consciousness, and there
is something that knows, the active **process** of knowing. This
distinction is taken further by Husserl in twentieth-century
phenomenology and developed to *noema* (the ideal content of
consciousness) and *noesis* (the intentional process of consciousness, its act). Therewith also the notion of experience at once is
more centralized in conscious processes, and differentiated.

In the twentieth century, phenomenology developed into *the*
stream of thought in which experience is central. The *Stanford Encyclopedia*, for instance, defines phenomenology as "the
study of structures of consciousness as experienced from the
first-person point of view" (Smith 2013). Likewise, in analytical
philosophy, phenomenology is considered to be concentrating
upon the "what it is likeness" of sensations and experiences.
Phenomenological research methods in the social sciences
are empirical qualitative research methods that pertain to the

meaning people give to their lives, as expressed by them in qualitative interviews. These streams of thought relate all in different ways to the notions of "experience" and "intentionality" as developed by Husserl. The latter implies that consciousness is always of or about something. Phenomenology studies these contents of consciousness (*noema*), as well as its acts (*noesis*).

While thus centralizing the notion of experience, from the start Husserl also problematizes an overly simple notion of experience. He first of all distinguishes between *Erfahrung* (experience) and *Anschauung* (intuition), arguing that while we may experience cases that are at least supposedly real, in *Anschauung* things may also be imagined or recollected. For Husserl phenomenology does not analyze experience but *Anschauung*, phenomenological intuition. Furthermore, these intuitions have intentional quality, which implies that they are experiences of a certain type (hope, desire, memory, **affirmation**, doubt, etc.), and that they have an intentional matter: that what they are about. For Husserl, the latter, that which we perceive, the objects, are not experienced. What is experienced are our sensations and the acts that interpret or apperceive them (Husserl o.c. in Zahavi 2003, 27). As Zahavi exhibits, intentionality thus consists of "the interpretation of something *as* something" (27). Experience implies the constitution of something in our consciousness.

During the same period in which Husserl founded phenomenology, the beginning of the twentieth century, the notion of experience was severely criticized by the masters of suspicion, that is, by critical thinkers such as Karl Marx and Sigmund Freud. They further complicated the notion of experience by contending that human experience is constituted by economic structures and the unconscious. Instead of being certain of one's experiences and taking them as starting point for gaining knowledge of the world, in their analysis our experience appears to be influenced by what remains outside of it. Therewith they give way to twentieth-century streams of thought in philosophy that fundamentally question the centrality of the subject and inherit the difficulties with experience already prevalent in modern philosophy.

Notwithstanding the questioning of experience by Marx, Freud, and others, the notion today still remains relevant for critical thinking. In feminist theory, Scott's forceful rejection of the notion of experience, on the ground of its exclusivity (its being prototypical for white, middle-class women) and its being constructed by the power relations under critique, has led to defenses of women's experiences. In the context of cosmetic surgery, Kathy Davis (1997) secures the experienced body as a source of empowerment for women; Sonia Kruks (2001) argues that embodied experience for women who have faced physical violence can form an **affective** basis for solidarity. Yet, Scott's restraint about the social constructedness of experience cannot simply be put aside, presuming that there is some sort of pre-discursive embodied experience that escapes social construction and power relations. Instead, it should be contended that experience is historically and culturally specific through and through. As experience, however, it does not coincide with discourse and with prevailing power structures but can be thought of as what Johanna Oksala calls "a sense of disorientation and dissatisfaction" (2014, 396). In critical perspectives, experience itself can be critical, in the sense of exhibiting a gap with dominant cultural representations, a realization "no, these representations do not accord with the way I perceive/feel/sense myself."

References

Davis, Kathy. 1997. *Embodied Practices: Feminist Perspectives on the Body*. London: Sage.

Descartes, René. 2008. *Meditations on First Philosophy: With Selections from the Objections and Replies*, translated by Michael Moriarty. Oxford: Oxford University Press.

Kant, Immanuel. 1998. *Critique of Pure Reason*. Edited and translated by P. Guyer and A. Wood. Cambridge: Cambridge University Press.

Kruks, Sonia. 2001. *Retrieving Experience*. Ithaca, NY: Cornell University Press.

Oksala, Johanna. 2014. "In Defense of Experience." *Hypatia* 29 (2): 388–403.

54   Rohlf, Michael. 2014. "Immanuel Kant." In *The Stanford Encyclopedia of Philosophy*, edited by Edward N. Zalta. Accessed April 18, 2016. http://plato.stanford.edu/archives/sum2014/entries/kant/.

Scott, Joan. 1991. "The Evidence of Experience." *Critical Inquiry* 17 (4): 773–797.

Smith, David Woodruff. 2013. "Phenomenology." In *The Stanford Encyclopedia of Philosophy*, edited by Edward N. Zalta. Accessed April 18, 2016. http://plato.stanford.edu/archives/win2013/entries/phenomenology/.

Zahavi, Dan. 2003. *Husserl's Phenomenology*. Stanford: Stanford University Press.

Fable

Sam McAuliffe

The projections of the imaginary as they appear across the field
of modernity give rise to a series of questions for the work of
critique. A reality less and less distinguishable from fable, to
the point that the longstanding arrangement securing their
opposition begins to give way, disrupting in turn the wide array
of premises and certainties that rest upon this distinction; a
reality, above and beyond this, increasingly *derived from* and
conditioned by the processes of fabulation running through it:
this is, for Roger Caillois, the characteristic signature of a certain
experience of this modernity. Such experience not only testifies to the repositioning of the sphere in which the fabular
circulates but an intensification of its efficacy. Having ceased
to be situated at a distance from what is real, no longer casting
its shadow over lived reality from an indeterminate elsewhere,
it becomes instead the very material out of which the real is
composed. "The world in which everything, everywhere, is possible at all times, because the imagination has sent there its
most extraordinary enticements ahead of time and discovers
them at once – this world was no longer remote, inaccessible,
and autonomous. It was the world in which people lived" (Caillois
2003, 178). Now what brings this transformation to pass – Caillois
dates it to the first half of the Nineteenth Century – is the
emergence of the modern city, the city as backdrop to "a keen

commitment to *modernity*" (182). This shows itself above all in the representational forms devoted to urban experience, and the relation that subsists between the two. Why, then, does the cityscape constitute a privileged point of reference for the study of "the social processes of the imagination"? Because for the first time within modernity's scope the conditions emerge for a form of "mythic" experience that had otherwise fallen into dormancy. Myth, Caillois's preferred term here, is a strain of "collective property"; once it ceases to encompass the collective, pertaining to the individual alone and in isolation, it can no longer be understood as mythic, properly speaking (176). And the same must be said of any fabular phenomenon: it is a projection that necessarily extends beyond the private imagination, that circulates at the level of the *socius*, is even a means by which sociality is itself underwritten.

For Caillois the modern cityscape facilitates such conditions. Within its horizons a "collective mental atmosphere" is inculcated, exerting a "powerful hold", a "constraining force" over an imagination that exceeds the confines of individuated experience. Yet it is one that offers up the city as setting in a particularly paradoxical form, inasmuch as the mythic projection concerns neither the real nor the imaginary in isolation, but the real *as* imaginary: "the realist depiction of a clearly defined city (more integrated than any other in readers' actual lives) was suddenly exalted along fantastic lines" (177). Writing on the same context some time after Caillois, Michel Foucault will pick up the trail of the very same tendency: "For the attitude of modernity, the high value of the present is indissociable from a desperate eagerness to imagine it, to imagine it otherwise than it is, and to transform it not by destroying it but by grasping it in what it is" (Foucault 1997, 311).[1]

---

1   For both authors (and for Walter Benjamin too, of course), Baudelaire provides the exemplary figure of this "commitment" or "attitude" that confounds any simple opposition between reality and imagination.

Myth, fantasy, and fable, no longer concerned with a world beyond this one, are rerouted back through reality, so that the distinction between the real and the imaginary is reproduced on this side of reality itself. For the collective subject encompassed by this realignment of the spheres of experience in question, what is real seems increasingly dissociated from itself, appearing as its own vestige. "Under these conditions," Caillois writes,

> how could each reader fail to develop the intimate belief (still manifest today) that the Paris he knows is not the only one? Is not even the real one? That it is only a brilliantly lit decor, albeit far too *normal*, whose mechanical operators will never reveal themselves? A setting that conceals another Paris, the true Paris, a ghostly, nocturnal, intangible Paris that is all the more powerful insofar as it is more secret; a Paris that any-where and at any time dangerously intrudes upon the other one? (2003, 179–180)

Reality encompassed by fable appears to retreat behind its own façade, so that contact with it is always imminent, always prolonged – "everywhere, reality was contaminated with myth" (181) – and as Caillois suggests, this myth has yet to relinquish its hold.

It would be possible to plot across the terrain of modernity the new forms of "collective property" precipitated at the level of the imaginary by abrupt changes in social conditions, forms that each time draw the spheres of reality and fable into a zone of disarming indiscernibility. The series of phenomena and the range of contexts brought together in this way would no doubt bear little external resemblance to one another, but they would nevertheless be analogous at the level of structure and function, allowing critique to take stock of the implicit social process at work in the projections of the imaginary. In answer to where such a series would take us, it would no doubt have to pass through – and would perhaps reach its apotheosis in – a text closer to our own historical present, Jacques Derrida's "No Apocalypse,

Not Now." The nuclear age with which the latter is concerned is animated by an intrinsically aporetic circumstance, one that, as is the case with Caillois's Paris study, has acute implications for the relation between reality and the fabular.

The circumstance at stake here is that of nuclear war, the taking place of which raises for Derrida the specter of a properly total event. It brings with it the prospect of an act of destruction that would potentially be without delimitation, one that would withdraw the very ground from which it could be surveyed, an event without spectators, only participants, and as such it implicates "the whole of the human *socius* today" (Derrida 2007, 394). In other words, it traces out the conditions for an unprecedented instance of collectivity (the cityscape is, after all, a local setting, whilst the stage of this war is "nonlocalizable," global and, once underway, would by no means leave the stage itself unaffected).

This is the context in which Derrida begins to approach a disarming hypothesis: With this total event we are left facing "a phenomenon whose essential feature is that it is *fabulously textual*, through and through." Why is this so? Because something can be said of it only insofar as it has not yet come about, insofar as it remains in abeyance, a "non-event." Reference to it in any form is dependent upon its non-occurrence. "The terrifying 'reality' of nuclear conflict can only be the signified referent, never the real referent (present or past) of a discourse or a text." In this sense, it "has existence only by means of what is said of it and only where it is talked about. Some might call it a fable, then, a pure invention" (393). To be clear, this does not consign the destruction it threatens to a realm from which existence can consider itself protected, sheltered, or shielded. On the contrary, it is precisely as a piece of fabulation that the nuclear event acquires its force, that it becomes the "horizon" or the "condition" of all that is considered real.

> For the "reality" of the nuclear age and the fable of nuclear war are perhaps distinct, but they are not two separate

things…. "Reality," let's say the general institution of the nuclear age, is constructed by the fable, on the basis of an event that has never happened (except phantasmatically, and that is not nothing), an event of which one can only speak, whose advent remains an invention of men … The anticipation of nuclear war (dreaded as the phantasm of a remainderless destruction) installs humanity – and even defines, through all sorts of relays, the essence of modern humanity – in its rhetorical condition. (394, 396)

That there is nothing left of the order of reality that is not con-ditioned by the fable in question is, for Derrida, the signature of the nuclear age, and if this announces a new set of imperatives to which critique must respond, chief amongst them would be the following: should this circumstance be considered unique, singular, something without precedent, or is it the latest stage of a tendency apparently intrinsic to modernity, whereby the potency of the fabular appears to be increasing exponentially and hyperbolically (from the nineteenth century city to the twentieth century war), each time encompassing more and more of "reality"?

References

Caillois, Roger. 2003. "Paris, a Modern Myth." In *The Edge of Surrealism: A Roger Caillois Reader*, edited by Claudine Frank, translated by Claudine Frank and Camille Naish, 173–189. Durham: Duke University Press.

Derrida, Jacques. 2007. "No Apocalypse, Not Now (Full Speed Ahead, Seven Missiles, Seven Missives)." In *Psyche: Inventions of the Other*. Vol. 1, edited by Peggy Kamuf and Elizabeth Rottenberg, translated by Catherine Porter and Philip Lewis, 387–409. Stanford: Stanford University Press.

Foucault, Michel. 1997. "What is Enlightenment?" In *Ethics: Subjectivity and Truth: The Essential Works of Michael Foucault, 1954–1984*, edited by Paul Rabinow, translated by Robert Hurley et al., 303–319. New York: New Press.

Immanence

Leonard Lawlor

Since the time of Immanuel Kant, philosophers, and cultural
theorists (like Friedrich Nietzsche) have always engaged in
immanent critique. Most generally and negatively, immanent
critique criticizes on the basis of no transcendent idea or value.
Immanent critique therefore is undoubtedly a kind of relativism.
We must not be afraid of relativism. Depending on no transcendent value, immanent critique depends on immanence itself.
Immanent critique then looks to be paradoxical. It is. Immanent
critique is a difficult idea. It means a critique that does not appeal
to a transcendent or other worldly value or idea. It is a critique
that remains *within* experience but is done in the name of a
different kind of **experience** such as **responsibility** (Deleuze
1983, 91–93). In order to start to understand the immanence
found in immanent critique, we must distinguish immanence
from apparently related forms of thinking such as materialism
and naturalism. And we must distinguish immanence from
its opposite term, which is not just the transcendent but also
transcendence.

Immanence seems to have two senses. As we can see already, the
first sense of "immanence" must be opposed to the transcendent.
Abandoning the transcendent (and therefore certain forms of
religious belief), we are no longer concerned with a second,
heavenly **world**; we no longer gaze at an idea that lies beyond

our world and our experience. Our gaze is now turned back to this world and to our ideas. We are now concerned with our experience or experience in general. Phenomenological investigations have shown that experience is necessarily structured by time. While our experience is ours and while it is of this world, the fact that experience is fundamentally temporal opens experience to something that goes beyond it. The fact that every present moment of experience is retained makes the retained image repeatable. And this repeatability provides the retained image with a **powerful** form of potentiality. In other words, due to the structure of temporalization, there is becoming in experience. Becoming is the second and more profound sense of immanence. It is this second sense of immanence that we find in Gilles Deleuze and Félix Guattari.

Before we turn to the second sense of immanence as becoming, we must stress the definition of immanence as experience. Deleuze and Guattari themselves define immanence as experience: immanence is a "field of experience" (1994, 46–48). When they speak of a field of experience, Deleuze and Guattari ask us, however, to reverse the traditional way we think of experience. Usually, we think of experience as a relation between a subject who senses and an object that is sensed. Usually, we think of experience as vision and something seen. In this case, the experience and the thing seen are related back to the seeing subject who synthesizes the views of the thing seen. The synthetic activity of the subject is therefore prior to the experience and makes it possible. By asking us to reverse the traditional view of experience, Deleuze and Guattari ask us to imagine experience itself as being prior to subjects and objects. Thanks again to phenomenology, we can imagine such a subjectless and objectless field of experience. Maurice Merleau-Ponty has shown that, in our usual, everyday experience, our vision is oriented by the objects and the world that surrounds them. The thing seen presents profiles that motivate the viewer's synthetic activity, and the profiles appear against the background of a world that already makes sense. However, like Deleuze and Guattari, Merleau-Ponty also asks us to reverse this common under-standing of experience. He asks us, for example, to think of night-time experience, experience during a very dark night. In such an experience, we lose the orientation of the object and the world as its background. In fact, the night "envelops me, it penetrates me through all of my senses, it suffocates my memories, and it all but effaces my personal identity" (Merleau-Ponty 2012, 296). Merleau-Ponty himself compares the experience of the night to mystical experience, which implies that, when we follow the reversal of normal experience, we find ourselves in an unusual experience. Being in an almost mad experience is not something we should fear: only in such experience are we jarred out of our common sense opinions and beliefs. It opens our minds to other ideas and thought. Only through such a nearly mad experience are we able to enter into immanence. Only through such an experience are we able to engage in immanent critique. As Merleau-Ponty might have said, we enter into immanence only by trying to depersonalize experience. The required depersonalization explains why the idea of immanence is so difficult for us to understand.

With the transition through a nearly mad experience, we are now prepared to examine the second definition of immanence. In *What is Philosophy?*, Deleuze and Guattari define immanence as a plane with two sides, with the two sides being thought and extension, or consciousness and matter (1994, 48–49). And to this list of sides, we could add subject and object. In the plane with two sides, we must note that the plane of immanence is neither matter nor consciousness. Therefore, immanence cannot be immanent to matter or to consciousness. If Deleuze and Guattari call the plane of immanence at times "nature," they mean nature in a sense entirely distinguished from anything like a natural sub-stance. As they say in *A Thousand Plateaus*,

> [t]his plane [as opposed to the plane of transcendence] is necessarily a plane of immanence and univocity. We

therefore call it a plane of Nature, although nature has nothing to do with it, since on this plane there is no distinction between the natural and the artificial. However many dimensions it may have, it never has a supplementary dimension to that which happens upon it. That alone makes it natural and immanent. (1987, 266)

The plane of immanence "never has a supplementary dimension." Therefore, the plane of immanence is based on nothing but itself, which gives it the status of being that which is prior to the two sides. Only in the sense of priority to the two sides is the plane of immanence "natural" (or better, "vital"). It is not natural in the sense of objective laws, chemical processes and causes, or neuro-chemical processes and causes, material forces; all of these scientific entities would be "supplementary dimensions." To reduce the plane of immanence to these scientific entities (to reduce being to these beings, as Martin Heidegger would say) distorts the very concept of immanence. One misunderstands the conceptual core of Deleuze and Guattari's plane of immanence if one identifies their thinking with naturalism or materialism.

Through the quotation above we just mentioned transcendence, which leads us back to the second and more profound sense of immanence. Immanence is a becoming. It becomes because it has "no supplementary dimension." In other words, it is infinite, in the sense of having no absolute endpoint and no absolute starting point. It is based on no principle and on no purpose (no *arché* and no *telos*). In order to understand the infinite becoming of immanence, we must distinguish transcendence (which oriented so many phenomenological investigations) from the transcendent. As the literal meaning of the word indicates, with transcendence, we can say that the other (person) is beyond me, but in a sense that the other is still of this world or of this experience. The transcendence of the other indeed opens experience. Yet, it does not, according to Deleuze and Guattari, open it enough. In the transcendence of the other, we might conceive the other as another subject. In other words, we conceive the other as an always hidden subjectivity, the form of his or her experiences being always hidden from my gaze by the face, but still there somewhere like a secret. If we conceive the transcendence of the other in this way, then we have set up a starting point and an endpoint to becoming. Instead of the face as the expression of a hidden subjectivity – a hiddenness that implies a transcend subject – we can conceive the face as the expression of a possible world, with the eyes as portals through which I can see the other world and through which I can become other. The difference between transcendence and immanence therefore is the difference between the other and becoming-other: not just "alter," but alteration. Transcendence is a point at which we could imagine movement stopping (as if we were finally to reach the secret life of the other), while immanence is a vanishing point toward which one never stops moving (as if we always reach beyond ourselves). The unlimited movement of becoming is why we must really imagine immanence as a plane. On the vastness of this surface, it is possible to move and keep moving, especially if there are no objects or subjects at which to stop. On this surface, we are able to continue to fly. The image of incessant flight gives us an image of freedom. Perhaps to help others flee, escape, and be free is the highest form of **responsibility**.

References

Deleuze, Gilles. 1983. *Nietzsche and Philosophy*. Translated by Hugh Tomlinson. New York: Columbia University Press.

Deleuze, Gilles, and Félix Guattari. 1987. *A Thousand Plateaus*. Translated by Brian Massumi. Minneapolis: University of Minnesota Press.

Deleuze, Gilles, and Félix Guattari. 1994. *What is Philosophy?* Translated by Hugh Tomlinson and Graham Burchell. New York: Columbia University Press.

Merleau-Ponty, Maurice. 2012. *Phenomenology of Perception*. Translated by Donald Landes. London: Routledge.

The Inhuman

Veronica Vasterling

In *The Inhuman* (1991) and *Postmodern Fables* (1997) Jean-François Lyotard outlines an anthropology of the inhuman that takes its cues from psychoanalytical theory and Kant's notion of the sublime. Starting from the standard observation that humans are not born human as, for instance, cats are born cats, Lyotard relates the inhuman to infancy (Lyotard 1991, 3). Infants lack language, common reason, locomotion, in short, they lack almost everything that is considered to be typically or essentially human. In contrast to humanist anthropology, Lyotard maintains that the initial inhumanness persists in adulthood as an irreconcilable remainder that haunts and agitates the soul.

The import of Lyotard's anthropology of the inhuman is not simply its critique of anthropocentric humanism. Critique of the latter is a common goal of poststructuralist philosophers and new materialists like Karen Barad (2012). Lyotard's critique stands out from the others in that it reflects on the point of view of the one who does the criticizing. His anthropology decenters the human point of view but also acknowledges that critique always involves a human point of view. Instead of eclipsing the human viewpoint, Lyotard's critique, therefore, attempts to account for the critical potential of a decentered human perspective.

In the history of Western philosophy, from Aristotle onwards, the initial inhumanness of human life has been interpreted in two ways. It has been understood either as a potentiality that will develop into human maturity, or as a first nature that is compensated by a second acquired nature, also known as culture. This teleological view persists to this day, both in the sciences and in common sense understandings of human nature. Criticizing the essentialism inherent in developmental models, which take humanness as their *telos*, twentieth-century continental philosophy has provided a dialectical-hermeneutical reinterpretation of the teleological view of human nature. The re-interpretation emphasizes, in Jean-Paul Sartre's famous formula, that existence precedes essence (Sartre 2007). Sartre's existentialist account of the human is reworked in Maurice Merleau-Ponty's phenomenological account of the human body-subject. Despite its non-essentialist character, the anthropology of Sartre and Merleau-Ponty does not constitute a break with humanist tradition. As Lyotard points out, essentialist and non-essentialist anthropologies are humanist in that the heterogeneity of the inhuman and human is reconciled and unified without leaving any remainder. The seemingly innocent unification of all human beings under the cloak of humanism hides the violent exclusion of many in the name of the fully human. The unifying gesture of humanism neutralizes and totalizes, transforming contingent heterogeneity into a (supposedly) meaningful whole, thereby opening the door to the closed systems of totalitarianism to be witnessed in modern European history and beyond. Humanism, moreover, was and is an important source of the "grand narratives" of modernity, the utopian blueprints for a better future that invariably end in hell, epitomized by Auschwitz and the Gulag in the last century, and perhaps by the expanding war and chaos of the Middle East in the present century.

Lyotard details the humanist character of Merleau-Ponty's chiasmic ontology of the flesh as "a congruence of mind and things" (Lyotard 1991, 11), suggesting the attunement of human flesh and flesh of the **world**. In contrast to Merleau-Ponty (1995), he emphasizes the ambivalence of **sensibility,** drawing attention to the disruptive openness of the human-world relation. Whereas sensibility, in Merleau-Ponty, enables the attunement of body and environment, sensibility in Lyotard is primarily affecta-bility. A sentient body is an **affect**able body in the sense of non-intentional, heteronomous, and vulnerable openness to the world. Sensibility in the sense of affectability implies the pos-sibility of becoming overwhelmed by what affects us. Lyotard's elaboration of sensibility in terms of affectability is inspired by Immanuel Kant's exposition of the sublime in *The Critique of Judgment.*

Kant describes the sublime as, "the absolutely great," as that which is in every respect and "beyond every comparison great" (1974, 91). Perceiving the overpowering greatness of nature gives rise to contradictory feelings. According to Kant, the reason of this ambivalence is that we are capable of an idea but not of a representation of the absolute. On the one hand, perception of something sublime gives rise to a feeling of pain because the faculty of imagination (*Einbildungskraft*) is incapable of rendering a representation (*Darstellung*) of the sublime. On the other hand, it also arouses a feeling of pleasure because the sublime reminds us of the limitless power of the faculty of ideas (*Vernunft*). Incapable of providing a representation of the absolute (the sublime), we are nevertheless capable of thinking the absolute, of having an idea of the absolute. In its humanist reading, the experience of the Kantian sublime is emblematic of human nature that compensates finite sensibility with infinite reason. In Lyotard's reading, the experience of the Kantian sublime is exemplary for the irreducible heterogeneity of human faculties, entailing a reconsideration of these faculties. Thought is no longer the faculty that overcomes or compensates the finiteness of the senses, of embodiment in general. What the senses – in collaboration with imagination – fail to grasp or conceive is not recuperated in thought but rather registered as an irrecoverable, inarticulable feeling which precisely for that reason incites us to think. The failure of the senses and imagination attests to the fact that the body is not necessarily attuned to what affects it. On a more primordial level sensibility is affectability to the point of violation:

> Sensation makes a break in an inert nonexistence .... What we call life proceeds from a violence exerted from the outside on a lethargy. The *anima* exists only as forced. The *aistheton* tears the inanimate from the limbo in which it inexists, it pierces its vacuity with its thunderbolt, it makes a soul emerge out of it. (Lyotard 1997, 243)

Instead of a body-subject in tune with the world, Lyotard's anthropology of the inhuman foregrounds a body-soul whose openness to excesses of affection is unmasterable. The excess of affection causes a breakdown of the capacity to process and articulate what affects me. The effect of unmasterable affectability is comparable to what Sigmund Freud calls "primary repression" (*Urverdrängung*; 1960). Something has happened, but the event is not and cannot be processed and integrated in the framework of **experience**. The feeling of pain and confusion evoked by the event is repressed and its cause – the event – remains unknown because it never became part of one's knowledge or experience in the first place. But what is repressed returns to haunt us: the soul remains hostage to the irrecoverable and inarticulable feelings evoked by the excess of affection. According to Lyotard it is "the task of writing, thinking, literature, arts, to venture to bear witness" (1991, 7) to this anguish of the soul. Haunted by the "sublime breakdowns" resulting from an excess of affection, the soul gives rise to "true thought": "If you think you're describing thought when you describe a selecting and tabulating of data, you're silencing truth.... Thinking, like writing or painting, is almost no more than letting a giveable come towards you." (18)

The unmasterable openness and affectability of infancy is the inhuman that inhabits humankind. Lyotard's anthropology of the inhuman replaces humanism's harmonious ontology of a body-subject whose existence is co-extensive with, and attuned to the world with the ontological heterogeneity and finiteness of a body-soul forced into life by a violently affecting exteriority. Inhabiting humankind as an unmasterable openness and affecta-bility, the inhuman provides the conditions of reflective critique. True, that is, critical thought and art is not taking and defending a point of view, it is bearing witness to what emerges in one's view. In "letting a giveable come towards you," thought and art require patient irresoluteness, waiting till "what doesn't yet exist, a word, a phrase, will emerge" (19).

References

Barad, Karen. 2012. "On Touching – The Inhuman That Therefore I am." *Differences: A Journal of Feminist Cultural Studies* 23 (3): 206–223.

Freud, Sigmund. 1960. "Psychoanalytische Bemerkungen über einen auto-biographisch beschriebenen Fall von Paranoia (Dementia paranoides)." In *Gesammelte Werke VIII*, 240–316. Frankfurt am Main: Fischer Verlag.

Kant, Immanuel. 1974. *Kritik der Urteilskraft*. Hamburg: Felix Meiner Verlag.

Lyotard, Jean-François. 1991. *The Inhuman: Reflections on Time*. Translated by Geoffrey Bennington and Rachel Bowlby. Stanford: Stanford University Press.

Lyotard, Jean-François. 1997. *Postmodern Fables*. Translated by Georges Van Den Abbeele. Minneapolis and London: University of Minnesota Press.

Merleau-Ponty, Maurice. 1995. *Phenomenology of Perception*. Translated by Colin Smith. New York and London: Routledge.

Sartre, Jean-Paul. 2007. *Existentialism Is a Humanism*. Translated by Carol Macomber. New Haven: Yale University Press.

Inner Voice

Sam McAuliffe

In a short text written in exile in 1941, Theodor W. Adorno identifies the emergence of a "new type of human being," and as a functional corollary of the administered world, it falls to critique to reconstruct the configuration of indices through which this incipient *Menschentypus* has been cast. Pursued to these ends, the resulting analysis repeatedly lays bare the following tendency: when modeled after this type, nothing of the interior world of the resultant individual is exempt from heteronomous determination; its inner space is permeated by the governing structures of external reality all the way down to its "innermost constitution" (Adorno 2009, 463). This process extends well beyond one of outside influence ("*'Beeinflussung' von außen*") acting upon an otherwise self-subsistent entity. As Adorno later writes in *Minima Moralia*, his expanded study of the typology in question, "there is no substratum beneath such 'defor-mations,' no ontic interior on which social mechanisms merely act externally" (Adorno 2000, 229). The seclusion of the subject's interior world has always already been breached. The social mechanism is at work and in force on both sides of the threshold that separates the inner world from outer (it engages the individual, whether the latter is aware of it or not, on either side of this division). Inwardness persists for this new human type as, at most, a semblance, shorn of whatever necessity it once had.

This is certainly the case when it comes to the position allocated to the heteronomous subject within its discursive field, the schema for which is drawn up by Adorno in much the same way in this text. Insofar as the administered world is composed of "a synthetic, essentially advertising-determined language," the terms of which circulate all the more readily the more opaque they are, the new type of human being is struck with a form of aphonia, "the wasting away of language [*die Verkümmerung des Sprachschatzes*] and the capacity for expression through language" (Adorno 2009, 464). So too, then, within this linguistic sphere is the subject expropriated of even the pretense of autonomy and intentionality. It is as if the synthesis that produces meaning, that guides the passage of what is said by determining the form of relation between words and things, and between words themselves, has always already been locked in place. The speech of this subject is *prefabricated*, reduced without remainder to the circulation of formula.

It is this that leads Adorno to identify the faltering of speech – the culminating point of which would be its falling away altogether – as one of the primary characteristics of the new type of human being, a privation encompassing all of its actions and passions, and one it would have no available means to counter; again, in *Minima Moralia*, he writes: "the *rigor mortis* of society is spreading at last to the cell of intimacy that thought itself secure. No harm comes to man from outside alone: dumbness [*das Verstummen*; falling silent, becoming mute] is the objective spirit" (Adorno 2000, 138). But what is surprising here, as this line of thought approaches its conclusion, is the specific instance of discourse invoked as evidence of this tendency, as well as the dimension of experience within which this privation is said to come into effect.

> The change in the body of language concerns the interior monologue most of all. So far, there has not been any investigation of the influence of this nascent speechlessness on the overall condition of the people who are made speechless. (Adorno 2009, 464)

The tendency towards speechlessness that accompanies the expansion of the administered world would first and foremost make itself known *within* the integral structure of the subject. No doubt this privation will have further consequences for the possibility of communication in general, but not before it has impinged upon the subject, in and of itself. What lapses into silence, ceasing not only to speak but to hear itself speak, is the monologue of the inner voice, the voice that addresses itself, that alone receives what it emits, and this disrupts, if it doesn't withdraw it altogether, the very condition of reflexive experience, the possibility of staging a relation between the self and itself in any given form. It would mean that the subject could no longer take up a position in relation to itself, not even one of estrangement, because the primary term of this relation has been dissipated: "there is no longer an 'ego' in the traditional sense," it no longer holds together as a point of reference (462).

At issue here is nothing less than a constitutive change in what Adorno elsewhere refers to as "the facticity of inwardness" (Adorno 1991, 32), that which, within the subject, takes the form of spontaneous, ever-present immediacy. Once the inner voice has ceased to speak, once the living support it appears to grant to experience is withdrawn, not only the formal cohesion but the material composition of the interior world finds itself fundamentally affected. This is one of the primary tasks that falls to a critique of "the new type of human being": to analyze the historical conditions for this lapse into speechlessness and to gauge the full range of its consequences, from the effect this silence has on the distribution of the individual's other faculties and the various spheres of psychic life, to its wider implications for the social categories in which the individual is embedded, the division between the public and private self, for example (consequences which are, no doubt, still unfolding today).

Such analysis may even show that the tendency in question is not entirely detrimental. It could well harbor a potential of sorts. Something of this is already apparent in the fact that the critical model developed by Adorno here at no point speaks in the name of the supposed integrity of subjective inwardness, as though the inner voice was a property that should be restored to the individual, even if this was indeed somehow possible. On the contrary, Adorno subscribes to a doctrine of the individual for which interiority is a condition that must be worked through and ultimately overcome: "the subject does not come to itself through the narcissistically self-related cultivation of its being-for-itself but rather through externalization, by devotedly abandoning itself to what is not itself" (Adorno 1998, 164). There is always a danger, after all, that the inner voice impedes the process of externalization on which the subject's realization is said to depend here, that it leaves the subject estranged from itself by confining it within itself, locking it into its accidental particularity. Interior monologue is a resource that can always lead the subject to mistake inwardness as a value in and of itself, thus suspending the process of self-reflection by which "the ego becomes transparent to itself as a piece of the world" (Adorno 1973, 73). Conversely, then, a model of language from which the structural possibility of interior monologue had been withdrawn, a language given over entirely to externalization, at all points transparent in its mediations: would not such a language necessarily draw the subject out of its self-seclusion, so that, in speaking, the latter would be left "transparent to itself as a piece of the world"? And would this not offer the prospect of a new form of sociality, a revised social relation between its speakers? In his essay on the totally administered society of Huxley's *Brave New World*, Adorno does in fact entertain such a possibility, when he writes: "Through total social mediation, from the outside, as it were, a new immediacy, a new humanity, would arise" (Adorno 1967, 106).

In any case, an intimation of where this question would take us is given intermittently in Adorno's subsequent critical writing. From the radio's phantasmatic mediation of the living voice to the popular cult of biography; from the talking cure in psychoanalysis to the psychotechnical procedures underwriting administered life (the aptitude test, the questionnaire, and so on): once viewed from within the scope of this question, it would be possible to treat these widely disparate yet historically convergent phenomena as so many prostheses for the absent voice, so many attempts to make speak what has fallen silent, the subject's interior monologue.

References

Adorno, Theodor W. 1967. "Aldous Huxley and Utopia." In *Prisms*, translated by Samuel and Shierry Weber, 97–118. London: Spearman Press.

Adorno, Theodor W. 1973. *The Jargon of Authenticity*. Translated by Knut Tarnowski and Frederic Will. Evanston: Northwestern University Press.

Adorno, Theodor W. 1991. "The Position of the Narrator in the Contemporary Novel." In *Notes to Literature*, Vol. 1, translated by Shierry Weber Nicholsen, 30–36. New York: Columbia University Press.

Adorno, Theodor W. 1998. "Gloss on Personality." In *Critical Models: Interventions and Catchwords*, translated by Henry W. Pickford, 161–165. New York: Columbia University Press.

Adorno, Theodor W. 2000. *Minima Moralia: Reflections on Damaged Life*. Translated by E. F. N. Jephcott. London: Verso.

Adorno, Theodor W. 2009. "The Problem of a New Type of Human Being." In *Current of Music: Elements of a Radio Theory*, edited and translated by Robert Hullot-Kentor, 461–468. Cambridge: Polity Press.

Metaphor

Annemie Halsema

Metaphor is not only one of the most commonly used figures of speech in everyday language, it also has attracted more philosophical interest than any other figure of speech. Metaphor is defined in the Merriam-Webster dictionary as a form of figurative language; it is "a figure of speech in which a word or phrase literally denoting one kind of object or idea is used in place of another to suggest a likeness or analogy between them." Besides, it also denotes the object or activity or idea of metaphor itself. Philosophically interesting about the notion is the possibility of using one word or phrase instead of another, which introduces analogy, similarity, displacement but also imagination and **creativity** into language and, for some philosophers, into everyday life.

Metaphors are of interest to philosophers in the Anglo-American analytic tradition, because they escape the accepted conditions for determining the truth value of statements, yet cannot simply be set aside as not meaningful. Consequentially, analytic philosophers such as Max Black (1962, 1979) and Donald Davidson (1984) aim to define the function of metaphor as heuristic and as inspirational and guiding our insight, and not as related to truth. Especially Black (1979) develops a theory of metaphor in which the interaction between the two subject terms explains its meaning, thereby at once alluding to the conventions within a linguistic community as leaving some space for creating new meaning.

Continental philosophers do not so much tackle metaphor in a linguistic context but rather consider it in a broader sense. Philosophers such as Friedrich Nietzsche ([1873] 1999) and Jacques Derrida (1982) point critically at the metaphorical character of all concept formation and of metaphysics in particular, while others, such as Paul Ricoeur, understand metaphor more positively in terms of our abilities to see things anew making use of imagination. In *The Rule of Metaphor* (1977), Ricoeur draws together insights from Kantian philosophy, notably the notion of productive imagination, and linguistic philosophy (i.e., the ideas of structuralists such as Ferdinand de Saussure, Émile Benveniste, Roman Jakobson, but also of the father of analytical philosophy, Gottlob Frege), in order to describe metaphor as the stimulus of change in both the linguistic and ontological or existential field. Metaphor for Ricoeur makes us *see* things differently, because of its **transformative** aspect, which at once disturbs the logical order while begetting it in a new form. Living, as opposed to dead, metaphors cannot be simply **translated** into existing terms; understanding them requires a novel way of perceiving reality. As such they create new reality. Metaphors, in other words, pertain to sameness *and* difference, they refer to reality while at the same time redescribing it.

Derrida in "White Mythology" (1982) uses this ambiguous character of the metaphor to critique philosophy, while at the same time affirming it. He relates metaphor to philosophy itself, claiming that philosophy is nothing more than a **process** of metaphorisation. Philosophy, he writes in a Nietzschean fashion, aims at a ruling metaphor, at similarity, and in its deepest dreams at reducing all significations to a principal, fundamental, or central metaphor. But metaphoricity in itself implies multiplicity, and philosophy expresses itself in texts, which implies that meaning can never be exhausted. He detects two trajectories in philosophy, that he both calls self-destructive and that are closely related: One is the metaphysical sublation of the metaphor into the proper sense of being in which metaphor implies a detour and loss of meaning, but one in which the literal, proper sense can be appropriated in the end (Derrida 1982, 270). In the other, the opposition between metaphoricity and the proper itself is set aside, an opposition foundational for metaphysics. Thereby metaphysics in the end sublates itself.

Since metaphor in the analytical and continental tradition of philosophy is already described in detail in other sources (e.g., Hills 2012; Theodorou), here we can further concentrate on the notion of metaphor as influential in critical forms of theory, notably in psychoanalysis and feminist theory. Jacques Lacan famously introduced the notion of metaphor, in distinction to metonymy, to reinterpret the central workings of the Freudian unconscious. Both notions play an important role in the French psychoanalytically inspired feminist theories, such as Julia Kristeva's and Luce Irigaray's. The latter is especially critical of Lacan's use of metaphor and develops notions such as the "two lips" and "the mucous" with the aim of rewriting and recreating the symbolic. These notions are either interpreted as metonymic (Whitford 1991, 180) or as subverting the binary metonymy/metaphor (Fuss 1990; Joy 2013).

Lacan introduced the notion of metaphor in his rereading of the processes of repression and displacement, both of which are for Freud the basic functions of the unconscious. As is well known for Lacan Freud's discovery anticipates modern linguistics (Lacan 2006, 578). He uncovers a relation between the laws governing the unconscious and the laws of the signifier: repression is related to metaphor, and displacement to metonymy. He thereby draws upon Jakobson's distinction between selection and combination, which in itself is a reinterpretation of a similar distinction made by de Saussure, and was related to Freud already by Jakobson himself. Lacan reorders the terms: metonymy corresponds to Jakobson's "combination," that is, it relates two terms *in presentia*. Metaphor, in contrast, relates two or more terms *in absentia.* Lacan defines the two terms as follows: Metonymy indicates "that it is the signifier-to-signifier connection that allows for the elision by which the signifier instates lack of being in the object-relation, using signification's referral value to invest it with the desire aiming at the lack that it supports" (Lacan 2006, 428). Metonymy, therefore, refers to the replacement of one term for another: it defers meaning, but in itself cannot explain the process of a sign gaining meaning. Lacan follows de Saussure in understanding language as not referring to reality but rather as a system in which there are no positive terms, only differences between signs. Metonymy thus characterizes the process of signification in language.

Yet, on the basis of metonymy alone language would not have any meaning: every sign would be replaced by another, in a continuous process. Metaphor for Lacan is then – surprisingly, and according to some inconsistently – the mechanism that explains the creation of a specific meaning. Metaphor indicates "that it is in the substitution of signifier for signifier that a signification effect is produced that is poetic or creative, in other words, that brings the signification in question into existence" (429). Metaphor refers to the process of substitution between signifiers that in themselves do not have a fixed, "natural" meaning. It forms, in other words, a momentary stop in the incessant gliding of signifiers, but a stop that is always unexpected and not predestined in the signifier.

Although critical of Lacan, the notions of metaphor and metonymy in French feminist philosophy come to play a part in the context of rewriting the (phallic) symbolic in order to create more possibilities for women to articulate their subjectivity. Irigaray's strategy of mimesis, for instance, in her early works, that aim at subversion of the phallogocentric discourse, can be seen as a metonymic strategy. Figurations named above, such as the two lips and the mucous, are part of this mimetic strategy. Irigaray herself writes that mimesis includes copying "anything at all, anyone at all, ... receiv[ing] all impressions, without appropriating them to oneself, and without adding any" (Irigaray 1985, 151). Margaret Whitford accordingly interprets Irigaray's philosophy as rejecting metaphor, because it fixes and puts the signifying process to a halt, while metonymy "allows for process" (Whitford 1991, 180). Irigaray, in Whitford's interpretation, would suggest a maternal genealogy based upon metonymic identification, instead of the paternal (Lacanian) genealogy based upon paternal metaphorization. Morny Joy, in contrast, names Irigaray's strategy one of displacement of the metonymy/metaphor scheme. Irigaray, instead of alluding to metonymy, would aim at metamorphosis. Her new verbalizations of the female body "realign the terms of reference regarding sameness and otherness" (Joy 2013, 78). Yet, as Judith Butler writes in *Bodies That Matter*, one can also ask whether Irigaray's strategy does not lead to a renewed consolidation of the place of the feminine, albeit as "the irruptive *chora*, that which cannot be figured, but which is necessary for any figuration" (Butler 1993, 48). Does the feminine in this interpretation not figure as the nonidentical, and is it not miming the excluding violence of the phallogocentric discourse, repeating it once again? Read as such, Irigaray's strategy would remain close to Lacan's metaphorization. On the other hand, however, naming the nonidentical metaphorically, identifying it as that which cannot be figured ("a volume without contours," as Irigaray writes in *Speculum*), seems to blow up the entire process of metaphorization in itself. The critical engagements with metaphor in feminist theory as such continue its operations.

References

Black, Max. 1962. *Models and Metaphors*. Ithaca, NY: Cornell University Press.

Black, Max. 1979. "More about Metaphor." In *Metaphor and Thought*, edited by Andrew Ortony, 19–41. Cambridge: Cambridge University Press.

Butler, Judith. 1993. *Bodies That Matter: On the Discursive Limits of "Sex"*. New York: Routledge.

Davidson, Donald. 1984. "What Metaphors Mean." In *Inquiries into Truth and Interpretation*, 245–264. Oxford: Oxford University Press.

84　Derrida, Jacques. 1982. "White Mythology: Metaphor in the Text of Philosophy." In *Margins of Philosophy*, translated by Alan Bass, 207–271. Chicago: University of Chicago Press.

Fuss, Diana. 1990. *Essentially Speaking: Feminism, Nature, and Difference*. New York: Routledge.

Hills, David. 2012. "Metaphor." *The Stanford Encyclopedia of Philosophy*. Accessed August 2015. http://plato.stanford.edu/archives/win2012/entries/metaphor.

Irigaray, Luce. 1985. *This Sex Which Is Not One*. Translated by Catherine Porter and Carolyn Burke. Ithaca, NY: Cornell University Press.

Joy, Morny. 2013. "Explorations in Otherness. Paul Ricoeur and Luce Irigaray." *Études Ricoeuriennes/Ricoeur Studies* 4 (1): 71–91.

Lacan, Jacques. 2006. *Écrits*. Translated by Bruce Fink. New York: Norton & Company.

Merriam-Webster Dictionary. n.d. "Metaphor." Accessed August 2015. http://www.merriam-webster.com/dictionary/Metaphor.

Nietzsche, Friedrich. (1873) 1999. "Über Wahrheit und Lüge im außermoralischen Sinn." In *Sämtliche Werke. Kritische Studienausgabe in 15 Bänden*. Vol. 1, edited by Giorgio Colli and Mazzino Montinari, 873–890. München: dtv.

Ricoeur, Paul. 1978. *The Rule of Metaphor*. Translated by Robert Czerny with Kathleen McLaughlin and John Costello. London: Routledge and Kegan Paul.

Theodorou, Stephanie. n.d. "Metaphor and Phenomenology." *The Internet Encyclopedia of Philosophy*. Accessed August 2015. http://www.iep.utm.edu/met-phen.

Whitford, Margaret. 1991. *Luce Irigaray: Philosophy in the Feminine*. London: Routledge.

Parrhesia

Kári Driscoll

Red Peter, the protagonist of Franz Kafka's "A Report for an Academy" has been summoned by the titular learned society to give an account of himself, or rather of his "previous life as an ape [*äffisches Vorleben*]" (Kafka 2007, 76). As he is quick to point out to the "esteemed gentlemen," however, it is also *their*, i.e., mankind's, simian prehistory:

> To speak frankly [*offen gesprochen*], as much as I like to employ figurative images for these things, to speak frankly [*offen*]: Your apedom [*Affentum*], gentlemen, to the extent that you have something of the sort behind you, cannot be more remote from you than mine is from me. (77)

Whereas Red Peter had described his transition from ape to man in the form of an elaborate, extended **metaphor** of human evolution as a horserace, now that he has reached the finish line, so to speak, it is important to speak frankly, lest the assembled scholars abrogate his hard-won post-simian status. In order to justify his inability to acquiesce to the Academy's request, he thus explicitly sets aside metaphor, and hence rhetorical embellishment, and instead stylises himself as someone who can – is able and permitted to – speak frankly or openly.

Red Peter is thus making use of *parrhesia*, the ancient Greek practice of frank speech, whereby the speaker, addressing an authority figure, issues a critique in the form of the unadorned truth about himself or another, at significant personal **risk**. Because the *parrhesiastes* is always in an inferior position to his interlocutor, who may be hurt or angered by the truth, *parrhesia* must be predicated on a sort of agreement or "contract," whereby the sovereign, "who has power but lacks the truth" (Foucault 2001, 32), promises not to punish the speaker, who does not, strictly speaking, have the authority to speak the truth with impunity, unless the sovereign grants it to him. There is always a risk that the sovereign will renege on this agreement, however, in which case he reveals himself to be a tyrant. *Parrhesia* is thus always a "game" (17) between the one who speaks the truth and the one who has the power to punish. Hence, in the most extreme case, *parrhesia* is a "'game' of life or death" (16). Thus, although *parrhesia* is cast as antithetical to rhetorical persuasion (12), and Red Peter constantly disavows any rhetorical embellishment in his speech, the report is rhetorical through and through, precisely in the way in which it establishes the speaker *as a subject* and demands that the sovereign body to whom the report is addressed recognise him as such. This performative aspect of this parrhesiastic contract is clearly evident when Red Peter, following his demurral, begins the account of his transition from ape to man by recalling his first lesson: "The first thing that I learned was to shake hands; the handshake signifies openness [*Offenheit*]. Now, today, at the high point of my career, let frank speech [*das offene Wort*] be coupled with that first handshake" (Kafka 2007, 77). The emphatic repetition of "*offen*" finds an echo in the ascription of "*Affen*tum" to the gentlemen of the Academy – a phonetic contagion that recurs thematically later on when Red Peter mentions, as an aside, that one of his first teachers had become apelike even as he himself was learning to become human (83). Thus, Red Peter's transition from animal to human is figured by a vocalic shift from *A* to *O*, "*Affentum*" to "*Offenheit*," but in laying claim to openness in this privileged sense, his ape(n)ness (animality) begins to haunt the text, attaching itself metaphorically to everyone else: from the members of the Academy, whose "apedom" Red Peter invokes in his own defence, to the "monkey" who gave him his "repulsive" name (78), and the hack journalist [*Windhund*, lit. whippet] who had dared to question whether Red Peter's "ape-nature" is truly fully "suppressed" (78), citing the latter's habit of pulling down his trousers to reveal the wound he suffered during his capture. The *parrhesiastes* not only tells the truth about himself and others, he also shows himself "in his natural nakedness" (Foucault 2010, 287). This nakedness is linked to a valorisation of animality, which is "taken up as a challenge, practiced as an exercise, and thrown in the face of others as a scandal" (Foucault 2011, 265). In exposing himself, the *parrhesiastes* challenges others to do the same, and to consider their own relationship to the truth. In the case of Red Peter, this is especially evident in his insistence that "I have the right to lower my pants in front of anyone I like; there is nothing to see there ... Everything is open and above board; there is nothing to hide; where it is a question of truth, every large-minded person casts off the fanciest manners" (Kafka 2007, 78).

Etymologically, *parrhesia* derives from *pan*, meaning "everything" and *rhema* or *rhesis*, "word, statement, or utterance," and means "to say everything." Hence, the *parrhesiastes* is "someone who says everything he has in mind: he does not hide anything, but opens his heart and mind completely to other people through his discourse ... The word *parrhesia*, then, refers to a type of relation-ship between the speaker and what he says" (Foucault 2001, 12). This relationship is characterised by a series of correspondences, first and foremost between the speaker's life (*bios*) and his words (*logos*). *Parrhesia* is thus linked to the art of living and the care of the self, of constructing a "straight life" (Foucault 2011, 265) or *bios philosophikos* in which *bios* is in complete harmony with *logos* – almost to the point of the radical honesty and openness attributed to the non-linguistic animal, which "conceals nothing and at every instant appears wholly as what it is" (Nietzsche 1997, 61). In the context of Red Peter's report, it is interesting to note that the first element in the word *parrhesia*, i.e., *pan* ("everything"), is also the name of the Greek god of nature, Pan, who is typically depicted as half-human, half-beast, and it is for this reason that *"Pan"* is also the name of the taxonomic genus that includes chimpanzees (*Pan troglodytes*) and bonobos (*Pan paniscus*) (see Tyler 2006). Hence, given the taxonomic confusion at work in Kafka's text, one might be so bold as to read *parrhesia* (Pan-rhesis) as "chimp-speak." This is particularly important given the link between *parrhesia* as self-care and as a response to the Delphic imperative to "know thyself" – which, as Giorgio Agamben notes, was the original species marker for man in Linnaeus's *Systema naturae*. The "knowledge" implied in *Homo sapiens* is thus a veiled imperative: "man is the animal that must recognize itself as human to be human" (Agamben 2004, 26). In asking the members of the Academy to recognise him as one of their own, Red Peter effectively hijacks the "anthropological machine" – which is a device for producing the recognition of the human through the inclusionary exclusion of the animal (33–38).

Parrhesia forms a nexus for the three fundamental axes of Foucault's philosophical endeavour, namely truth, power, and the subject. Furthermore, it stands at the root of the "critical tradition" (Foucault 2001, 170), precisely because it calls the subject into question, and, in this respect, represents one of the arts of "not being governed quite so much" which Foucault (2007, 29) defines as the basic gesture of the critical attitude (45). This is linked to "virtue" (43) – telling the truth, about oneself and about others, and specifically having the courage to position oneself as someone who tells the truth, is a virtuous (and in this sense *critical*) act of "desubjugation" (47), which does not imply total freedom from any coercion, but rather a critical re-assessment of the fundamental question of what I can become, given the "contemporary order of being" (Butler 2005, 30). This is why Red Peter is so adamant about the critical distinction between "freedom" and a "way out" (Kafka 2007, 79–80): in seeking a "way out" of his confinement, the best he can hope for is not to be governed "like that, not for that, not by them" etc. (Foucault 2007,

44). In this sense, *parrhesia* represents a critical repositioning or reconstitution of the self within the reigning discourse of power, which, in turn calls that discourse into question. Hence, *parrhesia* involves "problematisation" (Foucault 2001, 170), and, conversely, new opportunities for frank speech become available in moments of crisis, when certain forms of knowledge/power/subjectivity have become problematic, as was the case with the category of the human as the *zoon logon echon* at the time when Kafka wrote this text. In having Red Peter assert his ability and right to speak openly, the text in turn opens up an indeterminacy about who can speak in the first place – an indeterminacy which is of course inherent in the very history of *parrhesia*, since the freedom of speech it originally granted applied only to natural born male citizens; not women, children, immigrants, and certainly not animals. This is why it is impossible to separate *parrhesia* from rhetoric and performativity, since in claiming the right to speak freely, one presupposes the ability to speak and be heard, and, what is more, one obliges, by means of the *parrhesiastic* contract, the sovereign (in this case, man), to listen. The "risk" thus reveals the inherent precarity of everyone's right to speech – not only that of the *parrhesiastes*, the "beast," but that of the sovereign as well.

References

Agamben, Giorgio. 2004. *The Open: Man and Animal*. Translated by Kevin Attell. Stanford: Stanford University Press.

Butler, Judith. 2005. *Giving an Account of Oneself*. New York: Fordham University Press.

Foucault, Michel. 2001. *Fearless Speech*. Edited by Joseph Pearson. Los Angeles: Semiotext(e).

Foucault, Michel. 2007. "What Is Critique?", translated by Lysa Hochroth. In *The Politics of Truth*, edited by Sylvère Lotringer, 23–81. Los Angeles: Semiotext(e).

Foucault, Michel. 2010. *The Government of Self and Others: Lectures at the Collège de France 1982–1983*. Edited by Frédéric Gros and translated by Graham Burchell. Basingstoke: Palgrave Macmillan.

Foucault, Michel. 2011. *The Courage of the Truth (The Government of Self and Others II): Lectures at the Collège de France 1983–1984*. Edited by Frédéric Gros. Translated by Graham Burchell. Basingstoke: Palgrave Macmillan.

90   Kafka, Franz. 2007. *Kafka's Selected Stories*. Translated and edited by Stanley Corngold. New York: W. W. Norton.

Nietzsche, Friedrich. 1997. *Untimely Meditations*. Edited by Daniel Breazeale. Translated by R. J. Hollingdale. Cambridge: Cambridge University Press.

Tyler, Tom. 2006. "Four Hands Good, Two Hands Bad." *Parallax* 12 (1): 69–80.

Perspective

Esther Peeren

What is the perspective of critique? This question not only asks
from what perspective (point of view or standpoint) practices
of critique are developed, but also what perspective (outlook
or prospect) such practices offer. The Kantian notion of critique
saw it emerging from an externalized, superior view presumed
to be universal and comprehensive, and offering disinterested
judgment. In today's condition of global **entanglement** – "being
twisted together or entwined, involved with" (Nuttall 2009, 1) –
the claims to completeness and objectivity that inhere in this
notion of critique are more problematic than ever. At the same
time, concluding that such entanglement renders perspective
as a particularized point of view or standpoint irrelevant and
perspective as outlook or prospect impossible would play into
neoliberal discourses that present globalization as an ungras-
pable process for the excesses of which no **responsibility** can be
assigned and to which there is no alternative.

While perspective as point of view or standpoint remains relevant to mark the embodied situatedness of critique, it needs
to be redefined from a stable point of view that preexists and
remains separate from what it perceives to something dynamic
that enters into a reciprocal relationship with what it perceives
and is therefore subject to constant feedback and re-vision. As
outlook or prospect, moreover, it should be seen as **speculative**

and open rather than as offering a determinate **vision** of what will be. No perspective can oversee global entanglement to obtain a full, independent picture of its present status or future, but at the same time global entanglement is not undifferentiated. There are perspectives *of* entanglement – human and nonhuman – that mark differences, distances, possibilities, and tensions within it. Perspective also shifts as soon as matters move and is always multiple: global entanglement appears differently from the Global South than from the Global North, even if these per-spectives only emerge in their "intra-action" (Barad 2007, 33).

A text that marks the importance of acknowledging differences in perspective as catalysts for **immanent** critique in a particularly clear and forceful manner is Virginia Woolf's epistolary essay *Three Guineas* (1938), which stages a feminist, pacifist, and (to some extent) anti-colonial intervention in the context of the unfolding Spanish Civil War and the looming threat of German and Italian fascism. Woolf begins by insisting to her interlocutor, introduced as "an educated man" who had written her asking for a donation to help prevent war, that "though we look at the same things, we see them differently" (Woolf 1996, 109 and 111). This statement, which summarily rejects the possibility of absolute judgment or complete consensus, resonates with Mikhail Bakhtin's phenomenological contention that, because two people cannot be situated in exactly the same place at the same time, "there are as many different worlds of the event as there are individual centers of answerability, i.e., unique par-ticipative (unindifferent) selves" (Bakhtin 1993, 45). At the same time, it ties these **worlds** or "faces" of the event (45) to collective social positions, which Woolf proceeds to elaborate in terms of structural gender inequality.

Thus, she has the "educated man's daughter," having obtained her own income ("the sacred coin"), ask herself: "What shall I do with it? What do I see with it?" (Woolf 1996, 123). In answering this question – "Through that light we may guess everything she saw looked different" (111) – Woolf initially envisions perspective as something separate from the eye, interfering with what it registers. However, the rest of "Three Guineas," especially in its recurring references to several photographs she has received portraying dead bodies from the Spanish Civil War, suggests that it is not a question of choosing or being made to see the world *through* a certain light that is, as it were, added onto a universal way of seeing. Instead, it is a question of one's way of seeing emerging *as* a particular light on the world due to one's entanglement in gender, class, and colonial relations. Such a perspective can be expressed and brought into negotiation with other perspectives, but it cannot simply be transferred or relinquished. In Bakhtin's terms, since it emerges from an active participation in "Being-as-event," one is bound to this perspective by a fundamental answerability or *"non-alibi-in-Being"* (Bakhtin 1993, 31 and 40). It is, then, not merely that everything looks different to the educated man's daughter after she secures "the sacred coin," but that, as an educated man's daughter, she already participated in and thus saw the world differently from others.

When Woolf first describes the Spanish Civil War photographs (which, significantly, are not reproduced in the text), she notes that "photographs, of course, are not arguments addressed to the reason; they are simply statements of fact addressed to the eye" (Woolf 1996, 117). She continues to detail how, when looking at the photographs, via the physiological trajectory that connects eye to brain to nervous system, "some fusion takes place within us; however different the education, the traditions behind us, our sensations are the same; and they are violent" (118). Four aspects, however, immediately disrupt the alleged facticity of the photographs and their supposedly unitary and unifying interpretation through the universally shared physiology of human sight. First, the rhetorical overkill of the interjection "of course," more than confirming the validity of Woolf's statement, incites the reader to question it. Second, her remark that it is the Spanish Government that sends these photographs "with patient pertinacity about twice a week" invests them with a particular, partial perspective on – or "face" of – the Civil War (117). Third, the speculative description of one of the photographs – "This morning's collection contains the photograph of *what might be* a man's body, or a woman's; it is so mutilated that *it might*, on the other hand, *be* the body of a pig" (117, emphasis added) – installs doubt as to photography's objective nature. Finally, there is the formulation of the last sentence of the photographs' first textual appearance: "For now at last we are looking at the same picture; we are seeing with you the same dead bodies, the same ruined houses" (118). This makes explicit the temporal dimension that inhabits the fusion of perspectives that is said to take place; seeing the same thing in a photograph is not a self-evident consequence of the medium, but an interpretative process involving the echoing of the other's words whose end-point – "at last" – is unstable – "for now."

The fusion that is really a delayed echoing of another's perspective becomes subject to fission – splitting – as alternative connections are "brought out" between the dead, mutilated bodies in the photographs and the "prostituted culture and intellectual slavery" (213) of women. These connections are not visibly present in the photographs, but emerge as a result of a sustained engagement between them and the perspective or "face" brought to bear on it. Illuminated by the light of Woolf's way of seeing as an educated man's daughter, the photographs are made to show more than they previously did and become critical tools, no longer statements of fact, but openings for discussion and dissent.

Accordingly, the final appearance of the Spanish Civil War photograph with the dead bodies reveals it as no longer showing the same: "as this letter has gone on, adding fact to fact, another picture has imposed itself upon the foreground" (266). The dead bodies and ruined houses have been superimposed by "the figure of a man" or even "Man himself" – "called in German and Italian Führer or Duce; in our own language Tyrant or Dictator" (266). The connections unearthed by looking at the world from the perspective of the daughters of educated men, a perspective that claims difference and validity, materialize in the photograph, which now "suggests" (a notably nonfactual term) "that we are not passive spectators doomed to unresisting obedience but by our thoughts and actions can ourselves change that figure. A common interest unites us; it is one world, one life. How essential it is that we should realize that unity the dead bodies, the ruined houses prove" (267).

There is indeed a common interest, but this interest is not served by the fusion of perspectives or by an insistence on the photograph's unequivocal factuality. As Woolf notes, "opinions differ" on the man (Hitler? Mussolini?) who has invaded the pictorial plane and she only has her addressee's letter "to prove that *to you* the picture is the picture of evil" (267, emphasis added). Even if they could agree that what the photograph shows is indeed evil and that this evil must be destroyed, their ways of going about this may be – *must be* – different, as they arrive at their critical perspective (as point of view or standpoint) and at the perspective (as outlook or prospect) it yields with **regard** to how to prevent war in the future from differently situated entanglements that also make them answerable in divergent ways.

This brief reading of "Three Guineas" shows how accepting that "critique is always of the world, it is always situated and expressed from within worldly engagements – and as such also always itself an expression of the world" (Kaiser, Thiele, and Bunz 2014) does not do away with the question of the perspective of critique, but makes it more urgent. Critique is an expression of the world, yet emerges from a particular position and moment within this world's becoming. Recognizing, with Bakhtin, that the events through which this becoming unfolds always have many "faces" that may yield different critiques and answerabilities is imperative, especially as it has become clear that even in a world widely recognized as globally entangled, certain of these "faces" continue to be privileged and dominant, while others are obscured, overlooked, or disavowed.

References

Bakhtin, Mikhail. 1993. *Toward a Philosophy of the Act*. Edited by Vadim Liapunov and Michael Holquist. Translated and notes by Vadim Liapunov. Austin: University of Texas Press.

Barad, Karen. 2007. *Meeting the Universe Halfway: Quantum Physics and the Entanglement of Matter and Meaning*. Durham: Duke University Press.

Kaiser, Birgit Mara, Kathrin Thiele, and Mercedes Bunz. 2014. "What is Critique in the 21st Century? Discussing *Terra Critica*: A Conversation between Birgit Mara Kaiser, Kathrin Thiele and Mercedes Bunz." *Terracritica.net*. Accessed November 15, 2015. http://terracritica.net/interview/.

Nuttall, Sarah. 2009. *Entanglement: Literary and Cultural Reflections on Post-Apartheid*. Johannesburg: Wits University Press.

Woolf, Virginia. 1996. *A Room of One's Own & Three Guineas*. With an introduction by Hermione Lee. London: Vintage.

Plastic/ity

Jennifer A. Wagner-Lawlor

In an essay entitled "Plastic," appearing in his seminal collection, *Mythologies* (1957), cultural philosopher Roland Barthes takes a hard look at what he presciently recognizes as the visible form of the modern death drive: plastic. This bold claim might seem incommensurate with both the brevity of his essay (barely four pages) and with its celebratory, even triumphalist tone. But irony lies just below the rhetorical surface. Barthes's essay is at once a celebration and a condemnation of this artificial material, invented a century before, but suitable for use as a consumer product material only after World War II. By the mid-1950s the petroleum, chemical, and manufacturing industries, foreseeing unprecedented profits, promoted plastic as the signature material of modernity, and enlisted the genius of the bourgeoning advertising industry to tell the story of this remarkably versatile, durable, "miraculous" substance (Barthes 1957, 193).

This story, as much as the substance itself, is Barthes's subject: the myth, in short, of plastic. It is at once an origin myth of a consumer imperium, and a cultural myth of manifest destiny. The philosopher's interest in "mythologies" resides, however, in the way such narratives disguise a barer reality. Obscured by the symbolic economy of a "plasticized" (195) world of consumers, buoyed by innovation and so-called convenience, Barthes sees a toxic underside: a world of users with an instrumentalist attitude toward other human beings, toward nature, toward life itself. It is not just the aesthetics of plastic that Barthes rejects. While he clearly does dislike things made of plastic – cheap, lifeless, fake copies of things once made with natural material – at stake is clearly something more abstract: the "conceptual matter" of plastic, which is to say the plasticity, of the individual and the social mind, in the post-war, modern age. Barthes apprehends that plastic and plasticity can reveal a great deal about freedom and unfreedom in a modern mass culture. Intending, as he says, to "live to the full the contradiction of my time" (xii), Barthes's examination of plastic as at once miraculous and utterly banal is exemplary of "myth today," which will always, upon scrutiny, "give the lie" to ideological rhetoric. Acknowledging there is no complete escape from ideology, Barthes can at least hold out his project as a kind of embodied critique.

Fifty years on, philosopher Catherine Malabou is producing a series of studies concerning plasticity grounded in her earliest work on Hegel. Her research into neuroplasticity is laid out in *What Should We Do with Our Brain?* (2004) and its sequel, *Ontology of the Accident: An Essay on Destructive Plasticity* (2009). Malabou rarely speaks of plastic products per se, with the exception of the explosive *plastique*, as a counter-figure to plastic's flexibility. In her essay "The Living Room: Plasticity and Hospitality" (2013), though, she does point toward the "range of meanings" the words plasticity and plastic can embrace, including "all the various forms of 'plastic' in our world [from the 'plastic arts' to plastic wood, plastic money, plastic explosives]" (n.p.). She acknowledges Barthes's warning that "plastic's ability to become anything at all may reduce anything to nothing by dissolving all differences.... Because plastic never presents itself without form, plastic is always thought as a factor of identification, standardisation, globalisation, and never as a possible welcome of the other" (n.p.).

Both philosophers see in the unique materiality of plastic a visual metaphor for the ontological paradox of plasticity. While of different generations in French philosophical thought, Barthes and Malabou face a common enemy: late-capitalist universalism. This universalism realizes itself through replication of the same, rather than through (re)production of the same with-a-difference (in Kantian terms, the difference between a reproductive and productive imagination). Malabou also follows Barthes in associating plastic's economic and political dimensions to a certain form of corporatized aesthetic, expressed in the "goods" of the market, and in the market's drive for "more and better" (Atwood 2003, 296). More and better stuff engendering more and better consumers is the contemporary dream of a consumer utopia – its microcosm materialized in each and every super-market (the bigger and cheaper, the better). All this Barthes discerns already in his essay's closing remarks, which posit that "the world" of nonhuman things, including the domain of nature, "*can* be plasticized" (Barthes 2011, 195); speaking of more and better, "even life itself" (195), with the invention, in the 1950s, of plastic aortas. A world with a hard plastic heart.

Barthes's description of plastic's mythic vitality and "quick-change talent" (194) heralds Jane Bennett's characterization of "the enchantment of modern life" (Bennett 2010, xi–xii). Barthes would have understood Bennett's emphasis on the power of such "enchantment" to turn us in two directions: "The first toward the humans who *feel* enchanted and whose agentic capacities may be thereby strengthened" (Bennett, xii). Think of the powerful pull of "pride of ownership" among owners of luxury products (even plastic ones). Luxury consumers or not, the urge for owning the latest model, the valuing of novelty and replacement is part of the magic. Here is Barthes:

> Thus, more than a substance, plastic is the very idea of its infinite transformation…. Plastic remains *completely impregnated by this astonishment*: it is less an object than the trace of a movement. And since this movement is here virtually infinite … plastic is, ultimately, a spectacle to be deciphered. (1957, 193)

The "idea of [plastic's] infinite transformation" (193) is our enchantment with ourselves, astonished by our capacity to transform, as if alchemically, the natural into the manmade. Barthes illuminates, over fifty years before Bennett, the entanglement of what Bennett calls "fantasies of a human uniqueness ... of escape from materiality, or of mastery of nature" with a "philosophical project of naming where subjectivity begins and ends" (Bennett, ix). The second direction Bennett indicates is "toward the agency of the things that *produce* (helpful, harmful) effects in human and other bodies" (xii). The overall pessimism of "Plastic" and one or two related *Mythologies* pieces may derive from Barthes's underdeveloped notion of *material agency*, which both Malabou and Bennett strive to provide. Without a notion of material agency, where can Barthes look for hope that our culture would get past the specter of modernity's instrumentalized usage of the earth, its universal dis-**regard** of the nonhuman? Wherein would lie an elemental force of critique, beyond mere words?

Malabou theorizes being itself – life – as plastic. This may sound metaphorical but it is not. Malabou's philosophical project materializes the vital agency of "gray matter" in its resistance to negative plasticity – that is, of hardened forms. Neuroscience reveals the brain's positive plasticity in its capacity for repair and resiliency. Neuroplasticity *means*, Malabou can claim without irony, that plasticity *is life*. Brain plasticity and the faculty of imagination must be co-constitutive; hospitality, the welcoming of the other, depends upon both. With the advantage of science that Barthes did not have, Malabou elucidates his ironical presentation of the "alchemical" (thus magical, mystical, mythical) essence of plastic/ity as the idea of transformation. Because the concept of plasticity embraces the work of making meaning (in the process of taking form) and of resisting meaning (in the potentiality for deforming, reforming), Malabou locates firmer ground for critique. Plasticity does not motivate but does allow for, make space for, criticality.

Barthes's language of magic and myth metaphorizes what Malabou would make as literal as possible: the paradox of plasticity as at once informing and deforming, as well as *re*forming and transforming. Recognizing the social dimension of this analysis of plasticity, Malabou can address cultural remediation quite specifically, throwing down "the plastic challenge" (2004, 82) in contemporary terms. Her work thus extends Barthes' sublimated perceptions of a plastic future that is not a capitalist caricature of utopia, or any other vision of a perfect(ed) and thus permanent ideological hegemony. This is not what our brain wants. "Between the upsurge and the explosion of form, subjectivity issues the plastic challenge," Malabou says, *"to do what they undoubtedly have never done: construct and entertain a relation with their brain as the image of a world to come"* (82, emphasis added). Nor is it, Bennett proposes, what "the world" wants. "The world" – or matter – has agency as well, a vitalism that resists humanity's "earth-destroying fantasies of conquest and consumption" (2010, ix), which is so blatantly figured in our toxic love affair with plastic (Freinkel 2011).

References

Atwood, Margaret. 2003. *Oryx and Crake*. New York: Anchor Books.

Barthes, Roland. (1957) 2011. *Mythologies*. Translated by Richard Howard and Annette Lavers. New York: Hill and Wang.

Bennett, Jane. 2010. *Vibrant Matter: A Political Ecology of Things*. Durham: Duke University Press.

Freinkel, Susan. 2011. *Plastic: A Toxic Love Story*. Boston: Houghton Mifflin Harcourt.

Malabou, Catherine. 2000. "The Future of Hegel: Plasticity, Temporality, Dialectic," translated by Lisabeth During. *Hypatia* 15 (4): 196–221.

Malabou, Catherine. 2004. *What Should We Do With Our Brain?* Translated by Sebastian Rand. New York: Fordham University Press.

Malabou, Catherine. 2009. *Ontology of the Accident: An Essay on Destructive Plasticity*. Translated by Carolyn Shread. Cambridge, UK: Polity Press.

Malabou, Catherine. 2013. "The Living Room: Hospitality and Plasticity." *Springerin.at*. Accessed July 23, 2014. http://www.springerin.at/dyn/heft.php?id=80&pos=1&textid=2732&lang=en.

Play

Sybrandt van Keulen

What does it take to apprehend how playing goes? Playing games seems to be about the only way to find out how even language games go, yet it is a mistake to think that the dynamics of inventing and performing play can be understood purely through doing games. Moreover, philosophy of play is anything but game theory.

Immanuel Kant's famous conception of play might function as an opening gambit. Distancing himself from the tradition of the *je ne sais quoi*, a tradition emerging from Gottfried W. Leibniz's *Monadology* and revolving around the epistemological status of so-called confused perceptions and ideas (see also Kaiser 2011, 17), Kant argues the following: Although it is not of the order of knowing what sets our powers of cognition into play, the related state of mind has everything to do with an undeniable "feeling of life" (*Lebensgefühl*; Kant 2000, § 1). To understand how this force touches us, we should not so much heed *what* exactly affects us but rather perceive that this "élan" (*Belebung*; § 9) is an effect of a particular "relation between those powers to each other" (§ 9). With this "free play of the powers of representation" (§ 9) a specific reciprocal relationship is meant: a relationship in which **powers** are brought to swing and thus play with each other.

To be able to weigh Kant's words "free" and "power," it should be pointed out that we are not dealing in any case with a power-free relationship. However, the way those powers or forces interact with each other could be called free of domination, with the specification that "free" does not mean an *absence* but rather a certain *dynamical distribution* of dominance: None of those powers should dominate in a static, autocratic sense; they are engaged in a complex drama and, until the final showdown, so to speak, they should remain evenly matched. This implies that the particular feeling the action of playing brings about is intertwined with duration, that it is not similar to an immediate **affect**, moreover, that it is not controlled by any particular instant profit. It may be noted that the energy that nourishes the playful élan for a significant extent, is drawn from the deferral of a final closure. One could speak of a successfully executed **process** of unbalance and rebalance, as long as pleasure lingers.

Now I have touched upon some dynamical aspects of playing, attention could be given to a few characteristics of the force that sets up the playground. In one way or another we talk about a force that establishes the necessary confines to let that specific élan happen, or which operates as supervisory authority of constitutive contours. In this respect the words "free" and "power" acquire their full meaning. In Kantian parlance the idea of a well-tempered free play can only take place within the limits of an arena carefully designed by the supervisory power of reason. This Kantian use of "free" comes close to the English meaning of "fair": free from self-interest, prejudice, or favoritism (Merriam-Webster dictionary).

Free play and the limiting force of reason are two sides of the same coin. According to Kant playing any game can only be pleasurable – that is, rewarding in the lively activity itself – if the intended relationship is not determined by any partiality. The implied supervision of reason resides in her assumed exclusive arbitral power to keep the actions of the playing parties within required limits. This could be called the condition of unconditionality, with reason as its sole superintendent. Free play has to do with a state of affairs that cannot be effectuated in one go, which is perhaps why reason cannot do anything else but meticulously repeat itself in her limitative activity. However, play equals the sense of going on *without end*, animation forever.

Kant has a keen eye for a variety of powers, such as intuition, productive imagination, and spirit (*Geist, esprit),* producing the wealth of life, yet he also strongly suggests that he is terrified of those powers embodied in one source named *genius* that sets free a poetico-**metaphorical** overabundance; a confusing waver, perhaps for Kant's feeling even potentially a threatening power – like a swarm of bees – that requires censorship and containment. As soon as the reasonable Self fears no longer being able to maintain his lofty arbitral position, being as it appears overwhelmingly surrounded by at least equally powerful forces, the sharing game *needs* to end. The power of genius turns out to give Kant the impression of a dangerous, because unsubduable, anarchistic source of "lawless freedom, nothing but nonsense"; it therefore should be brought "in line with the understanding" by "clipping its wings and making it well behaved or polished"; hence, "if anything must be sacrificed in the conflict of the two properties in one product, it must rather be on the side of genius" (§ 50). In the end genius seems to impel the fellow player from before, so-called understanding (with the power of reason in the background, because the collaboration of understanding and reason goes per definition *without* play) to a unilateral, eliminatory intervention. That is to say, a crucial proof of incapacity with regard to the power of reason seems to be that reason *itself* is unable to take part in a reciprocal, playful relationship without end or purpose. Playing *according* the rules of reason – so the command seems – and not playing *with* them. Gradually framed by reason's drive for mastery, the character or persona called genius is endowed with a subordinate role in a *logocentric configuration* – finally genius is stripped of any access (which is an excess in Kant's perspective) to political ruling power.

To what end? What else could there be in and beyond the game of reason?

Michel Foucault's analysis of the agonistic structure of the classical Greek erotics of the fourth century B.C.E. provide the terms required to problematize the consequences outlined above. Foucault's aim is not forging universally valid imperatives in order to curtail efflorescent unilateral power, he rather wants to provide an understanding of the stakes of "the purposeful art of a freedom perceived as a power game" (1990, 253). The complexity of this game is based on the reciprocal dynamics of an "elliptical configuration" (203) comprising two parties that are both becoming the centers of a "possible conversion – an ethically necessary and socially useful one – of the bond of love (doomed to disappear) into a relation of friendship, of *philia*" (201). The purpose of this rocking game seems apparently not a state of dominance of one party over the other but rather a permanent exercise in self-mastery combined with a certain care for the other. The principle of regulation should be sought in the relation itself, in "a sharing of thoughts and existence, mutual benevolence," culminating in "cultivation of indestructible friendship" (201). The point at issue can clearly be understood as critical towards the Kantian framework of reason, because it is not "... the sense of measure that one brings to one's own power, but the best way to measure one's strength against the power of others while ensuring one's own mastery over oneself ..." (212). Foucault's findings imply a critical stance in particular with regard to Kant's unilateral view on political power: In Foucault's mind good governance up to the highest level should take the shape of elliptical relationships.

As appealing Foucault's ideal of indestructible friendship might be, it is at the same time only a fraction less problematic as Kant's lofty game of reason. In order to understand *any* friendship as deconstructable, two questions of Derrida in his reading of Kant – also with regard to the consensus between reason and genius I already referred to above – seem relevant:

What can deeply bind the two opposing parties and procure for them a neutral ground of reconciliation for speaking together again in a fitting tone? In other words, what do they together exclude as the inadmissible itself? (Derrida 1999, 142).

In the case of the Greek friendship the inadmissible is evidently feminine: women did not have access to political governance. Yet in order to preserve the value of the notion of "configuration," this binding structure could be critically understood as a relationship without *one* end, referring to both hetero- and homosexual relations, and relations from another nature, yet unknown to us. The critical impulse, which gets hegemonic power relations at play, cannot be single – neither exclusively human, nor miraculous or accidental. Thus the sense of the notion of end comes to the fore as an opportunity to problematize the difference between closure and end. The activity of play could effectively happen under the condition that the so-called "neutral" playground can never be regarded as a *fait accompli*. Hence, a play without cognitive certainty, a friendship without a determined goal, and admiration without one eschatological end: an "end without end" (168). The immediate art historical association could be *l'art pour l'art* or *Dada*, yet an extension of this association would be purposiveness in its daring multiplicity. The *telos* of deconstruction, assumed that there is one, would be then to both instigate and welcome *divining configurations* of perhaps even hazard games between so-called secular and religious players, to effectuate instances of timely and untimely suspension.

References

Derrida, Jacques. 1999. "On a Newly Arisen Apocalyptic Tone in Philosophy," translated by John Leavey Jr. In *Raising the Tone of Philosophy: Late Essays by Immanuel Kant, Transformative Critique by Jacques Derrida,* edited by Peter Fenves, 117–171. Baltimore: The Johns Hopkins University Press.

Foucault, Michel. 1990. *The Use of Pleasure.* Vol. 2 of *The History of Sexuality.* Translated by Robert Hurley. New York: Vintage Books.

108   Kaiser, Birgit Mara. 2011. *Figures of Simplicity: Sensation and Thinking in Kleist and Melville,* New York: Suny Press.

Kant, Immanuel. 2000. *Critique of the Power of Judgment.* Translated by Paul Guyer and Eric Matthews. Cambridge: Cambridge University Press.

Power

Leonard Lawlor

It seems that there are two senses to the word "power." The first sense consists in having the force to oppress and repress others. Here, as indicated by the verb "have," power is a possession, and it aims at possession. If critique aims its weapons at anything, it is this sort of possessive power. As we shall see, repressive and possessive power appears to be a reaction to what in power cannot be controlled, predicted, and programmed in advance, like freedom.

Indeed, repressive power always implies some modicum of freedom; no one exercises power over another unless the other has possibilities of action (Foucault 2000, 342). There is no reason to repress and possess, unless the other is able to do something arbitrarily. Because all human and nonhuman animals have at least a modicum of freedom, we are very familiar with regimes of power that repress. However, thanks to Foucault, we know that forces do not only repress (1977, 27). The very same forces are able to produce. Through a kind of technique, these forces are able to make forms of subjectivity, they make an interior life or a soul, through which a person represses his own powers. These are techniques of habituation. These techniques can be so powerful that the habits they form, including habits of thinking, work upon us almost unconsciously. Through the idea of habituation techniques, Foucault famously reverses the traditional relation of the body and the soul (30). Under a regime of productive power (an educational system, for example), it is not the body that is the prison of the soul. It is the soul that is the prison of the body, of what the body can do. For Foucault, both repressive and productive powers require a kind of "micro-analysis" (or genealogy), which would disclose the complex relations through which power passes; it would disclose a whole "microphysics" of power (29).

Through the productive side of repressive power, we come to power's second sense. The second sense of "power" is potentiality. We must not immediately associate the word "potentiality" to the Aristotelian schema of potentiality-actuality. Of course, like Aristotle, we must speak of the actualization of power. However, in this sense of power, the actualization is not teleological. Because actualization is not aimed at a determinate purpose, Gilles Deleuze, for instance, calls actualization "counter-actualization" (1990, 148–153). Counter-actualization outstrips any possibility we are able to imagine (148–153). The non-teleological nature of counter-actualization gives the word "power" a profound sense. To understand this more profound sense, we must turn to Sigmund Freud.

"Power" is not part of Freud's psychoanalytic lexicon (Jean Laplanche and Jean-Bertrand Pontalis do not list "power" in their account of Freud's vocabulary [1973]). Instead, Freud speaks of drives (*Triebe*, a term also translated into English as "instincts") and "forces" (*Kräfte*) (Freud 1997, 83–103). Freud shows how unconscious drives and their force set up barriers but also break through the barriers (128–134). These forces are unconscious, that is, they are not given to consciousness. They never present themselves as such in visibility. Never present as such, the forces grant us access to them only through their effects. Our access to them is only ever mediated. Because our access to the forces is only ever mediated, we cannot control them. Out of our control, the forces seem to run on their own. Here, we can appropriate dream **experience**, which, for Freud, is the crucial example of our

access to these forces. In dreams, of course, the images that are
produced come from elsewhere; we cannot make or consciously
will dream images to come to our minds while asleep. In addition,
the images that do appear in dream never fail to surprise us. The
forces that produce dream images seem to be like **technologies**
– especially our contemporary technologies –, which all too
frequently run against our conscious desires and will, producing
effects we could have never predicted. Power in the sense of
potentiality, therefore, produces effects that we can neither control nor predict.

The potentiality sense of power produces effects that go
beyond our own forces and powers. The effects that the above-
mentioned technologies automatically produce are like texts
that continue to produce readings that the author cannot control
and could not have predicted. As Derrida would say, like writing,
power, in the sense of potentiality (a kind of "archi-writing"),
effectuates or actualizes itself; and, it actualizes itself without a
purpose and never entirely (2011, 73). Like the machines that run
without human intervention, potentiality always has a reserve of
virtual effects. Therefore, we can see now that the second sense
of power involves two components.

On the one hand, there is the automatic component; on the other,
there is the unpredictability component. Potentiality happens
on its own, and it happens in unforeseen ways. Happening on its
own, potentiality, when it is experienced, forces us to ask what
happened. And, happening unpredictably, potentiality makes us
ask the question of what is going to happen. But we do not know
with certainty the answer to these two questions. What "might
be" is a question that remains unanswered and unanswerable
in any definitive way. With its sense of chance, "perhaps" is the
only answer we can formulate. In fact, in order to have even a
sense of the potentiality sense of power, we must, with Derrida,
imagine that what remains virtual in power is something that is
impossible. The impossible within the possible is the meaning
of the word *"peut-être"* for Derrida (1997, 28–29). Therefore,

including the possibility of what is impossible, power seems to be even more powerful than a collection of pre-formed possibilities simply waiting for realization. We come now to one of the most important conclusions of the analysis in which we have been engaged: through its automaticity and through its unpredictability, the experience of potentiality is at once both the experience of power and the experience of powerlessness. It is the experience of power because when one produces a repeatable form (as in writing), one knows that it will produce unforeseen events; it is the experience of powerlessness because the events, being unforeseeable, cannot be controlled. Powerlessness in the face of unpredictable power is power's most profound sense.

If the potentiality sense of power is really powerlessness, then one question becomes pressing. What sorts of reaction are possible to the experience of that which we cannot dominate and predict? This question is the question of critique. As we have seen already, one reaction is the negative reaction of repression. It strives to control, predict, and program in advance that which cannot be controlled, predicted, and programmed. This negative reaction is a sort of counter-actualization. But here the word "counter" is taken in its most destructive sense. It is a reaction of hatred. Thankfully, there is another reaction, which is **affirmative**.

The affirmative reaction looks like this: the work of critique consists in unearthing or deterritorializing the unconscious techniques that function in us. They must be made thinkable, even if only in a mediated mode. We must bring to light the ways we have been controlled, how we have been made to control ourselves, and especially how we have compromised with the forces of destruction. Through this process of deterritorializing, we experience pain, anguish, or perhaps shame. In fact, there is no deconstruction without the experience of pain. Pain is even perhaps the sign of a "successful" deconstruction. Then, as conscious or at least semi-conscious, the techniques themselves must be investigated. We must investigate them in order to bring to light what still lies potential or virtual within them. For example, any natural language contains possibilities of speaking, which are latent within the taught and imposed forms of the language. As Deleuze and Guattari have shown, a major and dominant language like English must not be treated in terms of constants and universals. It must be treated in terms of variables and variations (1987, 75–110). When we expose latent possibilities of variation, when we make a language "**stutter**," as Deleuze and Guattari would say, we experience the variations as beyond our control. When we experience this powerlessness, we must not repress the possibilities; we must release them and let them go as far as they are able to, farther than any possibility we can imagine. "Perhaps," they will go so far as to actualize the impossible, producing a counter-actualization.

Like the repression of the forces, the liberation of them is a counter-actualization. But here the sense of "counter" is not that of repression but of "up against." We must make ourselves be exposed, and come to be as close as possible to what the techniques are able to produce. We must put ourselves in the closest proximity to the possibilities as possible – in order to release them and let them be free. Letting the forces be free is the true meaning of affirmation. And it might be the true meaning of **responsibility**.

References

Deleuze, Gilles. 1990. *Logic of Sense*. Edited by Constantin Boundas. Translated by Mark Lester with Charles Stivale. New York: Columbia University Press.

Deleuze, Gilles, and Félix Guattari. 1987. *A Thousand Plateaus*. Translated by Brian Massumi. Minneapolis: University of Minnesota Press.

Derrida, Jacques. (1977) 1997. *Politics of Friendship*. Translated by George Collins. London: Verso Books.

Derrida, Jacques. 2011. *Voice and Phenomenon*. Translated by Leonard Lawlor. Evanston: Northwestern University Press.

Freud, Sigmund. 1997. *General Psychological Theory*. Edited by Philip Rieff. New York: Touchstone Simon and Schuster.

114   Foucault, Michel. 1977. *Discipline and Punish: The Birth of the Prison*. Translated by Alan Sheridan. New York: Vintage.

Foucault, Michel. 2000. *The Essential Works of Foucault 1954–1984*. Vol. 3, *Power*. Edited by James D. Faubion. New York: The Free Press.

Laplanche, Jean, and Jean-Bertrand Pontalis. 1973. *The Language of Psychoanalysis*. Translated by Donald Nicholson-Smith. New York: Norton.

Process

Melanie Sehgal

Critique strives for change, which classically has been thought of in terms of radical disruption. Today, hope for a revolution, for changing everything at once, seems in blatant mismatch with a world of tightly interlocked processes that traverse the political and natural, the individual and collective. One could say that critique in its modern face presupposed a particular spatiotemporal constellation that no longer seems to hold: a static world in which it was possible to practice critique in the sense of *krinein* – to separate and select, to discern between good and bad, to dispute, to judge (see **Symptomatology**). Critique in this sense implies a position that is distinct from, outside of the situation it is looking at. Only from this position is it possible to effect, in an all-encompassing move, radical change. Rethinking critique beyond modern parameters implies rethinking this spatiotemporal constellation – it implies a metaphysics of process instead of a metaphysics of static and simple location. It is thus necessary to reconsider the notion of process itself.

To conceptualize process was always a difficult task for philosophy from antiquity onwards. Within modern habits of thought an implicit generalization of Newtonian physics rein-forced a privilege of the static over process. Matter, following Newton, is self-identical and simply located, it is in one place at one moment. The most fundamental and concrete aspect of nature is considered to be devoid of process. Such a metaphysics of simple location and its spatio-temporal coordinates inform modern strategies of critique: experience – which implies movement – is separated from reality itself, and this reality can then only be disclosed by knowledge. The movement of critique in this sense disqualifies experiential knowledge in favor of what conditions it and what, from this perspective, is "really real."

The turn of the twentieth century, however, saw radical challenges to the Newtonian framework, most notably by quantum physics. In consequence, new philosophical attempts at thinking process have been made, for example, by Henri Bergson and Georges Canguilhem, by the German *Lebensphilosophien*, and the American Pragmatists. At the core of these attempts lies the problem whether and how conceptual knowledge of processes is actually possible. Do concepts necessarily fail to capture the time-bound, fleeting nature of processes, fixating what is in flux and hence missing the essential feature they wish to represent? It seems that thinking about processes automatically implies an anti-intellectualist stance. The mind is, following Bergson's famous metaphor, like a cinematograph that takes stills of the flow of reality, but – in its attempt to piece them together after the fact – is bound to fail. It is due to this nature of the mind, that we need to "invert our accustomed habits of thought" in order to adequately represent reality as it is: in process. Bergson does not question two central presuppositions, however, that are implicit to his argument: The assumption that reality is something that needs to be *represented* as well as that it is simply given, rather than something that within a theoretical construction needs to be *posited*.

Can we conceive of process without falling into such a constitutional anti-intellectualism? Can we think of it not as "radical change" or "disruption," but in terms that are more adequate to the interlocked processes we experience today, and in terms that also give us tools to make use of these processes – in order to actively shape them and give them the directions we desire?

When rethinking critique as a situated practice, we need to think about different ways of conceptualizing process as well as to reconsider the status and function of conceptual knowledge, its procedures and givens. In other words, the question of "process" implies an ontological and a methodological dimension. Alfred North Whitehead, as a reader of Bergson and in contrast to him, develops a **speculative** notion of process that also opens up a possibility of a non-modern practice of critique. According to Whitehead "there is a becoming of continuity, but no continuity of becoming" (1985, 35). Process in the sense of continuity, in a speculative vein, is not a given. It cannot be taken for granted as in the Bergsonian *durée*. Process is *made*, it *has* to be made, bit by bit. And not all processes are equal – some create continuity, some disruption. If there is continuity, from the perspective of the one that desired it, it is an achievement. In order to conceptualize process in this way, Whitehead invents a concept: the actual entity. Actual entities are "the final real things the world is made up of" (18). They designate the concrete, just as the Newtonian concept of matter did. In contrast to it, however, actual entities are not devoid of temporality. Actual entities *become* – but their temporality is not a continuous but an "atomic" one. It is only through their concatenations that processes with a duration and a common pattern are formed. It is in this sense that the concept of the actual entity is speculative: actual entities are not experienced as such, but designate what is *presupposed* by experience, the experience of processes and interlocked societies. Processes are formed through the intertwining "intra-actions" (to borrow a concept from Karen Barad) on the micro-level of actual entities. Processes are not given, they have to be made, on the level of actual entities, that is: bit by bit.

Such a speculative concept of process is crucial for situated practices of critique, because it shows how change firstly happens on the micro-level of the actual entity; the actual entity constitutes the real and on its level "decisions" – a Whiteheadian term which doesn't imply consciousness – are being made.

Through the way in which actual entities "prehend" one another, continuity and commonality is constructed. Change can never be abrupt, or happen in a stroke. Change on the experental macro-level needs to build up, as many actual entities need to "decide" to change their way of becoming.

Speaking of the speculative nature of the concept of actual entities then leads to the second, but not less crucial methodological dimension of the attempt to rethink process. Here it becomes apparent that to speak of macro- and micro-levels of processes could be misleading. "Actual entities" are speculative, precisely because we cannot experience them. They are not part of experience, not even on an imagined micro-level, but *conceptually required* in order to conceive of a becoming of continuity. This is how they avoid an anti-intellectualist stance. Introducing this speculative dimension implies a pragmatic image of thought that does not attempt to *represent* reality but rather invites process and speculation into its very construction. It means taking the situated aspect of critical thinking into account: theory itself is part of the construction of changing realities.

In Whitehead's metaphysics novelty (and thus real change and process) depends on what he terms "conceptual feeling" – the prehension of eternal objects, the realm of pure potentiality – as well as on "propositions," the realm of an "impure potentiality" that is already entangled with a specific historical actuality. Were actual entities only to prehend one another – that is past and present experiences – this would entail a **world** of processes which simply reproduce the same in different combinations but cannot foster any real change. By means of selecting from these potentials, the actual entity decides *how* it inherits its past. Here, propositions should not merely be considered in the usual linguistic sense of the term and in respect to the possibility of being *judged*. For Whitehead, they are a category of existences whose primary function is *entertainment*. Propositions, like all entities, need to manifest themselves in experience; they need to be embodied. This is why "in the real world it is more

important that a proposition be interesting than that it be true"
(Whitehead 1985, 259). Hence the importance of false and "non-conformal" propositions. Despite the strong "pull," however, a proposition might exert, being a "lure for feeling," even it cannot *determine, decide* the way it is taken up. The truthfulness of a proposition is not immanent; it rather depends on the determinate actual entities from which it is an incomplete abstraction. Depending on them to prehend them, a proposition "is a datum for feeling, awaiting a subject to feel it" (259). It is *as* such a datum that a proposition has "relevance to the actual world" (259). The efficacy of propositions is thus a suggestive one: They elicit interest, divert attention and propose a way something is taken into account and what is likewise eliminated. In this way, they account for difference and divergence in the various processes of intra-action and thus are crucial for a speculative notion of critique. Different subjects – in the metaphysical, non-humanist sense of the actual entity – will feel and respond to a proposition differently. Thus, it is the social environment, the historical and experiential world, which decides on its *relevance*. Propositions have an empiricist bias. Always told after the fact, propositions take up the past of certain actual entities and divert their trajectory. As "the tales that *perhaps might* be told about particular actualities" (256, emphasis added), they are one possible way of making sense of a situation, and at the same time they lure it into a new becoming. Propositions entail a speculative notion of critique because they divert accustomed processes, all the while taking their inheritance into account, and introduce difference and change. Operating on the speculative level of the actual entity, they eventually affect experiential processes. By means of the lures of propositions, processes might change their conformal continuity into a different kind of becoming.

References

120   Barad, Karen. 2007. *Meeting the Universe Halfway: Quantum Physics and the Entanglement of Matter and Meaning*. Durham: Duke University Press.

Whitehead, Alfred North. 1985. *Process and Reality: An Essay in Cosmology* (Corrected Edition). Edited by Donald W. Sherburne and David Ray Griffin. New York: The Free Press.

Regard

Jennifer A. Wagner-Lawlor

Susan Sontag loved the word *regard* for its multivalent res-
onance. It is a noun, and it is a verb. As a noun it describes is a
kind of attention, a kind of looking; it is also a kind of love or care,
or a kind of esteem, admiration. *To regard* is to look "intensively":
etymologically the word derives from *re-*, intensive prefix, + O.Fr.
garder "to look, heed"; *garder* corresponds to Frankish **wardon*,
which refers to a "collective sense of 'a keeping, a custody,'" and
gives us our word *ward* (as in, a ward of the state). The word
evolves in English to connote "consideration, appearance, kindly
feeling," and a kind of "esteem, affection" (*Merriam-Webster's
Collegiate Dictionary*). Behind this shift is a valuation that becomes
clear when we remember that the words *regard, guard,* and
guardian are closely related. One guards only what one "regards"
as valuable. No wonder Sontag, an admirer by constitution and
indeed by profession, was attracted to the word. Her lifework as
a critic was devoted to regarding those writers, artists, and film-
makers whose **work** she valued most. There was no point in her
writing otherwise. The title of Nancy Kates's 2015 documentary of
Sontag is pitch-perfect: *Regarding Susan Sontag*.

Regard is a particular form of attention: intensive, evaluative,
care-ful. It might be, as Jane Bennett puts it in a slightly different
(but not unrelated) context, a perceptual style (5). "To hold in
regard" connotes not just a "holding close," a protecting from

harm but also a holding out as exemplary. Regard links the individual and the collective in an *affective* economy which frankly disregards the economy of profit and financial accounting. Regard is thus related to an aesthetic, a **sensibility** (certainly for Sontag), a "sensible cognition" (Largier 2010, 536) that gives shape to value(s). Regard enables us to *recognize* objects, people, ideas, and concepts that are exemplary, not just "held close" but "held out" to view, for others. But exemplary of what? An aesthetic, in the sense of the beautiful or the good? Or, more artlessly, in the sense of touching and being touched?

We can regard forms of evil, particularly when such forms become visible by expression or act; indeed sometimes we cannot help but see, or are even forced to look. But regard cannot be forced in those ways. Regard requires intention, a willing- ness to look carefully, with patience, toward a critical estimation of that expression or act. In that sense, holding something in regard need not suggest "esteem"; "estimation" is more apt. Holding something "in regard" can mean holding it in esteem, but our evaluation may change, or be forced to be reconsidered, reestimated, revalued, according to terms that are unstable. As Margaret Atwood's reluctant heroine, Offred, puts it in *The Handmaid's Tale*, "context is all" (1985, 190). Offred, a prisoner of a modern theocracy, should know. When one can only see the world through glimpses, without either the time or the space for sustained attention and for understanding relationships of self to other or of here to elsewhere, regard is impossible.

In *Terra Critica* each of us shares a commitment to *relationality*, which calls for perceiving, describing, advocating for, and dwelling in difference, particularly with regard to our selves and others. Which calls, in other words, for critique. In a critical context, regard, as an embodied, sensible cognition, is not only aesthetic work but political and ethical work as well, for all these world-**perspectives** feed into the processes of estimation. Regard thus engages us in a *visual ethics*. Kaja Silverman proposes (in *The Threshold of the Visible World*) that an ethics of vision is "an active gift of love" conferred by the eye "upon bodies which have long been accustomed to neglect and disdain" (1996, 219). Regard is, as Silverman proposes, a gesture of generosity. Only in the performance of these gestures – small and large, individual or national or international – do we even think of making productive "a human society that wasn't just disgust" (180), as Jeanette Winterson puts it in *The Stone Gods*. Disgust is a kind of embodied opposition to regard; it makes us turn away from the sight, even from the presence of the object of disgust. A human society that "wasn't just disgust" is one that is committed to turning toward one another. Similarly, Hélène Cixous also wonders "what a completely different couple relationship would be like, what a love that was more than merely a cover for, a veil of, war would be like" (1981, 44).

This "love," or what I prefer to call "imaginative sympathy," is the relational incentive of regard, and it might even be the ethical core of the "work" in the active sense, of art. As Sontag writes, a work of art must be "an extension of my sympathies to other selves, other domains, other dreams, other wor[l]ds, other territories" (2007, 147). I and Thou. By acknowledging, welcoming, and regarding the differences, "the strange(r)" even, in ourselves and in others, we can think again about an *economy of regard*, a moral economy that assumes the possibility of relationality, not the likelihood of division. Regard points toward the importance of **response-ability**. As Mieke Bal observes, looking is "also a mediation between collective and individual, between culture and subject" – a "form of socialization" (1997, 61). Regard is that and more: the recognition and visualizing of something exemplary to be shared.

In his work on heterotopias, Tobin Siebers extends Cixous's speculation, imagining such a community as "[rivaling] any worldly republic … that can be realized on the strength of the desire for community inspired by its very imagination. It is not a pure community – one purified of conflicting interests – but a community with many different stories" (1995, 19–20). The willingness to listen to these stories is, itself, a gesture of regard, opening social relationships to the kind of hospitality that welcomes community based on difference rather than sameness, conversation rather than compliance. Toni Morrison calls this an "endless work" (1997, 316): of dwelling among networks of affiliations; of extending hospitality toward a **vision** of community that becomes itself a kind of living, desiring entity; a corporation based not on an economy of calculation but an economy of regard. An economy of regard is related not to mastery and the production of sameness, but to the **play** of difference, diversity, and heterogeneity. Not a simple transaction of one thing for another, but an inter-action, an engagement, between equal (equally regarded) agents. Such a moral economy drives the (hetero)**utopian** vision of community and citizenship that Siebers pursues. We can also associate this economy with care ethics theory that "views the self as a being immersed in a network of relationships with others" (Benhabib 1992, 149).

Finally, this definition of regard invites us to extend our regard to the nonhuman, the "object" of general disregard. An economy of regard must be also ecological, an extended relationality that, too, is maintained through generous gestures of (self-)critique and care that come from seeing the other. Attending to what we see, regarding it, allows us to "articulate the psychic and aesthetic conditions under which we might be carried away from both ideality and the self, and situated in an identificatory relation to despised bodies" (Silverman 1996, 2). Through this "sensible cognition," which involves the body's and the brain's critical faculties, we might approach an economy of regard in which ecosystems might profit. An economy of regard frankly contradicts the dominant economy of profit and financial accounts. An economy of regard would require a different accounting. Not of simple "exchange," but of much more complex transaction, its currency, as noted above, in the generous gesture. Regard is a sustained commitment to the kind of critique that intensifies sensible cognition interacting with imaginative sympathy, which is necessary (but not sufficient) for co-creating conditions for moral maturity. As Sontag observed at her acceptance speech for The Jerusalem Prize (2000), "I think there is no culture (using the term normatively) without a standard of altruism, of regard for others" (2007, 147).

References

Atwood, Margaret. (1985) 1998. *The Handmaid's Tale*. New York: Anchor Books.

Bal, Mieke. 1997. "Looking at Love: An Ethics of Vision" (book review) *Diacritics* 27 (1): 59–72.

Benhabib, Seyla. 1992. *Situating the Self: Gender, Community and Postmodernism in Contemporary Ethics*. Cambridge: Polity Press.

Cixous, Hélène. 1981. "Castration or Decapitation." *Signs* 7 (1): 41–55.

Harper, Douglas. "Guard." *Online Etymology Dictionary*. Accessed November 22, 2015. http://dictionary.reference.com/browse/guard.

Harper, Douglas. "Regard." *Online Etymology Dictionary*. Accessed November 22, 2015. http://dictionary.reference.com/browse/regard.

Largier, Niklaus. 2010. "The Plasticity of the Soul: Mystical Darkness, Touch, and Aesthetic Experience." *Modern Language Notes (MLN)* 125 (3): 536–551.

Merriam-Webster's Collegiate Dictionary. 2003. 11th ed. Springfield, MA: Merriam-Webster.

Morrison, Toni. 1997. *Paradise*. New York: Vintage Books.

Regarding Susan Sontag. 2014. Film directed and produced by Nancy Kates. Question Why Films.

Siebers, Tobin. 1995. *Heterotopia: Postmodern Utopia and the Body Politic*. Michigan: University of Michigan Press.

Silverman, Kaja. 1996. *The Threshold of the Visible World*. London: Routledge.

Sontag, Susan. 2007. *At the Same Time: Essays and Speeches*. Edited by Paolo Dilonardo and Anne Jump. New York: Farrar Straus Giroux.

Responsibility

Leonard Lawlor

The most tangible reason that philosophers in the twentieth century have devoted themselves to the reformulation of the concept of responsibility lies in the extreme violence of the contemporary **world**. A piece of evidence for this claim lies in the fact that Emmanuel Levinas dedicates his *Otherwise than Being or Beyond Essence* "to the memory of those who were closest to the six million assassinated by the National Socialists" (1981). Levinas is not alone in attempting to rethink responsibility. Jacques Derrida and Gilles Deleuze have also devoted a lot of their thinking to the problem of responsibility (Derrida 1998, 26; Deleuze 1983, 85; Deleuze and Guattari 1994, 108–109). When these philosophers criticize contemporary political and philosophical ideas, the critique frequently calls for others to be responsible, and more responsible. Critique is done in the name of an increased responsibility, perhaps a hyperbolic responsibility.

If we think of tangible suffering, we are able to formulate one principle for the brief investigation into responsibility that follows: what is fundamentally at stake in all recent, philosophical discourses on responsibility is empathy. In fact, empathy is at the root of all the recent, philosophical discourses on alterity. Since Edmund Husserl's *Fifth Cartesian Meditation*, no philosopher has been able to speak of the phenomenon of the other (any sentient being) without relying on the idea of empathy (Husserl

1977, 108–120). Empathy is not sympathy. While sympathy is the conscious feeling of the pains of others, empathy is the virtually unconscious feeling of being "paired," as Husserl says, with others. Empathy is something like an unconscious form of compassion. Even though Husserl is a twentieth century Descartes in regard to the unity of the "I think," he still places nearly unconscious empathy at the fundamental level of all **experience**. It is this fundamental empathy that requires us to formulate a new or different concept of responsibility, one that is different from the traditional one that we find, for example, in Kant. We shall turn to the distinction between the new and the traditional concepts of responsibility in a moment. But we should note now that critique done in the name of an increased responsibility intensifies the experience of empathy.

The traditional concept of responsibility revolves around the primary, everyday sense of the word "responsibility." The primary, everyday sense consists in being responsible, that is, taking responsibility for one's actions. The everyday sense of responsibility appears when we chastise our children, saying, "You made this mess. Who else could be responsible for it?" The everyday sense of "responsibility" essentially depends on the freedom of oneself. In other words, it depends on the Kantian idea of autonomy. Therefore, being responsible for oneself assumes that the subject of responsibility is unified and the self-identical, like the Cartesian "I think." Only if one is self-identical is one capable of receiving praise or blame for an action. However, with this conception of the self as self-identical, we can see that there is no alterity here, and we can wonder if there could ever be any empathy. So, following so many critiques of the subject in the twentieth century, we must abandon this alterity-less subjectivity, and with it the traditional concept of responsibility. Now, the new concept of responsibility that we are about to outline includes three components: first, a "responsibility to" (others in general); second, a "responsibility for" (others in general); and third, a "responsibility before" (others in general) (Derrida 1997,

250–252). It is "responsibility before" that will return us to the idea of being responsible for oneself, and therefore we shall conclude with a few words on guilt.

There are two paths into being "responsible *to*" others. On the one hand, there is the path of a "deconstruction" of interior monologue (see **Inner Voice**). To simplify what the word "deconstruction" means, one could say that, in deconstruction, one needs to pay attention to what lies under or is implicit in our discourse. Or, one could say that one has to crack open the words of our discourse. In this case, we would need to split open the words of our interior monologue. If one is able to crack open the words, then one hears that the words one uses in all discourse and in particular in interior monologue are words of a natural language, like English, French, or Mandarin Chinese. As words of a language that everyone shares and no one invented, the words refer to other uses of the words and therefore to others. Cracking the words open a little more, one hears the phonemes or the sounds of the words. One hears their arbitrariness and therefore their kinship with animal sounds and even with the rustling of leaves in the wind. In short, one must pay attention to the murmur within or below one's interior monologue, turning that monologue into a true dialogue. This turns auto-affection into hetero-affection. If one is able to crack the words open this far, then one has to say that the other (even trees), the "hetero," is in me, in my "auto." The other in me is a **specter** from which I am unable to avoid or run away from; my very freedom is in jeopardy. The cries in me demand – like a police interrogation – that I *respond to them*. They call out to me and put me in question (Levinas 1969, 178–179, 244).

The other way into the obligation of "responsibility to" others (and to nonhuman animals, for example) takes place through the experience of fascination (Deleuze and Guattari 1987, 239–254). In this case, with fascination, one finds oneself unable to stop looking at, say, a pack of animals. The fascination with the pack even leads this person to become fascinated with one of the animals in the pack. The fascination is always with an animal that stands a bit apart from the pack, as its leader or stray member. This stray animal is not abnormal; it is the anomalous, that is, it is that which remains at the border of the pack, outside the pack's *nomos* or order. When the fascinated self finds this anomalous figure in the pack, the anomalous animal infects the self. It is as if the one who is fascinated comes to be demonically possessed by the anomalous animal. One is infected with this animal, and, in a word, one has become the animal. When I have become the animal, I cannot avoid feeling the need to *respond to the animal*. Therefore, something like Kantian autonomy is at work here, but autonomy now fused with heteronomy: the animal inside of me, *the animal that therefore I am*, commands me or gives me an imperative to which I must respond.

With the component of "responsibility *to*" in place, we can turn to the conceptual component of "responsibility *for*." As we just **transformed** Kantian autonomy, we must also transform the traditional idea of being responsible *for someone else*. The idea of being "responsible for" that must be pushed aside is the idea in which we think the word "for" means that we *represent* others. But if "responsibility for" means representation, then it is clear that we have homogenized others down to a generality. If we think of the word "animality," for example, we see one obvious fact. The word "animality" homogenizes all the millions of forms of animal life down to one kind. How is it possible that elephants and amoeba could be compared to one another? In order not to insult the multiplicity of animal life, and of others in general, "responsibility *for*" must be conceived without any generalizing representation. The role of the anomalous already helped us to see that the other in me is singular not general: a singularity "blocks" all general concepts (Deleuze 1994, 12–13; see **Singularization**). However, in order to see what "responsibility for" means positively, we need to make use of a French expression. Of course, the relationship expressed in "responsibility *for*" makes use of the English word "for"; in German it would be "*für*," and in French the word is "*pour*." However, in French one can form the expression *"pour que"* (Deleuze and Guattari 1994, 109). A literal English translation of *"pour que"* would be "for that." But native English speakers say nothing like that. The standard English translation is "so that." Now if we can retain the idea of *"pour que"* and especially retain the *"pour"* or "for" within it, we can argue the following. Responsibility for others amounts *not* to representing them, which performs a kind of conceptual violence on them. "Responsibility for" really means responding to the others with which I am fascinated, this demon, or to the other within me, this specter – *pour que* (so that) the other might be able to become otherwise. Demonology or spectrality is always *responsibility for* the other's escape or flight from its misery. "Responsibility for" always means letting the other be free. And we could say that in genuine responsibility the freedom of the other must always come first.

Finally, we come to "responsibility *before*." In order to understand "responsibility *before*" others, one has to think phenomenologically again. But even more so, one has to reverse the phenomenological location of the gaze in the perceiver and place the gaze in the perceived – as if I, as the perceiver, experience myself under a gaze. Here, it is as if, in my fascination with others, I find myself before or in front of the ones with whom I am fascinated. They look back at me. And I experience this reversed gaze as a gaze of accusation. It is as if the others have laid down the law, and I am responsible before the law. "Responsibility *before*" means the experience of *standing before others* as if one is standing trial. Here we see the role of "responsibility," yet not *"for* others," but *"for* oneself." As we saw through the analysis of "responsibility *to*," the idea of a self-identical subject does not withstand any sort of deconstruction. However, here in being "responsible *before*," we must see that still, even as deconstructed, there is something like a self here, the very one put in question by others. It is this interrogated "I" that is on trial.

If I am standing trial before others, then at least I have been accused. More likely, I am guilty. Indeed, even if I have never made animals suffer, for example, I am complicit in the world-wide suffering inflicted on animal life in the name of food and fuel production. Certainly, I cannot escape the charge of a conceptual violence against others since I would be able neither to speak of them nor to speak to them without using general terms and concepts, without using representations, which violate the singularity of every single other. The experience of responsibility before others is therefore the experience of a conscience that is never at rest. Standing before the suffering of others, in front of their accusatory gaze, I suffer too – from guilt or, perhaps better, shame. Shame is the intensification of the empathy with which we started. Only under the condition of the feeling of shame is genuine responsibility possible. But we cannot stop here. This suffering that I undergo must be exaggerated. It must be exaggerated to the point that the experience of a disturbed conscience approximates either madness or the sublime. This exaggeration is infinite responsibility (Levinas 1969, 244). Thus, if we criticize contemporary philosophical and political ideas in the name of responsibility, we find that our demand for increased responsibility can never be complete.

References

Deleuze, Gilles. 1983. *Nietzsche and Philosophy*. Translated by Hugh Tomlinson. New York: Columbia University Press.

Deleuze, Gilles. 1994. *Difference and Repetition*. Translated by Paul Patton. New York: Columbia University Press.

Deleuze, Gilles, and Félix Guattari. 1987. *A Thousand Plateaus*. Translated by Brian Massumi. Minneapolis: University of Minnesota Press.

Deleuze, Gilles, and Félix Guattari. 1994 *What is Philosophy?* Translated by Hugh Tomlinson and Graham Burchell. New York: Columbia University Press.

Derrida, Jacques. 1997. *Politics of Friendship*. Translated by George Collins. London: Verso.

Derrida, Jacques. 1998. "Faith and Knowledge, translated by Samuel Weber." In *Religion*, edited by Jacques Derrida and Gianni Vatimo, 1–79. Stanford: Stanford University Press.

Husserl, Edmund. 1977. *Cartesian Meditations*. Translated by Dorian Cairns. The Hague: Nijhoff.

Levinas, Emmanuel. 1969. *Totality and Infinity*. Translated by Alphonso Lingis. Pittsburgh: Duquesne University Press.

Levinas, Emmanuel. 1981. *Otherwise than Being or Beyond Essence*. Translated by Alphonso Lingis. The Hague: Nijhoff.

Risk

Rosemarie Buikema

Cultural critique emerges from the need to face the **entan-glements** of the cultural and geopolitical risks and dangers which surround us. At the same time cultural critique in a glob-alized and neoliberal **world** has become a practice in which the inherent intertextuality of every symbolic act implies a willing-ness to account for unforeseen and uncontrollable effects. Critical inquiries therefore require an attitude or willingness to take a chance, to be challenging, to be risky – to be convincing whilst neither searching for the ultimate truth, nor striving for objectivity. Cultural critique is thus a balancing act by implication, an exercise in the praxis of negotiation, **response-ability** and accountability. This is particularly true for cultural critique which addresses feminist and postcolonial agendas. Since Virginia Woolf's *A Room of One's Own* (1929) and *Three Guineas* (1938) foregrounded the issue that the first wave feminist struggle for first-class citizenship unavoidably included the risk of becoming complicit in the dark sides of that first class citizen's national his-tories (that is: imperialism, colonialism, and war) and since critical race and critical whiteness studies have elaborated on this kind of intersectional analysis *avant la lettre* ever since, the interrelated-ness of these discourses can hardly be ignored again.

However, the almost innately claimed necessity of thinking through the interrelated legacies of raced and gendered violence notwithstanding, the effective analysis of the raced and gendered entanglements of inclusion and exclusion at empirical, symbolic, and institutional levels is still easier to claim as a manifesto for cultural critique than to effectively enact. Practicing the feminist mantras of diversity, solidarity, and democracy has become an increasingly risky enterprise in a geopolitical context in which feminism is consequently framed as the combined achievement of Western post-World War II emancipatory narratives, cultural, and social developments and liberation movements. In the last two decades, feminist critique has been increasingly equated with the achievements and the core values of Western civilization whilst that same civilization is very reluctantly coming to terms with its different pre-World War II histories of violence, imperialism, and colonialism. As such, the feminist project now seems hijacked by both the neoliberal and the post-secular as well as emerging contemporary anti-Muslim discourse.

The task of twenty-first-century feminist and postcolonial cultural critique is therefore to face the risk that the achievements of the movement for women's liberation at large threaten to become disconnected from its initial manifestations of equality for all, understood as transnational solidarity. It has to think through the possible danger that the outcome of two feminist waves mainly serve neoliberal capitalism, patriarchy, and racism and the concomitant individualization and marketing of the process of emancipation and social participation (Scott 2011). As Nancy Fraser suggests, this risk of female empowerment becoming the handmaiden of global neoliberal capitalism might have been implicated in the movement from the start. Virginia Woolf's brilliant first wave example notwithstanding, Western second wave feminist goals and strategies in the end seem to have been ambivalent and thus susceptible for two different elaborations. The initial, deeply political commitment to participatory democracy and social justice for all included goals which, in hindsight, simultaneously served the neoliberal vocabulary of

autonomy, choice, and meritocratic advancement (Fraser 2013).
Contrary to the feminist postcolonial and post-socialist project,
which situates the female subject as submitted to patriarchal,
racist, and capitalist structures, neoliberal feminisms seem to
promote participation in both capitalism and patriarchy and show
a striking neglect for either structural or intersectional analysis.

Contemporary feminism is therefore at risk of being the servant
of the neoliberal status quo and, in that process, helping to
reduce subjects to economic actors, to servants of **capital**,
encouraged to invest in their own individual liberation and autonomy instead of striving for social justice for all (Brown 2013).
Further to this, when the neoliberal definition of freedom and
emancipation happens to get framed as the achievement and
even core value of Western civilization as is happening in populist
political analysis, any feminist form of self reflexivity and critical
thinking is in danger of being perceived as betraying one's own
political or national community.

This is exactly what recently happened in the Netherlands when
a young female daily newspaper journalist started a discussion concerning the deployment of half naked female bodies
in lingerie advertisements displayed on billboards in the public
space. She aimed to unravel the question of whether the use of
non-stereotypical, nearly naked female bodies (i.e., non-white
bodies, non skinny-bodies, bodies with scars) in commercials for
ladies' underwear would serve the liberation of women. For that
purpose, she interviewed women from several corners of the
feminist enterprise in the Netherlands and reported their views.

Addressing the issue of the representation of the female body in
advertisements in a newspaper article meant that three "good
old" feminist issues were put center stage at the same time and
implicitly or explicitly also popped up in the online discussion
following the publication of the article. In the first place, the
overdetermined sign of the female nude as subject of feminist
cultural critique became the subject of online and offline debates

again. In the second place, the campaign's alleged attempt to open up stereotypical representations of the female body as smooth, skinny, and white was recognized and pointed out as the problematization of the hegemonic beauty myth. Thirdly, the deployment of the female body as an object of exchange in a capital driven imagery has been central to the feminist agenda ever since Gayle Rubin's influential essay "Traffic in Women: Notes on the Political Economy of Sex" (1975) and triggered feminist public attention again. The controversy following the implicit re-entry of these topics into the contemporary feminist agenda not only served to provide an interesting insight in the mantras of both neoliberal feminist critique and radical feminist and postcolonial critical theories today; it also happened to brilliantly illustrate the fact that the mantras of neoliberal feminism risk being hijacked by populist and even ethnocentric discourses.

Please allow me to unravel this conundrum by analyzing the implications of liberal, radical and postcolonial feminist critique.

What Nancy Frazer would label as a neoliberal feminist take on the issue of the female nude unsurprisingly came down to the claim that it is every woman's free choice to be portrayed half naked on a billboard and it is everybody's free choice to resent this or not (see http://stellingdames.nl/). Self-proclaimed feminist women claimed it to be their right to wear miniskirts and/ or to play with their sexuality and stated they were unprepared to give in on that acclaimed freedom of expression. Men who joined the debate repeated the mantra that Western civilization equates emancipation and liberation of women. Radical feminist critiques informed by, for example, the feminist analyses of Joan Scott and Frazer, immediately pointed at the fact that notwithstanding the laudable attempt to counter the stereotypical representation of female bodies and thus the attempt to deconstruct the racist and sexist beauty myth, the advertisements did not offer an alternative to the sexist tradition of deploying female bodies in order to stimulate consumerism. The essence of the radical feminist claim thus reads: white or black, skinny or not so skinny, smooth or scarred, the female body in the imagery of so-called innovative advertisements is still serving as a **metaphor** for the circulation of capital. The postcolonial feminist's take on the matter concurred with the critique of radical feminism, emphasizing moreover the ethnocentrism of the Western compulsion to decorate the public space with images of naked female bodies and consequently claim this to be freedom of expression. They highlighted research exposing the phenomenon that the pornification of Western society inspires certain groups of women to increasingly cover themselves, not as a sign of religious commitment but rather as a sign of cultural critique (Buikema 2015). Postcolonial radical feminists emphasized the need for a new imagery that would be more fitting for a multicultural and post-sexist society (Smit 2015).

In the fierce online and offline discussions summarized above the good old feminist critique, that the framed image of a female body is an icon of Western culture, a symbol of civilization and accomplishment (Nead 1992) was abundantly illustrated by both male and female participants in the debate. In particular in those posts which pushed the postcolonial link between feminism and multiculturalism in the context of the 2016 refugee crises, the online discussions got overtly violent and turned into torrents of hate mail aimed at the defenders of postcolonial feminism. The suggestion that alternatives to the pornification of Western culture ought to be considered, because this imagery might be unpleasant for both women and people with different cultural values, was equated with collaborating: "You are a disgrace to this country" was an often articulated comment to the postcolonial radical feminists who had made that argument. In such a polarized context it proved to be very hard to get back to the initial cornerstones and structural analysis of feminist theory without getting entangled in a heated controversy concerning the unconditional freedom of expression as the core value of Western civilization.

140   In light of this exemplary case, the challenge for twenty first century feminist and postcolonial critique is to develop and practice a form of critique which continues to truly connect the local and the global, the private and the public, the personal and the political, the empirical and the symbolical. To parry the risk of being perceived as a traitor of Western democratic practices when turning to structural analysis of the sexist and racist risks and dangers which are surrounding us, twenty first century feminist and postcolonial critique should embark on a return to the history of feminism and a re-location of the definitions of emancipation, liberation, and solidarity. Inspirational texts of first and second wave feminism – most notably Simone de Beauvoir's *The Second Sex* ([1949] 1989) and bell hooks's *Ain't I a Woman* (1981), for example – already theorized liberation as a concept which not only referred to the individual but also to the simultaneous desire for a freedom for the other(s). This ethical-political second wave nuance – one geared towards justice for all rather than merely to equality and individual emancipation – needs to be reactivated and practiced in the context of twenty first century feminist critique and activism; what we need is a return to the envisioned futures of the past in order not to risk being disconnected from our rich and critical potential.

References

Beauvoir, Simone de. (1949) 1989. *The Second Sex*. Translated by Constance Borde and Sheila Malovany-Chevallier. New York: Vintage Books.

Brown, Wendy. 2013. "Reclaiming Democracy: An Interview with Wendy Brown on Occupy, Sovereignty, and Secularism." In *Critical Legal Thinking*, an interview with Robin Celikates and Yolanda Jansen. Accessed January 7, 2015. http://criticallegal-thinking.com/2013/01/30/reclaiming-democracy-an-interview-with-wendy-brown-on-occupy-sovereignty-and-secularism/.

Buikema, Rosemarie. 2015. "Waarom is dat naakt uberhaupt nodig?" *NRC Handelsblad*, December 19.

Fraser, Nancy. 2013. "How Feminism Became Capitalism's Handmaiden." *The Guardian* online. Accessed January 7, 2015. http://www.theguardian.com/commentisfree/2013/oct/14/feminism-capitalist-handmaiden-neoliberal

hooks, bell. 1981. *Ain't I a Woman*. Boston: South End Press.

Nead, Lynda. 1992. *The Female Nude: Art, Obscenity and Sexuality*. New York: Routledge.

Poel, Romy van der. 2015. "Als dit normaal is wat ben ik dan?" *NRC Handelsblad*, December 19.

Rubin, Gayle. 1975. "Traffic in Women: Notes on the Political Economy of Sex." In *The Second Wave: a Reader in Feminist Theory*, edited by Linda Nicholson, 27–62. Routledge: New York.

Scott, Joan W. 2011. *The Fantasy of Feminist History*. London: Duke University Press.

Smit, Maxime. 2015. "De blote vrouw op een bushokje is dat nou westerse beschaving?" *Parool*, December 24.

Woolf, Virginia. 1993. "Professions for Women" In *A Room of One's Own/Three Guineas*, edited by Michele Barrett, 356–361. London: Penguin Books.

Woolf, Virginia. 1938. *Three Guineas*. London: Hogarth Press

Woolf, Virginia. 1929. *A Room of One's Own*. London: Hogarth Press.

Semi-agency

Birgit Mara Kaiser

Unlike other terms in this vocabulary, semi-agency is not an
established expression with a critical heritage. It is not even listed
in the *Oxford English Dictionary* – and, hence, is not really an English word. Regardless, it cropped up in *Terra Critica*'s discussions
(see Kaiser 2012) and therefore made its way into this volume.
What does feature in the OED is the prefix "semi-" meaning
in common use "half, partly, partially, to some extent." When
coupled with "agency" here and with the **perspective** of critical
practice in mind, however, the prefix points to something else
than merely a quantitative halving. This entry explores both sides
of the term – "semi" and "agency" – with recourse to feminist
theory, to argue that "semi-agency" signals not so much "half of
something" but rather a kind of (boundary) articulation, always
entangled with the **affective**, material, circumstantial forces it
emerges from.

Let us begin with Toril Moi's description of Hélène Cixous's
work, especially Cixous's poetico-theoretical writings from the
mid-1970s, as "theoretical (or semi-theoretical)" (Moi 1985, 102).
The hesitation that Moi's proviso in parenthesis seems to betray
is that Cixous's work is not "really" theoretical but something
slightly different. And indeed, in the course of her argument,
Moi is highly critical of Cixous's theoretical work and she thus
indeed employs "semi-theoretical" to signal a deficiency. Moi

judges Cixous's work to be marred by its "lack of reference to recognizable social structures as by its biologism" (126) – a misreading of Cixous's project, as Peggy Kamuf has shown. Moi dismisses Cixous's project as a less than theoretical "textual jungle" (1985, 102) in which style and poetry stand in the way of real theoretical – that is, for Moi also always politically effective – **work**, which makes references to "recognizable social structures."

When Kamuf zooms in on Moi's use of "semi-theoretical" in regard to Cixous ten years later, she points out that, used in Moi's way, the prefix "semi-" adheres to an unquestioned "familiar set of distinctions that includes expression vs. thought, style vs. substance, **metaphoric** vs. literal, and poetic vs. theoretical" (Kamuf 1995, 73; bold added). Moi uses "semi-" to express indeed a diminishing (a halving) of the desirable faculties of thought that promise political empowerment. What might we gain, Kamuf asks, if we run with Moi's assertion of a "semi-theoretical" work but were instead to treat the nomination in less conventional and depreciative ways? Is not "theory" in its distinction from and critique of the traditions of Western metaphysics the very assertion that acts of thinking "uncontaminated by contingency, particularity, or experiential differences" (73) are impossible? Thus, is theory not by definition semi-theory? Is it not, Kamuf suggest, the very **affirmation** that affective, material, circumstancial, existential factors cannot be sidelined as irrelevant to thought and that thought cannot be kept uncontaminated by those forces? If this is the case,

> then there is no telling absolutely when and where the semi-theoretical and semi-political may shade off into the semi-poetic or semi-fictional or some other semi-recognizable mode since such distinctions are rendered rather dubious by the contaminating non-category of the "semi-." (74)

It is these contaminations that Moi finds politically, feministically unproductive – and that, on the contrary, Kamuf (with Cixous) affirms as precisely politically, feministically productive.

Importantly, the consequence of the possible multiplication of "semi-"modes of thinking and of their blurry distinctions Kamuf points to (and something that Cixous's writings indeed enact) does not repudiate the effectiveness of these modes nor is it a surrender to their murkiness. Rather, they are openings "onto a responsibility to that which is only glimpsed beneath the effacement of the prefix *semi-* on all names and general concepts" (74). Thus, if we follow Kamuf, prefixing a name or concept with "semi-" can signal something that is "not altogether there, it does not name a presence, nothing that *is*; rather, it calls for something to present itself otherwise" (74). In this sense, Kamuf precisely affirms Cixous as a semi-theoretician, whose work calls for "theory" and "thinking" to present themselves (always again) otherwise, and otherwise than in the traditions of Western metaphysics and the Cartesian subject.

It is from this angle, that "semi-" is attached here to agency. If we were to start from the conventional understanding of agency as the "ability or capacity to act or exert power" (OED), then semi-agency is not half of that capacity; that would retain implicitly either the desire for the full capacity, or the acceptance of a diminished part of it, with the full capacity still as a yardstick. Both of these options continue to adhere to a metaphysics of presence. Following the angle described by Kamuf instead, the non-category of "semi-" calls for agency "to present itself otherwise" (1995, 74) than within a logic of presence. Here, semi-agency is closer to the other (in fact: the first) definition of agency that the OED gives, namely that of "a person or organization acting on behalf of another." *I is another*, we might say, to echo Arthur Rimbaud's countering of the Cartesian idea of a willful, self-transparent subject in his *Lettres du Voyant* already in 1871.

With this in mind, let us then return to critical discourse, where agency as a term has surfaced over the past decades, especially in work that questions subjectivity as sovereign consciousness. In this vein, for example, Judith Butler speaks from a social constructivist perspective about subjectless, performative agency that is bound to the discursive formations in which it emerges. We can locate agency, she writes already in *Gender Trouble*, "within the possibility of a variation on that repetition" (Butler 1990, 145) upon which any identity understood as practice is based; that is, within the difference permitted by the iterability of signs, an iterability upon which any signification depends. And later, in *Excitable Speech*, Butler explains that agency and sovereignty must not be confused: "[a]gency begins where sovereignty wanes. The one who acts (who is not the same as the sovereign subject) acts precisely to the extent that he or she is constituted as an actor and, hence, operating within a linguistic field of enabling constraints from the outset" (1997, 16). Agency, therefore, has purchase in contemporary critical discourse precisely to the extent that it questions and reroutes conceptions of sovereign intentionality, and that it foregrounds praxis, action, and reiteration within discursive fields as inscribing difference and inventing "new" habits. It would, however, not be wise to abandon agency for action altogether, as Tim Ingold suggests in *The Life of Lines*.

Worried that agency continues to "separat[e] the doer from the deed" (Ingold 2015, 145) and thus adheres to traditional forms of the sovereign Subject (a worry that seems to ignore precisely the work feminist theory has done on the term), Ingold wants to let go of it. He suggests focusing on *"action without agency"* (145) instead in order to stress what he calls "the doing-in-undergoing of humanifying" (152). What we **risk** losing in such a move, though, are the *enabling* constraints (Butler) agency addresses, or – from a (new) materialist perspective – the "agential cuts" (Barad 2007, 175) crucial to any emergence of difference. Put otherwise, what we risk losing in the move Ingold suggests is the critical **transformation** that Butler, Karen Barad, and others foreground with *agency* or *agential*. Certainly, action is "doing-in-undergoing" as Ingold suggests, and the stale opposition of subject/object as well as the sovereign Subject are obsolete. But on the basis of a performative, quantum universe (which also underlies

Ingold's work), we also need to assess what comes to matter as a non-linearly-causal consequence of action. Crucially, as Barad stresses, "[d]ifferent agential cuts produce different phenomena" (2007, 175). What action is directed at-for and where action orients itself within-toward is therefore critical (in the sense of being decisive and interventionist). Agency permits precisely the pursual of this: what is effected, what is shifted and what is de/re-stabilized in the course of the actors' constitutive operations in discursive fields? In that way, action as intra-action remains tied to performative, material-discursive forms of agency, which are themselves a productive, **creative** mode of critical practice.

> Agency is a matter of intra-acting; it is an enactment, not something that someone or something has. Agency cannot be designated as an attribute of subjects or objects (as they do not preexist as such). *Agency is a matter of making iterative changes to particular practices through the dynamics of intra-activity* ... Agency is about the possibilities and accountability entailed in reconfiguring material-discursive apparatuses of bodily production, including the boundary articulations and exclusions that are marked by those practices. (Barad 2007, 214; emphasis added)

From this perspective, agency is not an attribute. Instead, the intra-actions and cuts create *specific* phenomena and practices and not others: "cutting together-apart" (Barad 2012, 46). Severing agency from action, as Ingold suggests, would loose this precision and the investment in rerouting practices and exclusions.

Ultimately, agency is then always already semi-agency, namely "nothing that *is*; [but that] calls for something to present itself otherwise" (Kamuf 1995, 74): a form of (boundary) articulation **entangled** with the affective, material, circumstantial forces that drive all intra-action; a form of enactment of **world** that makes a difference, that effects a change; the practice of acting within enabling constraints (Butler) or as intra-acting with-in a material-discursive field (Barad).

References

Barad, Karen. 2007. *Meeting the Universe Halfway: Quantum Physics and the Entanglement of Matter and Meaning.* Durham: Duke University Press.

Barad, Karen. 2012. "Nature's Queer Performativity." *Kvinder, Køn og forskning/Women, Gender and Research* 1–2: 25–53.

Butler, Judith. 1997. *Excitable Speech: A Politics of the Performative.* London: Routledge.

Butler, Judith. 1990. *Gender Trouble: Feminism and the Subversion of Identity.* London: Routledge.

Ingold, Tim. 2015. *The Life of Lines.* London/New York: Routledge.

Kamuf, Peggy. 1995. "To Give Place: Semi-Approaches to Hélène Cixous" *Yale French Studies* 87: 68–89.

Kaiser, Birgit Mara. 2012. "To Experiment and Critique with Kleist's Käthchen." *Terra Critica.* Accessed April 15, 2016. http://terracritica.net/wp-content/uploads/Kaiser_positionpaper.pdf.

Moi, Toril. 1985. *Sexual/Textual Politics: Feminist Literary Theory.* London: Methuen.

Sensibility

Timothy O'Leary

In *Daybreak* (1997, 103), Nietzsche explains that he denies both morality and immorality, not because morality is a sham and a self-deception, but because even though people genuinely *feel* they act morally and immorally, this feeling is not justified. Hence, he concludes, "We have to *learn to think differently* — in order at last, perhaps very late on, to attain even more: *to feel differently.*" Gilles Deleuze expands this point to a general characterization of Nietzschean critique: "The point of critique is not justification but a different way of feeling: another sensibility" (Deleuze 1983, 194). We can formalize these themes as the claim that critique is the transformative engagement with the (moral) sensibilities of our time. How far can we push this idea, by considering such simple examples as our changing feelings about plastic bags – and the TV series *Mad Men*?

One way of explaining the pleasure that many viewers experience while watching *Mad Men* is that the form of life it portrays is so close to our own and yet so distant. Unlike a series such as *Downton Abbey*, for example, *Mad Men* represents a world that many of us were born into and yet it seems to be significantly alien in many ways. That difference is one that could be described in terms of sensibility, and in particular of moral sensibility. It is not just a matter of our sensibility as the audience; that is, the ways in which we perceive, judge, praise, and condemn the social mores of the early 1960s. It is also the unavoidable sense we get that *their* experience of their own world is radically different from what our experience of it would be if we returned to it now. In other words, the series confronts us with an important fact: moral sensibility has a history, and that history is subject to quite rapid transformation.

The idea that we can identify the sensibility of an individual, a sub-culture, or even a whole era, and then track the transformations it may undergo, is not particularly new. It has appeared in different forms in literary studies, history, anthropology, cultural studies, and also in certain strands of philosophy (most notably in eighteenth-century and some contemporary moral theory). However, despite this long and varied tradition of thought (and perhaps *because* it is so long and varied), one could be forgiven for suspecting that the concept of sensibility has become so vague and inchoate that it creates as many confusions as it hopes to dispel. Hence, although it might seem acceptable to use it when casually discussing popular entertainment, as I have just done, one might question whether it is advisable to use it in a philosophically informed investigation of our contemporary ethical terrain, which is what I propose to do.

In this brief overview, I will try to show that the concept can indeed be useful in such an investigation. I will suggest that thinking in terms of moral sensibility allows us to understand important aspects of the relation between ethics, history, and critique that many philosophical approaches are incapable of taking into account. I will begin by proposing a rough, preliminary definition of the concept.

Sensibility is a concept that encompasses three elements: modes of feeling, perceiving, and valuing. All three must be given their place; and it must be recognized that all three are in constant mutual interaction. Sensibility, therefore, comprises: a) sensation and emotion; b) systems and practices of knowledge; c) moral and aesthetic appraisals. At every level, sensibility is profoundly historical. It is probably not necessary here to establish this claim with respect to b) systems of knowledge and c) modes of appraisal, but what about a) sensation and emotion? Surely the human sensations and emotions are constant – at least in the historical, if not in the evolutionary, sense. But even here, there has been a great deal of scholarly work in the fields of history and anthropology of the senses and the emotions that seems to firmly establish the case for continuous historical change in the way the human body engages with and experiences its environment. Sensibility, therefore, denotes constantly changing modes of receptivity and sensitivity towards the world. But it is not simply passive; it is also an active ability. It betokens an active engagement with the world: it is a set of abilities to perceive, discern, judge, and experience.

In 1966, in *The Order of Things*, Foucault pointed out that "At any given instant, the structure proper to individual experience finds a certain number of possible choices (and of excluded possibilities) in the systems of the society; inversely, at each of their points of choice the social structures encounter a certain number of possible individuals (and others who are not)" (2002, 415). In other words, at each particular place and time there is a certain range of subjective experience that is made more or less likely by the social structures of that time. And, as the social structures change, so too does the range of possible human experience. What this gives rise to, as Ian Hacking has pointed out, is the possibility of studying the historical transformations that open up and close off potential human experiences (2002, 23). And, if we do that in the domain of moral experience, we will be engaging in a critique of moral sensibility.

Let's take a simple and banal example from the increasing moralization of everyday consumption in many advanced economies around the world. Consider the way that the use of plastic shopping bags has come to be seen, and experienced, as an immoral form of behavior. How did it come about that the choice of a shopping bag could engage the moral sensibility of so many people today? I would suggest that this experience of buying the plastic bag is identifiable as ethical not only because it involves the practical application of previously accepted moral principles but also because it activates a whole range of concerns and practices relating to self-formation. These concerns and practices are activated within a broader framework that includes forms of knowledge about climate change and also an emerging set of norms of behavior that cajole us into "environmentally responsible" actions. At a basic level, therefore, we are being cajoled into becoming particular kinds of people: informed consumers who are guided by a new twenty-first century moral sensibility. The act of buying the plastic bag is not intrinsically moral in nature; hence, it is simply that recent shifts in moral sensibility have made it more likely that the experience will crystallize, or come into focus, as having a strong moral component.

What can we say about these observations, if we take moral sensibility as comprising the three elements identified above: a) sensation and emotion; b) systems and practices of knowledge; c) moral and aesthetic appraisals. In relation to the first element, we can ask how is the experience of, and our emotional response to, plastic transforming in contemporary societies? And, how do different forces, such as environmental activism and government policy, propel, and guide this transformation? In relation to the second element, what modes of knowledge (of varying degrees of scientific "certainty") inform our moral responses? What is the history of these knowledges, of their formation, dissemination, and, perhaps, contestation? In relation to the third element, what is the nature of the value judgments that are being made, how do the judgments of others relate to corresponding judgments of oneself, and how do moral and aesthetic elements intertwine in these judgments? What changes are these modes of judgment undergoing at the present?

Taking this perspective on our contemporary ethical terrain opens up the possibility of a new critical task: to investigate what we can now call the conduct of moral sensibility. The conduct of moral sensibility has two senses: first, the ways in which our sensibility is guided, formed, developed, expanded, narrowed, refined, and blunted, by a whole range of forces in the world and in ourselves; and second, the ways our conduct, that is, our behavior, is guided by the modes of moral sensibility we embody. These two aspects are in constant, mutual interaction. The investigation of this conduct gives us the basis for understanding the contemporary contest of moral sensibilities. In other words, it makes possible a genealogy of the moralizing and de-moralizing of the world, a critical, transformative engagement with the moral sensibilities of our time. Having learned to think our present differently, we might then come to meet Nietzsche's challenge – to *feel differently.*

References

Deleuze, Gilles. 1983. *Nietzsche and Philosophy.* Translated by H. Tomlinson. New York: Columbia University Press.

Foucault, Michel. 2002. *The Order of Things: An Archaeology of the Human Sciences.* London: Routledge.

Hacking, Ian. 2002. *Historical Ontology.* Cambridge, MA: Harvard University Press.

Nietzsche, Friedrich. 1997. *Daybreak: Thoughts on the Prejudices of Morality.* Translated by R. J. Hollingdale. Cambridge: Cambridge University Press.

Singularization

Singularization is the **processual** emergence of entities. It is, as Félix Guattari uses the term, always a *re*-singularization: a response to and redirecting of standardized, entrenched habits towards new, different modes of living. When thinking about (re)singularization, it is important to keep this **perspective** in mind, because the term singularity (and the related singularization) can also give rise to very different approaches and stakes. Therefore, first a brief word on singularity.

Singularity is an over-determined and contested concept, with a wide range of meanings and diverse theoretical and political investments. Apart from its mathematical usage, singularity has recently become a prominent term in fields ranging from philosophy (Badiou 2004; Derrida 1998; Deleuze 1990; Guattari 1996; Nancy 2000), literary and cultural studies (Attridge 2004; Clark 2005; Hallward 2002; Jameson 2002) to science and technology studies (Eden, Moor, et al 2012; Kurzweil 2005), with widely diverging implications. These span an understanding of singularity as uniform oneness (the singular as single in Fredric Jameson, or as non-relational absolute in Peter Hallward, who draws on Alain Badiou's [2004, 146–147] use of the singular as universal in his second thesis on the universal), as singularit*ies* in the sense of nonhuman forces constitutive of any process of individuation (Deleuze 1990), as well as a technological "event or phase that will radically change human civilization" (Eden, Moor, et al. 2012, 1) in techno-scientific or transhumanist debates, which aim to overcome human limitations by artificial intelligence.

Let us now zoom in on singular*ization*, a term that has, in its stress on the process of emergence, closest ties to the Deleuze-Guattarian use of the term singularity. For Gilles Deleuze and Félix Guattari, singularization brings into focus the formation of objects and subjects, or the **(trans)formation** of entities – unlike individuality or specificity, which are terms geared toward the classification of differences (as species or genres) that are already formed on a molar level. Contrary to this, Deleuze and Guattari interest in singularity and singularization lies in the terms' capacity to consider the transversal emergence of entities as the result of a relation of forces. For its critical potential, especially Guattari's use of (re-)singularization is of interest here.

In "Microphysics of Power/Micropolitics of Desire," Guattari discusses in this vein that – much like Deleuze's recourse to (Simondonian) individuation – the aim of Foucault's *Archaeology of Knowledge* (and other projects) is to move from "things," traditionally considered as anterior to discourse, to the formation of "entities" or "statements," which are "immersed in an enunciative field" (1996, 180). Singularization is, thus, not about the single, the (liberal) individual or the unique object, but about material-semiotic processes (to borrow Donna Haraway's term). Singularization describes the emergence of entities, and consequentially also the processes that undo (or deterritorialize) existing stratifications and in turn congeal (or reterritorialize) new modes of being. In that sense, Guattari employs the term in *The Three Ecologies* ([1989] 2008).

Guattari's argument in *The Three Ecologies* is anchored in a two-fold critique. On the one hand, as an analyst at La Borde (1955–1992), he is discontent with Lacanian structuralist psychoanalysis, which uses Freudian models of analysis focused on childhood experience and parental-familial structures. On the other hand, as a political activist, he is concerned about two socio-political developments observed at the time of writing: First, the "extreme complexification of social, economic and international contexts" (2008, 21) resulting from a decline of the dualist opposition USA–USSR in the late 1980s and what he calls "Integrated World Capitalism."[1] Second, the standardization of ways of life and a homogenizing of desires, largely promoted by the media (at the time, television as the prevailing medium). Guattari sees the "intoxicating and anaesthezising" (34) effects of (state-sponsored) media as intimately bound up with the production of signs and subjectivity, which he perceives as *modus operandi* of IWC. His hopeful excitement about new media and the Internet as possible openings are on the horizon of this critique in the late 1980s.

Singularization for Guattari is a counter-force to these formations, as it facilitates "new social and aesthetic practices, new practices of the Self" (45). In regard to his intervention into Lacanian psychoanalysis, he illustrates singularization in *Chaosmosis: An Ethico-Aesthetic Paradigm* (1995) with the example of a patient whose therapy got stuck and who was "going round in circles, and coming up against a wall" (17). Ultimately, the therapy moved forward not due to a Lacanian "symbolic hermeneutic centered on childhood" (18) but because of a schizoanalytic encouragement of unexpected, transversal practices: the patient suddenly desired to take up driving. This new habit fostered different fields of vision and enabled him to divert his problem into new directions. The driving lessons produced "active, processual ruptures within semiotically structured, significational and denotative networks" (19) and set into action different "existential operators capable of acquiring consistence and persistence," making possible new "existential orchestrations, until now unheard and unknown" (19). Concerned about analytic practice, Guattari holds that Freud's unconscious has

1   For Guattari, IWC is the post-industrial capitalism that moves from the production of goods to the production of signs and subjectivity, marked by its equally complexified effect on more than purely economic realms.

become an institution itself and in its "structuralist version, has been recentered on the analysis of the self, its adaptation to society, and its conformity with a signifying order" (10). It has lost its teeth, while schizoanalysis and ecosophy counter this reification to open up new passages, not only for analysis and "its theoretical scaffolding" (Guattari 2008, 27) but also for the socio-political problems that *The Three Ecologies* perceives. The real processes that set into motion such new "vectors of sub-jectification" (25), which are not directed at conformity with an established signifying order, is what Guattari calls singularization. The enactment, encouragement, and **affirmation** of such processes is in itself a critical practice.

The inventions of new "vectors of subjectification" are intimately bound up with Guattari's concern about contemporary forms of capitalist **power**.

> [C]apitalist power has become delocalized and deterritoria-lized, both in extension, by extending its influence of the whole social, economic and cultural life of the planet, and in "intension," by infiltrating the most unconscious subjective strata. In doing this it is no longer possible to claim to be opposed to capitalist power only from the outside, through trade unions and traditional politics. (33)

Given increasingly decentralized sites of power in neoliberal capitalism and the "introjection of repressive power by the oppressed" (32) that goes with it, the question arises how to modify or redirect the effects of such power. Or, in Guattarian terms: How to re-route desires that have come to turn in circles? How to activate "catalysts of existential change" (30)? Partly, Guattari's response is to note that – since an opposition only from the outside is not sufficient or feasible – it is "equally imperative to confront capitalism's effects in the domain of mental ecology in everyday life: individual, domestic, material, neighbourly, creative or one's personal ethics" (33). Therefore, "it will be a question in the future of cultivating a *dissensus* and the singular

production of existence" (33), the singularization of desires and
modes of living.

Importantly, processes of singularization and new subjectivities
are approached from an ecosophical perspective, inspired
by Gregory Bateson's *Steps to an Ecology of Mind* ([1972] 2000).
"Ecology" (of which human subjectivity is one of Guattari's
three ecologies, alongside social relations and the environment)
stresses that these existential modes are capable of morphing
or being "cultivated." They can "bifurcat[e] into stratified and
deathly repetitions or ... open ... up processually from a praxis"
(2008, 35), they can be constrained or opened (*de-* and *re-*
territorialized). Given Guattari's analysis of IWC as a stratification
and homogenization of existence for profit, the de-stratification
and differentiation of existence is key to any critical intervention
into these conditions. Dissensus is not articulated in the name of
an alternative general project; rather, it serves to re-singularize
existences (or proliferate difference) without presupposing a
telos. The subjective domain – human subjectivity – is viewed
neither (prescriptively) on the basis of structure (unconscious,
language, law) nor as possessing directionality or end (self-con-
sciousness, normativity, consensus). It is rather phrased as the
affirmation of **creatively** cultivating new existential refrains, the
desire for a "subjectivity of resingularization" (44) which exploits
"a-signifying points of rupture" (37) to care into existence hitherto
unimagined vectors, desires, and phantasms.

Literature plays a crucial role for Guattari in this: as a practice
that can explore **symptoms** and incidents outside the norm,
and mobilize vectors of subjectification that elude the mastery
of the self to **work** for a re-routing of refrains (in a similar way,
Deleuze's *Coldness and Cruelty* ([1967] 1991) makes use of the
literary analyses of sadism and masochism, linking the critical
and clinical). For this reason Guattari pleads for tapping the
"cartographies of the psyche" (2008, 25) that *poetic-literary* texts
offer. The critical and clinical work go hand in hand here, with
literary texts seen as critical manifestos "for effective practices of

experimentation" (24) to "bring into being other **worlds**" (44–45, bold added) and to critically intervene into and transform oppressive modes of living.

References

Attridge, Derek. 2004. *The Singularity of Literature*. New York: Routledge.

Badiou, Alain. 2004. *Theoretical Writings*. London: Continuum.

Bateson, Gregory. 2000. *Steps to an Ecology of Mind*. Chicago: University of Chicago Press.

Clark, Timothy. 2005. *The Poetics of Singularity: The Counter-Culturalist Turn in Heidegger, Derrida, Blanchot and the Later Gadamer*. Edinburgh: Edinburgh University Press.

Deleuze, Gilles. 1990. *The Logic of Sense*. Translated by Mark Lester with Charles Stivale. New York: Columbia University Press.

Deleuze. Gilles. 1991. "Coldness and Cruelty." In *Masochism*, translated by Jean McNeil, 9–138. New York: Zone Books.

Derrida, Jacques. 1998. *Monolingualism of the Other: Or, The Prosthesis of Origin*. Translated by Patrick Mensah. Stanford: Stanford University Press.

Eden, Amnon H., James H. Moor, Johnny H. Søraker, and Eric Steinhart, eds. 2012. *Singularity Hypotheses: A Scientific and Philosophical Assessment*. Berlin: Springer.

Guattari, Félix. 1996. "Microphysics of Power/Micropolitics of Desire." In *The Guattari Reader*, edited by Gary Genosko, translated by John Caruana. 172–184. London: Blackwell Publishers.

Guattari, Félix. 2008. *The Three Ecologies*. Translated by Ian Pindar and Paul Sutton. London: Continuum.

Guattari, Félix. 1995. *Chaosmosis: An Ethico-Aesthetic Paradigm*. Translated by Paul Bains and Julian Pefanis. Bloomington: Indiana University Press.

Hallward, Peter. 2002. *Absolutely Postcolonial: Writing between the Singular and the Specific*. Manchester: Manchester University Press.

Jameson, Fredric. 2002. *A Singular Modernity: Essay on the Ontology of the Present*. New York: Verso.

Kurzweil, Ray. 2005. *The Singularity is Near: When Humans Transcend Biology*. London: Penguin.

Nancy, Jean-Luc. 2000. *Being Singular Plural*. Translated by Robert D. Richardson and Anne E. O'Byrne. Stanford: Stanford University Press.

Skin

Asja Szafraniec

Critique today, in one aspect at least, forks out in two directions,
differing with regard to the analyzed "object." The first prong
remains faithful to the transcendental focus inherited from
Immanuel Kant's philosophy, addressing the categories in
which we lift the world out of chaos (the criteria, the dividing
lines, the modalities of thought). The critique that is affirmative
and nonetheless intervening is one which attends to the
appropriateness of those dividing lines and the way in which they
influence our understanding, in the hope of discovering spaces
for adjustment, for creative supplementation, for emphasis, for
affirmation. The second prong abandons the Kantian model as
detracting our attention from the empirical and proposes to
focus instead on the analysis of states of affairs. While its call for
getting closer to the "matters of concern" – a renewed empiricism
– is utterly convincing, it remains to be examined whether
attention to "matters of concern" requires an abandoning of the
transcendental inquiry (Latour 2004, 231).

This question becomes particularly urgent when it comes to
categories of "things" (not necessarily the scientific "objects"
examined by Bruno Latour) that seem to have the characteristics
of "matters of concern," but also function as categories in terms
of which we perceive other "things." Skin might be one example
of such a "thing," in which, on a micro-level, the critical tension

between the empirical and the transcendental plays out. Skin is a bodily organ that distributes stimuli and protects the inside from the outside. But it is also a name for a set of mental constructs, each of which is a dispositif we use to regulate our relation to the outside world. At its most extreme, skin is a name for any surface that topologically produces sense by the sheer trajectory it traces (which makes it a condition of possibility of what it separates – constituting the in- and outside) – a plane of **immanence**. Since the ways in which it is construed are multiple and complex and crucially impact our view of the world, skin must also be seen as a matter of concern. It is the figure for the most urgent political, ethical, and philosophical problems of our time: for our ethical and ecological relation to other beings endowed with (another, different) skin, for the political issues of integration or assimilation, and finally for the understanding of the origin of human subjectivity and the nature of our relation to the world. As a surface on which an organism negotiates between the inside and the outside skin is also a figure for "**work**" as artistic production. On how we understand skin – its degrees of permeability, its capacity for **affect**, its interaction with its inside and outside – depends what we will be able to say about both the organism and the world. Often misunderstood in terms of a neutral partition separating an organism from its environment, skin remains on the outskirts of critical discourse. But this phenomenal and semantic region and the tensions that it hosts, might be said to respond in many ways to the objectives contemporary critique sets for itself: to find out "who 'we' might be" (Kaiser, Thiele, and Bunz 2014) (Are we contained inside our skins? Is the outside really outside?). Also, different conceptions of skin lead not only to different ideas about the need for, the manner, and the desired degree and trajectory of any possible intervention, **affirmation**, re-orientation, etc. but also to different ideas about the way in which affirmation is also intervention, about what precisely should be affirmed and where (by what affirming instance).

Two currents of thought that critique draws on today refer to skin as a site of potentially affirmative receptivity: the French tradition (Deleuze, Derrida, Lacan) and a tradition influenced by a certain understanding of "Romanticism" (Wittgenstein, Cavell, Benjamin). They do so in seemingly opposed ways: on the one hand, the French investment in difference, on the other, the Romantic yearning for seamlessness. For the first current, skin is always an operator of difference, the place where difference is thematized, endorsed, and amplified. For the "Romantically" inflected philosophies, in contrast, skin, and analogous surfaces or textures are so many figures of yearning for effortless align-ment with the world, the site of a desire for seamlessness, for the closing of the skeptical gap – in other words for a dis-appearance or at least an attenuation of difference (Cavell 2002, 61; Benjamin 1999, 590). Each of those approaches suggests a possible response to the problems of our relation to the world (and to the pervasive question: How do we change the world?). And each does so through its concern with receptivity and with the production of sense. The response of the French-inspired approaches has often been taken to be "through difference" – through differing from the world, distancing or some form of collective negation of some aspect of the world (an affirmation of one aspect is usually a negation of an other). Against this backdrop, the response of the "Romantic" approaches, in terms of perfect alignment with the world, might be taken to suggest a form of (political) quietism: the absorption of the world as it is in its entirety, without negation.

Jacques Lacan's famous gloss on our embodiment, that we are "sacks of skin," when not properly contextualized, might be taken to invite a reading in which skin is seen as a boundary between the self and the world, an individuating container in which something inner (and deeper) is encapsulated (Bernet 2000). This initial interpretation of the sack's relation to the world (and to other "sacks") needs to be revised. Clearly, skin is not simply a continuous layer of tissue where impressions from the environment accumulate, but rather a *selective barrier* permitting economic exchange of information, including the emergence of information to the outside (pigment, wrinkles, sweat). But for some thinkers this "membranous" reading of skin in terms of transmission, recording, selection, and exchange also needs to be qualified: for Gilles Deleuze, skin is a transcendental surface (addressed by Deleuze's appropriation of Paul Valéry's statement that "skin is the deepest" [Deleuze 1990, 103]). As opposed to the understanding of skin in terms of "economic exchange," skin in this approach does not mediate between independently established entities (as in self and another self): instead, it constitutes them topologically as such – it is the origin of their sense. In so defining skin, Deleuze makes it an empirical figure for all immanent lines of discernment, critical partitions, for all "critical" surfaces.

A somewhat different course is charted by the "Romantically" inflected philosophies of skin (Wittgenstein, Cavell, and Benjamin). Among those authors, skin stands for the way in which the affinity between the world and me, as a being endowed with skin, is construed, be it skeptically, phantasmatically, or ordinarily. Unfathomability of the inner (and thus also of the outer) feeds skepticism, so it's preferable to focus on surface instead of depth. "Wittgenstein wishes an acknowledgment of human limitation which does not leave us chafed by our own skin, by a sense of powerlessness to penetrate beyond the human conditions of knowledge" (Wittgenstein 2003, 71; 2012, 238; Cavell 2002, 61). Consequently, the Romantics approach skin as a site of organic suture to the world, with the world conceived as the second skin, enveloping the first. This Romantic yearning for spiritual osmosis, being enfolded, seamlessness, and **plasticity** seems, on the one hand, the purest affirmation that we can have: it accepts that to our **terran** existence there is no alternative. But on the other hand, its potential for intervention seems to be attenuated – or at least an ethical rather than a political one.

Two points of convergence suggest that these approaches can be reconciled and that the Romantic approach can regain its potential for intervention. In some of the approaches (on both the French and the Romantic side), skin is not conceived as a membrane or a biological epidermis but rather a fabric (see Walter Benjamin's question whether it is to be seen as a "net" or a "mantle" [Benjamin 2006, 96] and Stanley Cavell's injunction to "word the world together" [Cavell 1994, 126] – so that it doesn't fall apart, so to speak), suggesting that affinity to the world comes from human actions and words, is fabricated or woven (see Benjamin's figures of glove, sock, etui, etc.). That those approaches meet in their understanding of skin in terms of language and "fabric" offers possibilities for affirmative intervention: "wording the world together" is not just letting it be as it is.

Another point of convergence between the two approaches that might contribute to the understanding of aspects of affirmation is their move away from thinking about skin as a border or a container so as to focus on the figure of reversibility or alignment in the negative. Walter Benjamin pleads for recasting the opposition between inside and outside: an important figure in his work is the "turning inside out" (Friedlander 2012, 104) where the inside reveals itself as its opposite (see also Mondzain 2015). It would perhaps be more appropriate to say that for both traditions, rather than "sacks of skin" (Lacan 2006, 282), we are reversible folds of the world (so that the inner is as political as the outer). The figure of "turning inside out" speaks to Baruch de Spinoza's question of "what a body might do." Suggestive of an unmediated, privileged interaction – on the "inner side" – with each and every aspect of the world, but also of the potentially unlimited reach of the "merely individual," it contests the opposition between the political and the ethical. It indicates that both the "we" of critique and its trajectory might need to be redefined.

References

Benjamin, Walter. 1999. "Ibizan Sequence," translated by Rodney Livingstone. In *Selected Writings*. Vol. 2, *1927–1934*. Cambridge, MA: Harvard University Press.

Benjamin, Walter. 2006. *On Hashish. Translated by Howard Eiland*. Cambridge, MA: Harvard University Press.

Bernet, Rudolf. 2000. "The Encounter with the Stranger: Two Interpretations of the Vulnerability of the Skin." In *The Face of the Other and the Trace of God: Essays on the Philosophy of Emmanuel Levinas*, edited by Jeffrey Bloechl, 43–61. New York: Fordham University Press.

Cavell, Stanley. 1994. *In Quest of the Ordinary*. Chicago: Chicago University Press.

Cavell, Stanley. 2002. *Must We Mean What We Say?* Cambridge: Cambridge University Press.

Deleuze, Gilles. 1990. *The Logic of Sense*. New York: Columbia University Press.

Friedlander, Eli. 2012. *Walter Benjamin: A Philosophical Portrait*. Cambridge, MA: Harvard University Press.

Kaiser, Birgit Mara, Kathrin Thiele, and Mercedes Bunz. 2014. "What is Critique in the 21st Century? Discussing Terra Critica: A Conversation between Birgit Mara Kaiser, Kathrin Thiele and Mercedes Bunz." *terracritica.net*. Accessed May 2015. http://terracritica.net/interview/.

Lacan, Jacques. 2006. *Le Séminaire XVI: D'un autre à l'Autre*. Paris: Éditions du Seuil.

Latour, Bruno. 2004. "Why has Critique Run Out of Steam? From Matters of Fact to Matters of Concern." *Critical Inquiry* 30 (2): 225–248.

Mondzain, Marie-José. 2015. *L'image, une affaire de zone*. Noisy-le-Sec: Éditions d-fiction.

Wittgenstein, Ludwig. 2003. "Movements of Thought." In *Public and Private Occasions*, edited by James C. Klagge and Alfred Nordmann. Lanham: Rowman & Littlefield.

Wittgenstein, Ludwig. 2012. *Wittgenstein in Cambridge: Letters and Documents 1911–1951*. Edited by Brian McGuinness. Oxford: Wiley-Blackwell.

Specters

Esther Peeren

Affirmation as an ambiguous critical mode would entail "not to simply love everything, but rather to really turn around both sides (love and hate), to avert the immediate (perhaps) natural tendency that you want to reject something if you do not agree or dislike it, and instead, to try it the other way around – to exercise a non-negation until space – a different spacing – will open up" (Kaiser, Thiele, and Bunz 2014). This resonates with Jacques Derrida's injunction that, when confronted with a ghost or specter (as a figure of radical alterity), we should not give in to the urge to exorcize it, but should instead learn to live *with* it (Derrida 1994, xxviii). Such living *with*, as the just way of dealing with a haunting, is not self-evident (hence the need to learn how to do it) or straightforward, for, in addition to not being negated, the specter should also not be forced to assimilate. Haunting is reconfigured as a relational dynamic of **responsibility** with unpredictable results and considerable **risks** that cannot be fully controlled by either party, as Hamlet and his father's ghost find out at great cost in William Shakespeare's tragedy, from which Derrida's *Specters of Marx* (1994) takes off.

Specters, then, put agency – as sovereign control over one's actions and their consequences – into question. What we are left with is not so much agency circumscribed or agency to a lesser degree – as **semi-agency**, in its reference to a quantitative halving, seems to imply – but agency itself rendered as ambiguous and ephemeral as the specter. For, Derrida insists, a specter is not half-alive and half-dead, but something that, in full, exists in apparently mutually exclusive states, oscillating unpredictably between life and death, visibility and invisibility, materiality and immateriality, as well as the past, present, and future. Rather than dividing itself between these states, the specter exemplifies how each is divided from itself by its others, which do not remain separate from it, but are always already **entangled** with it.

In Derrida's terms, a spectral "*living on* [sur-vie]" appears as "a survival whose possibility in advance comes to disjoin or dis-adjust the identity to itself of the living present as well as of any effectivity" (Derrida 1994, xx). Effectivity – the ability to have effects that constitutes agency – comes apart not into quantifiable parts, but is undone in a more fundamental manner by the specter as "*more than one/no more one* [*le* plus d'un]," as simultaneously multiple and heterogeneous (xx). The specter, then, does not merely do something to **temporality** by putting time out of joint, and to being by transforming ontology into *hauntology*. It also does something to doing by making agency ambiguous and dynamic, causing it to wander in time, in space, and between what or who haunts, and what or whom is haunted. As a result, haunting manifests as an insistent following – in Dutch, aptly, it is translated as *achtervolgd worden* (being followed) – that also indicates a fundamental dependency: as popular culture teaches, ghosts haunt because they need something from the living (revenge, justice, reparation, assistance) and, conversely, the living conjure ghosts because they want them to provide access to the past or to other **worlds**. In itself, following already combines the active and the passive as a deliberate, insistent, and insidious action that does not determine its own course. Thus, haunting can be said to stage an "entangled state of agencies" (Barad 2007, 23) where **power** and dependency are not clearly distinguishable. In the depersonalized form of the German *es spukt* ("it haunts"), moreover, which lacks an identifiable haunting agent or force, what appears is "an unnameable and neutral power, that is, undecidable, neither active nor passive, an an-identity that, *without doing anything*, invisibly occupies places belonging finally neither to us nor to it" (Derrida 1994, 172). Without being or doing anything determinable, the *es spukt* nevertheless constitutes a force that **affects** its surroundings and can make something happen.

The Derridean specter also figures the condition of being implicated, as it is impossible not to be haunted, even for ghosts. Thus, Karl Marx is not only seen to haunt us but is himself conceived as haunted, together with Max Stirner, by Hegel. According to Derrida, it is impossible not to receive inheritances from the past and such inheritances cannot be refused, even if they can also never completely be known and appropriated. Something must be done with these spectral inheritances in order to live *with* them, and this something marks a site of critical agency: "'One must' means one must filter, sift, criticize, one must sort out several different possibles that inhabit the same injunction" (16). That the spectral inheritance has the power to make one act does not divest such compelled acts from agency altogether, but redefines the latter as entangled and ambiguous – as spectral agency (Peeren 2014, 16–24).

While ghosts appear to wield considerable power – including in Derrida's account, which ascribes to them the intimidating visor effect (the ability to see without being seen) as well as the ability to put time out of joint and to hand down injunctions – their dependency on being acknowledged by the living ensures that they are never all-powerful. At the same time, they are also never powerless, not even when their ghostliness marks extreme dispossession and vulnerability to exploitation rather than a haunting ability to instill fear and fascination, as is the case for those inhabiting the necropolitical death-worlds of the colonial, postcolonial, and neocolonial regimes described by Achille Mbembe: "My concern is those forms of sovereignty whose central project is not the struggle for autonomy but the generalized instrumentalization of human existence and the material destruction of human bodies and populations" (Mbembe 2003b, 14). Even these "living-dead (ghosts)" are capable of making something happen, not necessarily deliberately or efficiently, but by the very condition of constant wandering and **transformation** that defines their spectral existence, which renders them simultaneously vulnerable and elusive (Mbembe 2003a, 1).

Antonio Negri, in his response to *Specters of Marx*, complains that Derrida's theory and the "new spectrality" of postindustrial labor renders spectrality so pervasive that nothing solid, not even the worker's body, can be set against it:

> The new spectrality is here – and we're entirely within this real illusion … There's no longer an outside, neither a nostalgic one, nor a mythic one, nor any urgency or reason to disengage us from the spectrality of the real … The subject is therefore unlocatable in a world that has lost all measure, because in this spectral reality no measure is perceived or perceptible. (Negri 1999, 9)

For Negri, the fact that spectrality now fully encompasses the worker removes any capacity to act: if the subject cannot even be located and is of the same ephemeral quality as the capitalist system, how can it do anything to challenge it? He links the inability to act with spectrality, even though he also describes the capitalist system as highly effective in establishing a "ghostly dominion" (10). Yet, if there can be a spectrality that signifies dominion (and thus, surely, a form of agency), might the spectralized subject not also partake of it? This is exactly what Derrida proposes. The ambivalent force of *es spukt*, invisible yet not beyond being perceived, potentially allows spectralized subjects – the living-dead – to struggle against the spectralizing system by which they are produced as exploitable and expendable. As the familiar horror film scenario shows, the ghost can indeed come to haunt or possess its conjurer, but it can do so only as a ghost and not by laying claim to an unambiguous visibility, materiality, presence, and aliveness.

Spectral agency can refer to ghostly acts or to acts in the face of ghosts. For Derrida, as noted, the latter ought to be aimed at living *with* specters rather than at their exorcism or assimilation. If not exactly advocating a *caring for* specters, in the double sense of taking care of and having affinity with, this does imply an affirmative relationality and responsibility that might also be a criticality. The specter, conceived as a haunting entity, confirms our implicatedness in the world, our inability to separate ourselves from our multiple and complex entanglements with it, but at the same time it also stresses the element of "one must." We may not be able to choose what or whom we must care for or about, as ghosts and their spectral inheritances press themselves upon us. Yet critical force may reside in how we give shape to our living *with* them.

References

Barad, Karen. 2007. *Meeting the Universe Halfway: Quantum Physics and the Entanglement of Matter and Meaning*. Durham: Duke University Press.

Derrida, Jacques. 1994. *Specters of Marx: The State of the Debt, the Work of Mourning & the New International*. Translated by Peggy Kamuf. New York: Routledge.

Kaiser, Birgit Mara, Kathrin Thiele, and Mercedes Bunz. 2014. "What is Critique in the 21st Century? Discussing *Terra Critica*: A Conversation between Birgit Mara Kaiser, Kathrin Thiele and Mercedes Bunz." *terracritica.net*. Accessed May 2015. http://terracritica.net/interview/.

Mbembe, Achille. 2003a. "Life, Sovereignty, and Terror in the Fiction of Amos Tutuola." *Research in African Literatures* 34 (4): 1–26.

Mbembe, Achille. 2003b. "Necropolitics," translated by Libby Meintjes. *Public Culture* 15 (1): 11–40.

Negri, Antonio. 1999. "The Specter's Smile." In *Ghostly Demarcations: A Symposium on Jacques Derrida's Specters of Marx*, edited by Michael Sprinker, 5–16. London: Verso.

Peeren, Esther. 2014. *The Spectral Metaphor: Living Ghosts and the Agency of Invisibility*. Basingstoke: Palgrave Macmillan.

Speculation

Melanie Sehgal

Philosophically, speculation seems to be the antidote to critical thinking - striving for absolutes, for truths beyond the realm of experience, beyond historicity and finite perspectives. Thus, with the birth of critique, speculative thought became subject to critique. One could say that speculation was the first object of critique – if one understands speculation as metaphysical speculation about objects beyond experience, beyond what one can safely know and critique in the sense inaugurated by Immanuel Kant. In this perspective, critique historically *replaced* speculation. This replacement of metaphysical speculation by the Kantian reversion to the conditions of possibility of knowledge marks the beginning of modern thought, it even mark its modernity. Even if the Kantian conditions of the possibility of knowledge have now been replaced by linguistic or cultural conditions, the movement of critique, its practice, still follows the Kantian turn: It is a move away from what is given in experience to its conditions. Thus, if we stick to the classical philosophical understandings of both terms, the relation between critique and speculation has been a difficult, even antagonistic one. However, rethinking both terms, critique and speculation, enables a different perspective.

From this perspective, speculation becomes a new form of critique, a method of critical thinking. Speculation then is not defined by its objects – objects beyond experience pertaining to the absolute as it has been the case throughout the history of philosophy as well as in current re-actualizations of speculation (for example within the context of so-called speculative realism). Instead, speculation is to be defined by its practice and to be understood as a method. How does this method work? And in what way is this focus on the practice of theory exhibiting speculation as a critical method?

This question reverberates with the crucial stake of rethinking critique today. Why critique matters is not because it enables judgment. Taking sides has in some cases become impossible, while in others it is simply redundant, because every one agrees in theory anyways. The crucial aspect in rethinking critique today seems to be about method, about the practice of theory itself: How do we do theory? How does theory position itself towards experience, including its present and its past, its predecessors? If the desire to relate to the **world** we live in, to be relevant to it, is at the core of critical thinking, then how do we conceive of the mode of functioning, the efficacy, or performativity of theory towards its outside? In other words, how do we think of the relation of theory to practice, given that theory itself is a form of practice? What does it mean practically to think critically?

Bruno Latour famously concluded that "critique has run out of steam" (Latour 2004) as traditionally critique is leading *away* from experience, away from the world towards its conditions. But Latour also emphasized the necessity to renew, to reconstruct the notion and, above all, the very practice of critique. For him, rather than a "critique of critique" there is "[t]he practical problem … to associate the word criticism with a whole set of new positive metaphors, gestures, attitudes, knee-jerk reactions, habits of thoughts" (Latour 2004, 247). What might these new critical metaphors, gestures, attitudes, and habits of thought look like?

In the first place, as Latour says, they are positive, they are
affirmative – and this is a point in method concerning the situated practice of theory itself. New critical gestures start out from
the simple observation that whatever becomes subject to critique
is repeated, given space, time and weight and thus is affirmed
– simply by means of one's own theoretical practice. From this
perspective, even the most judgmental and negative critique
implicitly starts out from an affirmation. A reconstructed form
of critical thinking thus begins with a simple gesture: it takes this
primary affirmation into account *methodologically*. It forms the
necessary starting point for speculation insofar as it *posits* its
factual starting point in its theoretical practice rather than taking
it as a given. And such a reconstructed practice of critical thinking
lets this unavoidable affirmation guide its choice of subject, its
way of constructing a problem.

This leads to the second aspect of a speculative practice of critical
thinking: It is engaged in the very construction of the problem.
As Henri Bergson emphasized, the task of philosophy at large is
not simply to find solutions for given problems. Its first task is to
find the problem and challenge its current formulations, and to
eventually recompose it.[1] A speculative approach to a problem
is to start out from a particular issue, this issue being what situates thinking, what pertains to the world and forces to think. But
this does not imply taking the formulation of the problem for
granted according to the immediate way in which the problem
seems to present itself. Rather, a speculative practice of critical
thinking actively creates an indetermination, so that a solution
doesn't necessarily follow from the way the problem has been
posed. Thus, as Isabelle Stengers puts it, actively creating an
indetermination "requires the transformation of what announced
itself as a foundation, authorizing a position and providing its
banner to a cause, into a constraint, which the solution will have

1   "But the truth is that in philosophy and even elsewhere it is a question of
finding the problem and consequently of positing it, even more then of
solving it" (Bergson 2007, 36).

to respect but to which it may, if necessary, confer a somewhat unexpected signification" (2011, 15). Defining a problem does not determine its solution, rather the problem is a constraint for constructing a solution critically and speculatively.

Thirdly, a speculative practice of critique constructs responses to a problem with regard to their consequences. In view of sketching out speculation as a form of critical thinking, I have implicitly been drawing on a lineage of thought that ranges from Deleuze and Stengers to the early pragmatists. For William James or Charles Sanders Peirce pragmatism was "a method only" (James 1975, 31) and – despite of the prejudices against pragmatism that have been predominant within critical theory – I would like to argue that pragmatism is essentially a critical method. In the first place, the pragmatic method is a method of evaluation: The meaning of a concept is to be searched for in its consequences in experience, not in its reference to some idea or abstract truth. Thus, while critique in a classical, Kantian or even post-Kantian sense implies a movement backwards towards conditions, be they understood as a priori or linguistic or cultural, speculation leaps forward. It evaluates a concept, an idea, a response to a problem in terms of its imagined consequences in future experience, in terms of what the idea might *lead* to.[2] These consequences lie in the future and can thus only be imagined they are inherently speculative. And because this speculation

2   This implies or presupposes a certain idea of knowledge, one that builds on the changes within physics from a Newtonian framework to one of relativity and quantum physics and on enquiries into the physiology and psychology of knowledge processes. From this perspective, knowledge can never be certain. If one looks at the way knowledge is constructed concretely, in a scientific experiment, for example, knowledge, partly because of its time-bound nature, is inherently speculative. There first is a hypothesis, an idea, that *then* needs to be verified. In addition, constructing the solution to a problem implies the belief that some solution is actually possible. Without this belief no solution can be found – thus *this* or more generally: *a* belief *precedes* the verification. In this way, from a pragmatic point of view, which builds on twentieth century physics and psychology, knowledge is per force inherently speculative.

is grounded in the experience it starts out from, it isn't "mere speculation." The pragmatic method combines speculation with immanence – remaining within the flat ontology of a philosophy of immanence and radical experience –, and it does so methodologically: It avoids a representionalist, dualist stance in its own method, its own practice. There is no transcendent viewpoint from which a claim to absolute truth can be made; instead, there is only the stream of radical experience to follow, through the consequences a hypothesis generates.

This is why the pragmatic method is not restricted to evaluating already existing ideas and concepts. It can also be used as a method of constructing new ideas, new concepts (see Lapoujade 1997, 10). It can be put to work in the construction of different kinds of concepts, putting ideas to the test in view of possible outcomes and effects in experience. What would this idea, this response to a problem lead to? How could this concept guide our experience, our action in this particular situation? How does this idea address its recipients? Who is included by it, who is excluded? Could this idea change the way a situation is taking its course? What if we would think about this situation, or that problem in other terms? These are pragmatic questions and pragmatic questions can only be answered speculatively: by imagining future outcomes and consequences. Thus, speculation pragmatically understood is an art of consequences, of effects and such speculation is never certain, but always situated. It is grounded in its claims without creating new foundations. It starts out from what is given in experience, a problem, a situation that forces one to think, then tries to actively change the terms of this problem or situation, in order to change the course of its con-sequences: What if this problem was answered in this way? What would this lead to?

Critical thinking understood speculatively thus involves three dimensions: it implies starting out from a practical, methodological affirmation of what is given in experience, simply by means of one's own theoretical practice. It implies actively constructing the problem and only then formulating responses, constructing new ideas, or putting forth concepts that are then to be evaluated by their consequences, by what they might lead to in experience. Borrowing a term from Alfred North Whitehead, critical speculation formulates, constructs "propositions". Propositions, understood pragmatically and speculatively, are not jugdments or statements about what is; they are "lures for feeling" *this* world – otherwise.

References

Bergson, Henri. 2007. *The Creative Mind: An Introduction to Metaphysics*. Translated by Mabelle L. Andison. New York: Dover Publications.

James, William. 1975. *Pragmatism: The Works of William James*. Vol 1. Edited by Fredson Bowers, Frederick H. Burckhardt and Ignas K. Skrupskelis. Cambridge, MA: Harvard University Press.

Lapoujade, David. 1997. *William James: Empirisme et Pragmatisme*. Paris: PUF.

Latour, Bruno. 2004. "Why Has Critique Run Out of Steam? From Matters of Fact to Matters of Concern." *Critical Inquiry (Special issue on the Future of Critique)* 30 (2): 225–248.

Stengers, Isabelle. 2011. *Thinking with Whitehead: A Free and Wild Creation of Concepts*. Translated by Michel Chase. Cambridge, MA: Harvard University Press.

Stutter

Esther Peeren

In everyday life, stuttering – clinically defined as "a speech disorder that involves frequent and significant problems with the normal fluency and flow of speech"[1] – garners sympathy but is also seen as something aberrant that ought to be overcome for everyone's benefit. Keeping stutterers from communicating clearly and efficiently, their halting speech is considered a burden on their interlocutors, who may "respond with embarrassment" or even "experience a kind of pain" (Gunn and Rice 2009, 217). At the same time, stuttering interferes with views of the subject as autonomous and fully in control of itself by at once impairing voluntary action (what it intends to say is not what is uttered) and constituting involuntary action (words or parts of words come out altered or repeatedly).

The connection between stuttering and a lack of sovereignty is literalized in the 2010 Oscar-winning film *The King's Speech* (directed by Tom Hooper), which follows the struggle of King George VI (1895–1952) to overcome his speech impediment in order to give a radio address worthy of a king after – it is suggested – having embarrassed himself and the monarchy at an earlier public speaking engagement. Helped by Lionel Logue, a speech

---

1   http://www.mayoclinic.org/diseases-conditions/stuttering/basics/
     definition/con-20032854.

therapist who uses a combination of physical exercises and psychoanalysis, the king ends up conquering his stutter to deliver a rousing radio address on the occasion of the British declaration of war on Germany. The implication is that his position as ruler of the British Empire is cemented not so much by what he says, but by the fact that he is able to say it fluently. In 2013, an episode of *Educating Yorkshire*, a Channel 4 reality television show set in a secondary school, went viral after featuring a pupil, Musharaf, who was helped to overcome his severe stutter for his oral exam by his English teacher; the latter used the same method employed by Logue of having the stutterer listen to music while reciting a poem. Here, too, overcoming a stutter is framed as gaining control of oneself and as facilitating unconstrained, effective communication, even when, as in *The King's Speech*, what is achieved is not a speaking *with* but a speaking *to* (an address rather than a dialogue) that is also a speaking to a script (and thus not autonomous). In both cases, moreover, the disappearance of the stutter indicates a return to and affirmation of the norms regarding what constitutes "normal" speech and proper social and political organization: Musharaf can participate in the oral exam without questions having to be raised about its exclusion of those with speech impediments and George VI shores up the British monarchy after it had been brought into crisis by the abdication of Edward VIII.

With stuttering, as a speech disorder, marking non-normative communication and, etymologically, indicating that which forcefully comes up against something else – "stutter" has the same Old High German root (*stôʒen*) as the modern German *stossen*, meaning "to knock, strike against, collide" (see *Oxford English Dictionary*, stutter, v. and stut, v.) – it is not surprising that it has been taken up **metaphorically** to configure a more general disruptive and potentially critical force. Most notably, Deleuze, in "He Stuttered," extends the stutter beyond speech by arguing that, by stuttering in language, authors like Herman Melville, Franz Kafka, Samuel Beckett, Gherasim Luca, and Charles Péguy make language itself stutter. Through various techniques – the use of inclusive disjunctions, asignifying particles or repeated substantives – the language system is made to strike against or collide with itself, rendering it "**affective** and intensive," and putting it "in perpetual disequilibrium or bifurcation" (Deleuze 1997, 107, 108; bold added). For Deleuze, the **creative** stutter is a figure of **immanence**; it is not a vacillation between or mix of different languages but operates within a singular language to modulate or "*minorize*" it (109). Rather than adding something external, it expands, rhizomatically, from within: "Every word is divided, but into itself (*pas-rats*, *passions-rations*); and every word is combined, but with itself (*pas-passe-passion*)" (110). The critical potential of this immanence is signaled by the parallel Deleuze draws between the way stuttering takes language to its limit, putting it in touch with its outside and with silence, and the "state of *boom*, close to a *crash*" that creates space for radical new insight in "pure science" (109).

This line of thinking has been taken up by Isabel Stengers, who invokes the stutter as that which, in science, can disrupt and destabilize "matters of fact" and "consensus" (Stengers 2005, 154, 158). Her reading of Deleuze and Guattari's *What Is Philosophy?* (1994) conjures an image of stuttering minorities. Their stutters, if not dismissed or taken as an affliction to be cured, but considered as **symptoms** of systemic problems, may go from being interruptions to staging interventions. The stutter then becomes a "counter-effectuation" that produces "active divergence" (Stengers 2005, 163) and thus a mode of critique. From a similar Deleuzian perspective, Simon O'Sullivan conceives of the stutter, which he equates to the glitch, as both breaking a **world** and making a world, as simultaneous negation and **affirmation**: "The glitch is then a moment of critique, a moment of negation – but also a moment of creation and of affirmation" (O'Sullivan 2009, 251).[2]

Returning to stuttering as a speech disorder, it may be seen as inducing slowness and retardation through excess, expanding in time through a form of repetition that, instead of reconfirming meaning, moves beyond making immediate sense into ostensible redundancy. In the face of this, "the listener – or spectator – must respond to the glitch, the affective-event, *as* an event, as the bearer of the potentiality of something else" (249). Such a response can only reproduce the hesitation of what it responds to and, hence, should proceed slowly, thoughtfully, patiently. In a similar vein to the arrest of stupidity that Giorgio Agamben argues is the scholar's permanent condition (Pollard 2012, 125), stuttering may well be what the scholar in our age of advanced globalization – marked by relentless acceleration and neoliberal capitalism's cult of 24/7 (Crary 2014) – should respond to, as well as the form this response should take and the effect it should have.

Conceiving of stuttering as at once the object, form, and effect of critique radicalizes Geoffrey Hartman's notion of literary criticism as inducing a stutter in the text:

> Criticism as a kind of hermeneutics is disconcerting; like logic but without the latter's motive of absolute internal consistency, it reveals contradictions and equivocations, and so makes fiction interpretable by making it less readable. The fluency of the reader is affected by a kind of stutter: the critic's response becomes deliberately hesitant. (quoted in Sprinker 1980, 221)

---

2   The stutter's and the glitch's modes of disruption can be differentiated. As a "surge of current or a spurious electrical signal … ; also, in extended use, a sudden short-lived irregularity in behaviour," a glitch is a less sustained, singular event lacking the stutter's association with repetition, fragmentation, and excess (see *Oxford English Dictionary*, glitch, n.).

Here, rather than inhabiting language, making it "trembl[e] from head to toe" (Deleuze 1997, 109), the stutter is primarily an effect of criticism, produced through it and imposed on the text. It may reveal contradictions and equivocations in the text, but only in the service of interpretation; there is no pushing of "language as a whole to its limit, to its outside, to its silence" (113). As a form of critique, the stutter is seemingly reduced to the delayed but systematic interpretation of hermeneutics that is never outside the critic's control – its hesitancy is deliberate, a sign of eloquence rather than of inarticulacy or uncertainty. It is the smoothness and comfort of the reader's experience that is interrupted by this display of expertise.

Hartman's stutter appears sterile. It leaves aside the stutter's exposure of the difficulties of enunciation and address, and locates the discomfort and frustration experienced by stutterers like George VI and Musharaf exclusively in the reader. In contrast, conceiving of stuttering as object, form, and effect of critique in the current planetary condition would emphasize and distribute these aspects. In addition, it would stress the "**entanglement** between body and language" (Gunn and Rice 2009, 218; bold added) that renders stuttering a material, embodied experience of ineffectiveness, indeterminacy, uncertainty, and **risk**. Scholarly stuttering should not be an affectation or something we seek to grow out of, but an unavoidable part of our critical practices. Recognizing this is particularly important at a time when the neoliberalization of academia and its preoccupation with quantifiable productivity and efficiency pushes us to speed up and to smooth over (or to avoid altogether) the meandering and halting that, as Deleuze suggests, is often precisely what opens up new ways of making sense.

References

Crary, Jonathan. 2014. *24/7*. London: Verso.

Deleuze, Gilles. 1997. "He Stuttered." In *Essays: Critical and Clinical*, translated by Daniel W. Smith and Michael A. Greco, 107–114. Minneapolis: University of Minnesota Press.

Deleuze, Gilles, and Félix Guattari. 1994. *What is Philosophy?* New York: Columbia University Press.

Gunn, Joshua, and Jenny Edbauer Rice. 2009. "About Face/Stuttering Discipline." *Communication and Critical/Cultural Studies* 6 (2): 215–219.

O'Sullivan, Simon. 2009. "From Stuttering and Stammering to the Diagram: Deleuze, Bacon and Contemporary Art Practice." *Deleuze Studies* 3 (2): 247–258.

Pollard, Natalie. 2012. "The Fate of Stupidity." *Essays in Criticism* 62 (2): 125–138.

Sprinker, Michael. 1980. "Hermeneutic Hesitation: The Stuttering Text." *boundary 2* 9 (1): 217–232.

Stengers, Isabel. 2005. "Deleuze and Guattari's Last Enigmatic Message." *Angelaki: Journal of the Theoretical Humanities* 10 (2): 151–167.

Symptomatology

Birgit Mara Kaiser

Symptomatology is generally understood as a branch of
pathology, studying the indications of illness and disease in order
to treat the illness that these symptoms manifest. Symptoms are,
according to the *Oxford English Dictionary*, "a (bodily or mental)
phenomenon, circumstance, or change of condition arising from
and accompanying a disease or affection, and constituting an
indication or evidence of it." In the modern medical use of the
term, symptoms – although signs of an illness – differ from signs
in so far as they denote a subjective indication of affection or
illness, one that is perceptible to the patient, "as opposed to an
objective one or sign" (OED). Symptoms are, thus, **perspectival**
and subjective. And while they require – very much like signs –
to be interpreted, their interpretation always has to take into
account the specific constellation in which they appear and to
whom they appear; that is, they are not readable in isolation
but only in constellation with other symptoms, and their mani-
festation and readability might differ according to the perspective from which they are interpreted. A set or convergence of
symptoms, the "concurrence of several symptoms in a disease"
(OED), is then, in medical discourse, called a syndrome.

In critical discourse, symptomatology was prominently used by
Gilles Deleuze, who built on this clinical usage as well as on the
term's associations in Friedrich Nietzsche's writings. As such, the

term first surfaced in Deleuze's *Nietzsche and Philosophy* ([1962] 1983), most explicitly in the chapter entitled "Critique." As Deleuze points out, symptomatology is one form of the "active science" (1983, 75) that Nietzsche sought to establish, alongside the two other forms typology and genealogy. In order to overcome the established passive or reactive science, which fails to examine the genealogy of forces underlying its objects of study, Nietzsche aspired to an active science capable of interpreting precisely these relations of forces. An example Deleuze uses to show this difference in perspective is Nietzsche's turn to linguistics. While traditional linguistics places emphasis on the recipient of language, judging language "from the standpoint of the hearer" (74) and with an eye on the meaning inherent in words, Nietzsche strives for an "active philology," which would pursue the relations of forces that an utterance sets in motion. "Active linguistics" abandons the "objective" study of words and instead

> ... looks to discover who it is that speaks and names. "Who uses a particular word, what does he apply it to first of all; himself, someone else who listens, something else, and with what intention? What does he will by uttering a particular word?" The transformation of the sense of a word means that someone else (another force and another will) has taken possession of it and is applying it to another thing because he wants something else. (74–75)

The task of Nietzsche's active science is to pose these questions of **power** and pursue the relations of forces that become evident by asking them. They are the real and "subterranean differential mechanisms" (157) that shape phenomena, and a symptomatology, consequently, is that part of active science that "interprets phenomena, treating them as symptoms whose sense must be sought in the forces that produce them" (75). That Deleuze outlines symptomatology in a chapter entitled "Critique" is crucial: Symptomatology is used as a critical tool, an activity to distil the relations of forces underlying the currently congealed order of things. It thus displaces a notion of critique as judgment and the search for conditions of possibility (Kant's transcendental principles) and instead stresses critique (as symptomatology) as the analysis of the "genetic and **plastic** principles" (93, bold added) that *form* the becoming of things. Practiced as such, Deleuze writes, "[t]he point of critique is not justification but a different way of feeling: another **sensibility**" (94, bold added).

In *Coldness and Cruelty*, his critical introduction of 1967 to the French translation of Leopold von Sacher-Masoch's *Venus in Furs*, Deleuze then **translates** a Nietzschean symptomatology for the analyses of art. He demonstrates how Sacher-Masoch's and the Marquis de Sade's novels isolated two different desiring structures (masochism and sadism). These were, however, conflated as complimentary sexual "perversions" by Richard Freiherr von Krafft-Ebing as "sadomasochism," a portmanteau formed from the two authors' names. As Deleuze argues, Krafft-Ebing's *scientia sexualis* and subsequently Freudian psychoanalysis erroneously united "very different disturbances under a misbegotten name, in a whole arbitrarily defined by nonspecific causes" (1989, 134). Therefore, by revisiting Sacher-Masoch and de Sade, he unravels how they described irreducibly specific symptoms of the different "disturbances" of sadism and masochism (giving a list of eleven symptoms for each).

Two things happen here: First, instead of approaching writers as patients, Deleuze takes them as clinicians themselves, whose diagnoses have isolated or brought to light certain forms of desire. Rather than attribute an "illness" to the authors de Sade and Sacher-Masoch, to which their writings allegedly give expression (as Kraft-Ebbing and Freud did), their works are understood by Deleuze as a way to disentangle particular ways of feeling, taking literally the Greek root of critique – *krinein* – which is "to cut, rift, separate, discriminate, to decide" (see Hansen 2000, 4; see **Process**). The works themselves thereby perform a symptomatological analysis. In *The Logic of Sense* (1968), a text that draws prominently on Lewis Carroll's *Alice in Wonderland*, Deleuze then explicitly holds that writers are "themselves astonishing diagnosticians or symptomatologists" (1990, 237). We find this approach throughout Deleuze's engagement with literature and the arts right up to *Essays Critical and Clinical* (1993), where the very title signals the meeting-point of medical and artistic diagnoses in the sense outlined (see also Lambert). Second, Deleuze proposes a particular method of critical analysis – a method not only of literary works (in the double genitive as analysis done *by* and *of* literary works) but a method of analysis applicable to phenomena at large. Not taking phenomena at face value, Deleuze writes in *Nietzsche and Philosophy*:

> We will never find the sense of something (of a human, a biological or even a physical phenomenon) if we do not know the force which appropriates the thing, which exploits it, which takes possession of it or is expressed in it. A phenomenon is not an appearance or even an apparition but a sign, a symptom which finds its meaning in an existing force. (3)

Symptomatology is therefore directed at the constellation of forces that form a certain phenomenon or way of existing. The specificity of this method, however, does not only lie in its being directed at the forces that a symptom signals but also in the way it proceeds. Such a procedure, which Nietzsche called "active" and Deleuze "**creative**," differs from a reading of signs; it rather involves an interpretation of symptoms in their constellation *and* it is – in the course of this interpretation – a rearrangement or a new grouping of such a constellation. In *The Logic of Sense*, Deleuze explains: "There is always a great deal of art involved in the grouping of symptoms, in the organization of a *table* where a particular symptom is dissociated from another, juxtaposed to a third, and forms *the new figure* of a disorder or illness" (237, emphases added). As much as the doctor, the symptomatologist does not invent the disorder but she "isolates" it: by distinguishing and disentangling components that had so far been erroneously clustered together ("sadomasochism"), therefore by destroying the cluster that had falsely been taken as unity, by specifying its components and subsequently regrouping them ("sadism" – "masochism"), by detecting the forces that form these new conditions. In the course of such a "differential diagnostics" (Smith, xviii) new figures emerge, disentangling a false cluster and bringing to light the new portrait of a desire, a way of feeling, a differently posed problem.

Such a new figure comes about as a result of "creative" or active critique (Deleuze 1989, 134). In that sense, Deleuze remarks in *Coldness and Cruelty*, "[s]ymptomatology is always a question of art" (14). An art of reading the symptoms of our contemporary, planetary condition, which would involve cutting, rifting, separating (*krinein*) the apparent clusters and reordering them in ways that make different constellations appear, different degrees of freedom imaginable. Critique as symptomatology is in that sense a clinical and "interdisciplinary" endeavor – "located almost outside of medicine, at a neutral point, a zero point, where artists and philosophers and doctors and patients can come together" (Deleuze 2004, 134, translation modified).

References

Deleuze, Gilles. 1989. *Coldness and Cruelty*. Translated by Jean McNeil. New York: Zone Books.

Deleuze, Gilles. 2004. "Mysticism and Masochism (Interview with Madelaine Chapsal)." In *Desert Islands and Other Text (1953–1974)*, translated by Michael Taormina, 131–134. New York: Semiotext(e).

Deleuze, Gilles. 1983. *Nietzsche and Philosophy*, translated by Hugh Tomlinson. New York: Columbia University Press.

Deleuze, Gilles. 1990. *The Logic of Sense*. Translated by Mark Lester with Charles Stivale. New York: Columbia University Press.

Hansen, Beatrice. 2000. *Critique of Violence: Between Poststructuralism and Critical Theory*. London: Routledge.

Lambert, Gregg. 1998. "On the Uses and Abuses of Literature for Life: Gilles Deleuze and the Literary Clinic." *Postmodern Culture* 8 (3). doi 10.1353/pmc.1998.0022.

Smith, Daniel W. 1997. "Introduction". In *Gilles Deleuze, Essays Critical and Clinical*, xi–liii. Minneapolis: University of Minnesota Press.

Technology

Mercedes Bunz

Technologies make **world**s appear. It is this capacity that has always interested the contemporary critic when turning to the concept of technology. In *The Human Condition*, Hannah Arendt, for example, discusses the effect technologies have on "the very worldliness of the human artifice" (1958, 150). Samuel Weber (1996) makes the same point – that technologies are "Upsetting the Set-Up" – when thinking through Martin Heidegger, who before him had remarked: "Techné belongs to bringing-forth, to poiesis. It is something poietic" (Heidegger 1977, 12). By adding new objects, by varying the measurements, by changing the perspectives, by linking what had been disconnected and connecting what had been apart, by providing destructive powers, by confusing the boundaries, technologies allow new and different movements of thoughts, things, and bodies into the human artifice.

Although all technologies have the forceful and fabulous capacity to **create** a different world, the worlds that appear do not automatically lead in any progressive direction. In other words, their technical realities are necessarily different, but not necessarily "better." Walter Benjamin's circular glasses were among the first to come across this: in his famous essay "The Work of Art in the Age of Its Technological Reproducibility" (1936), he discusses the divergent ways in which the new means of (re) production – photography and cinema – are affecting the masses, an affecting that can be twofold as the "increasing proletarianization of modern man and the increasing formation of masses are *two aspects of the same process*" (Benjamin 1936, 120; emphasis added). Technologies can be employed to manipulate the masses in the interest of fascist capital, or they can be employed to allow masses meet themselves thereby helping them to understand their own formation, and therefore their needs. As Benjamin makes clear in his essay, the actual appropriation, the usage decides which of those worlds will be created. To ensure an appearance of a world aligned against fascism, his essay introduces a specific take on the new technologies:

> In what follows, the concepts which are introduced ... are completely useless for the purposes of fascism. On the other hand, they are useful for the formulation of revolutionary demands. (102)

Here, Benjamin points out that technologies change the world that is in place. New technical realities "neutralize a number of traditional concepts – such as creativity and genius, eternal value and mystery" (101). As they "neutralize" the framework of the world in place, technologies create an opening that harbors a political moment. It is technology that makes this opening possible – a point Benjamin makes again in another text, where he describes "technical revolutions" as "fracture points": "[I]t is there that the different political tendencies may be said to come to the surface" (1927, 17). Years later, in "A Cyborg Manifesto," Donna Haraway embraces technology for the same reason: "The frame for my sketch is set by the extent and importance of rearrangements in world-wide social relations tied to science and technology" (1991, 161).

If technology has the capacity to question the world in place and if it offers difference, as Benjamin and Haraway write, technology is *in this world* but *not of this world*: It is alien to its conditions. Benjamin writes: "In every new technical revolution, the political

tendency is transformed, *as if by its own volition*, from a con-
cealed element of art into a manifest one" (1927, 17; emphasis
added). We certainly can work with technology and with the
political tendencies it has created, but we can neither control
nor predict technology and thus *which* tendencies it will create.
Technology follows its own, alien logic. Even in the twenty-first
century, in which prediction has become a paradigm, this is still
the case: In a field as closely guarded as the digital economy, we
are never certain what will be "the next big thing." We cannot
predict the future of the technology we have invented. Alien to
us, technology has the capacity to set up a truly different frame,
which makes a new world appear.

Philosophical explorations of this frame tracing technology's
alien-ness have started. Against the assumption that algorithms
are obstinate step-by-step procedures, Luciana Parisi (2013) discusses the blind spots of computers with Chaitin's constant, for
example, a number that is real but not computable. Parisi reads
those alien logics of calculation as symptoms of algorithmic
thought and uses them as a point of departure for an immanent
critique of algorithmic practices and methods. Benjamin Bratton
(2016), on the other hand, describes today's planetary-scale
computation as an alien political geography. Based on mineral
sourcing, it links the earth, the user, and technology in new ways
and is inhabited by meaningful users, "human and otherwise":

> It is with vestigial stupidity that we police the human/animal
> divide in the way that we do, and it is equally misguided to
> insist that computing machines are 'just tools' and not also
> co-*Users* along with us. (Bratton 2016, 349)

The theoretical challenge, of course, is then not to think of
them as "just subjects" either – a challenge we are not very
well equipped for. As Bratton points out, "we lack adequate
vocabularies to properly engage the operations of planetary-
scale computation" (xviii).

In our philosophical thinking of technology, the problem of vocabulary, however, has been central for quite a while – no lesser text than Heidegger's forceful essay asking "The Question Concerning Technology" (1954) is a good example of this. Although Heidegger aims "to experience the technological within its own bounds" (4), he leads out of those bounds looking for an answer by linking techné and poetry via classical Greek. Stating that "the essence of technology is by no means anything technological" (4), however, Heidegger might have sent us in the wrong direction – interestingly, this is exactly where Arendt turns the other way. Instead of finding an answer to technology in the human artifice, she points to the functioning of technology itself:

> The discussion of the whole problem of technology, that is, of the transformation of life and world through the introduction of the machine, has been strangely led astray through an all-too-exclusive concentration upon the service or disservice the machines render to men. The assumption here is that every tool and implement is primarily designed to make human life easier and human labor less painful. Their instrumentality is understood exclusively in this anthropocentric sense. But the instrumentality of tools and implements is *much more closely related to the object it is designed to produce*. (1958, 151; emphasis added)

The technical object, according to Arendt, is misunderstood as a means to human ends. Its instrumentality is always more closely related to another object than to a human subject. In other words, the immanence of technology, its own, "alien" logic, is a force, which is driven by an **immanent** – "closer" – relation.

At the very same time, Gilbert Simondon (1958) explores this immanence at work in his philosophical analysis *On the Mode of Existence of Technical Objects*. Studying steam-powered and combustion engines, cathodes, turbines, telephones, and other technical objects convinces the French philosopher of the same close, immanent relation, which he describes as a *"processus de*

concrétisation" or process of concretization (1958, 19), triggered
by the specific relation of a technical object with its environment.
Comparing the modern engine of his time of writing to an older
one from 1910, Simondon points out that the newer one is not
"better" but that it just functions better because it is more tightly
related to the rest of the car. This tight relation has changed
how the engine runs in and provides energy for the car, but it
has also made the vehicle more dependent on its environment.
The engine of 1910 is "*plus autonome*," or more autonomous, (20);
unlike the new one, it also functioned in fishing boats without
breaking down. This and other examples lead Simondon to a
number of interesting conclusions that today affect thinking
far beyond technology. For example, that the transformation
of matter (things, bodies, thoughts) is driven by *concrétisations*,
which can be explained via concrete technical relations with
their milieu, creating an immanent development, which is non-
directional. As Elizabeth Grosz points out:

> Matter has a positive property immanent in any of its
> particular characteristics – it is capable of being modelled,
> formed. Matter has what Simondon understands as **plas-
> ticity**, the capacity to become something other than what it
> is now, as its positivity, its openness, its orientation to trans-
> formation. (2012, 45, bold added)

Here Grosz points out a political – open – moment that marks the
start of something new. It marks, however, only the start. New
technologies, alien to the existing human artifice, offer a forceful
moment of upsetting the setup in unforeseen ways; this is why
understanding technology is crucial to the contemporary critic,
and this is the case more than ever in the technical realities that
mark the twenty-first century.

To understand the force of technology, however, means to
differentiate the opening of technology from its actual interpretation – too often technology gets blamed for capitalistic interests that hide in it all too well. It is, however, not the fault of the

mobile phone that we feel the need to be available for work on the weekend (Berardi 2009, 193). Instead, the connection of what was once free time to capitalistic interests has been installed by a human boss who wants his workers to be always available (Bunz 2014, 32); others have set rules in place to avoid emailing after working hours. The mobile phone, for example, could also be interpreted as an emancipative weapon as it also allows one to remotely be there for someone who needs care, a dear friend, a child, an old parent, which eases the work of social availability, a role that in this world is still mostly carried out by women.

While in this case technology has the force to change the set up of the human artifice – we all become potentially available – it does not dictate whose interests are put across. As Haraway once remarked: "Technology is not neutral. We're inside of what we make, and it's inside of us. We're living in a world of connections – and it matters which ones get made and unmade" (cited in Kunzru 1997). For this, we need to turn to technology, which starts with using and understanding it better and ends with coding or hacking it – different ways to appropriate it are possible and open to us all. Technology might be an alien force, but unsurprisingly we cannot sit back and let capitalism create the revolution.

References

Arendt, Hannah. (1958) 1998. *The Human Condition*. Chicago: University of Chicago.

Benjamin, Walter. (1927) 2005. "Reply to Oscar A. H. Schmitz," translated by Rodney Livingstone. In *Selected Writings*. Vol. 2, pt. 1, *1927–1930*, 16–19. Cambridge, MA: Harvard University Press.

Benjamin, Walter. (1936) 2006. "The Work of Art in the Age of Its Technological Reproducibility: Second Version," translated by Edmund Jephcott and Harry Zohn. In *Selected Writings*. Vol. 2, pt. 1, *1927–1930*, 101–133. Cambridge, MA: Harvard University Press.

Berardi, Franco. 2009. *The Soul at Work: From Alienation to Autonomy*. Los Angeles: Semiotext(e); Cambridge MA: MIT Press.

Bratton, Benjamin. 2016. *On Software and Sovereignity*. Cambridge, MA: MIT Press.

Bunz, Mercedes. 2014. *The Silent Revolution: How Digitalization Transforms Knowledge, Work, Journalism and Politics without Making Too Much Noise*. Basingstoke: Palgrave Macmillan.

Grosz, Elizabeth. 2012. "Identity and Individuation: Some Feminist Reflections." In *Gilbert Simondon: Being and Technology*, edited by Arne De Boever, Alex Murray, Jon Roffe and Ashley Woodward, 37–56. Edinburgh: Edinburgh University Press.

Haraway, Donna. 1991. "A Cyborg Manifesto: Science, Technology, and Socialist-Feminism in the Late Twentieth Century." In *Simians, Cyborgs, and Women The Reinvention of Nature*. 149–181. New York: Routledge.

Heidegger, Martin. (1954) 1977. "The Question Concerncing Technology," translated by William Lovitt. In *'The Question Concerning Technology' and Other Essays*, 3–35. New York: Harper & Row.

Kunzru, Hari. 1997. "You are Cyborg." *Wired Magazine* 5.2, 1–7. Accessed May 2, 2016. http://www.wired.com/1997/02/ffharaway/.

Parisi, Luciana. 2013. *Contagious Architecture, Computation, Aesthetics, and Space*. Cambridge, MA: MIT Press.

Simondon, Gilbert. (1958) 1989. *Du Mode d'Existence des Objets Techniques*. Paris: Aubier Editions.

Simondon, Gilbert. 2012. "Technical Mentality," translated by Arne De Boever. In *Gilbert Simondon. Being and Technology*, edited by De Boever, Arne and Alex Murray, Jon Roffe, and Ahley Woodward, 1–15. Edinburgh: Edinburgh University Press.

Weber, Samuel. 1996. "Upsetting the Setup: Remarks on Heidegger's Questing After Technics." In *Mass Mediauras*, 55–75. Stanford: Stanford University Press.

Temporality

Yvonne Förster

The concept of temporality is closely linked to modernity, postmodernity, and the contemporary *conditio humana*. The term covers a variety of related concepts such as finitude, progress, future, memory, or acceleration, to name just a few. Only with the modern era, the concept of care for the future emerged (Dux 1992). Temporality in its various aspects is a deeply historical concept. Though there is a more basic dimension of temporality at stake in the ontogenesis of time in living creatures, cultural aspects of time are dynamic and changing.

Postmodern concepts of time and temporality present a critique of modernity with its ideas of progress and homogeneous time. The idea that time is a universal flux from the past into the future or vice versa has long lost its credibility, with the horrors of the Second World War at the latest. That is the reason why the temporal concept of progress has been widely criticized in the humanities. Concepts of time, like the idea of a continuing progress of society or eschatological scenarios have always had an impact on culture and the value of life. With industrialization, urban life and the omnipresence of **technology** emerged. Within this historical atmosphere of the early twentieth century, time became more perceptible than before, because technology and industrial production produced new rhythms that structure life in different ways than before. Natural rhythms loose importance and technological rhythms became more important. Those technological concepts of time structure historical and biographical narratives as well as everyday life. Instead of a continuous flux of time, the twentieth and twenty-first centuries envision time as fragmented and **perspectival.**

How can the concept of time then be a tool of critique? The way time is conceptualized influences narratives of history and individual identities. One very influential concept of time and temporal becoming is the arrow of time. In this image, time is a continuous and homogeneous flux that is future-oriented, with which constant progress in history is associated. This image has been widely criticized. One of the pioneers of this critique is Walter Benjamin. In his considerations in *Theses on the Philosophy of History* (1940), which he wrote facing the threats of the Second World War, he uses Paul Klee's painting *Angelus Novus* to illustrate his critique of the concept of historical progress:

> A Klee painting named "Angelus Novus" shows an angel looking as though he is about to move away from something he is fixedly contemplating. His eyes are staring, his mouth is open, his wings are spread. This is how one pictures the angel of history. His face is turned toward the past. Where we perceive a chain of events, *he* sees a single catastrophe which keeps piling wreckage upon wreckage and hurls it in front of his feet. (1940, 257)

Benjamin's famous interpretation of Klee's work makes palpable how historical progress is a dangerous idea, oblivious of the catastrophes that human culture produces. His concept of *dialectical materialism* implies a concept of time that focuses on materiality and simultaneity. These features are absent in traditional concepts of time, as for example Immanuel Kant's transcendental concept of time exemplifies, in which time is essentially non-materialistic (subjective and ideal) and homogeneous (an inner form of intuition, Kant 1997, 426/A 369).

Historical time for Benjamin is not "empty time, but time filled full
by now-time [*Jetztzeit*]" (Benjamin 1940, 261).

The notion of empty time implies an abstract structure, which
can be filled by projects and ideas. Empty time is an intellectual
construct that is suited to modern ideas of human self-creation
and perfection, of rationality and progress. Benjamin contrasts
this notion of time with an image of material temporality. His idea
is that the historical moment is a compound of past, present, and
future within historical materiality. He compares history to the
temporal aspects of fashion, which represents a form of historical
materiality, a material phenomenon, which is in itself temporal:
"The French Revolution viewed itself as Rome incarnate. It evoked
ancient Rome the way fashion evokes costumes of the past.
Fashion has a flair for the topical, no matter where it stirs in the
thickets of long ago; it is the tiger's leap into the past" (261). This
tiger's leap suggests discontinuity as well as material simultaneity.
Benjamin's idea of historical time implies the simultaneous
presence of different layers of time, all present in the actual
moment. A historical chain of events appears as progress
because these events are represented in a certain narrative
that makes sense of the "piles of wreckage," as Benjamin puts it.
Benjamin's aim is to show how the apparent ratio and continuity
of history is a product of a narrative that links events causally.
What historians ought to do, according to Benjamin, is to understand the temporal constellations that events are made of and
how the present comprises past times or "chips of messianic
time" (263).

For another model of non-homogeneous temporality we might
turn to cinematic time. Cinema experiments with various spatio-
temporal forms of representation, such as the French movement
Nouvelle Vague did. This allows for a representation of different
temporal and perceptual strata in one scene. These techniques
of montage do not adhere to rules of narrativity anymore,
but invent a form of temporal clustering, which represents
a critique of linear narration. Gilles Deleuze (1985) presents

two different conceptions of the cinematic image: One that is structured through movement (movement-image) and hence constitutes a continuous representation of the world; and one that is structured by time, what he then calls time-image. The time-image, according to Deleuze, is representative of precisely the cinema of his time, because techniques of cinematic representation also changed with the Second World War. Similar to Benjamin, who criticized the conception of historical time that orders events along a continuous causal chain, Deleuze diagnoses a change that occurred in the production of images.

New techniques of montage and camera-use create images, where time is not the measure of movement anymore. The time-image is a compound of past, present, and future as well as a presentation of different modes of consciousness. The driving logic in those images is neither simple action, nor a causal chain of events that leads to a certain result, but rather it is time itself. Film becomes a critique of the logic of progress, and it furthers an idea of original production (primacy of non-propositional subconsciousness) as opposed to capitalistic production, which creates a sense of need, negativity, and estrangement. The time-image is constituted by means of montage-techniques and can simultaneously represent different times and modes of perception, such as a memory of the past within an image of the present or the co-presence of undiscernible layers of the actual and the virtual, such as Orson Welles' *The Lady from Shanghai* (USA 1947). The time-image thus makes visible layers of time which are neither tantamount to the present moment nor do they simply represent the history that led to one individual moment in present time. Cinematic images become a medium that is able to make visible fragments of time and their intertwining. Not only past, present, and future, but also actuality and virtuality, reality, and possibility can be represented in their **entanglement** through techniques of montage. This way cinema becomes a critique of simple, progress-oriented ideas of time and history and proposes a view of the temporal process, which integrates varying perspectives, fragmentation, plurality, and discontinuity.

Within the twentieth and twenty-first centuries, the concept of time has been developed along the lines of cultural critique, where the above-mentioned aspects – plurality, discontinuity, and simultaneity – are central alongside a focus on temporal becoming and procedural ontology. The emphasis on becoming and the notion of **process** are the reasons for this entry dedicated to temporality. Contemporary concepts stress the dynamic and procedural aspects of time. This is what is captured by the term temporality.

Contemporary theories as put forth by Bernhard Stiegler (1994) or Mark B. N. Hansen (2004) focus on a temporality constituted by **technology**. Hansen understands human perception of time as embedded or informed by machine time (Hansen 2004, 235). That means that technologically constituted temporalities figure as ontological structures, which are not perceptible themselves but inform human perception of time. A plurality of temporalities is constituted by technology that does not necessarily relate or adapt to human perception. Technology is seen as the formation of consciousness-independent layers of temporalities. Contemporary art and cinema use knowledge of neuroscience research on human perception and the impact of digital technologies to induce experiences that affect the viewers on a perceptual level (see Hansen 2004, Pisters 2012). The various technological temporalities within our contemporary digital culture are described as being fundamental to human perception, yet they are of heterogeneous origin and thus introduce a transcendent element into human perception. This ontological view can be seen as a prolonged critique of the Kantian definition of time as an inner form of intuition and hence as a category specific to the humanities.

References

Benjamin, Walter. (1940) 1969. "Theses on the Philosophy of History," translated by Harry Zorn. In *Illuminations*, 253–264. New York: Schocken.

Deleuze, Gilles. 1985. *L'Image-temps: Cinéma 2*. Paris: Les Éditions de Minuit.

Dux, Günter. 1992. *Die Zeit in der Geschichte*. Frankfurt: Suhrkamp.

Hansen, Mark B. N. 2004. *New Philosophy for New Media*. Cambridge, MA: MIT Press.

Kant, Immanuel. 1997. *Critique of Pure Reason*. Translated by P. Guyer and A. Wood. Cambridge: Cambridge University Press.

Pisters, Patricia. 2012. *The Neuro-Image: A Deluezian Film-Philosophy of Digital Screen Culture*. Stanford: Stanford University Press.

Stiegler, Bernhard. 1994–2001. *La Technique et le Temps*, Tome 1–3. Paris: Galilée.

Terra

Birgit Mara Kaiser and Kathrin Thiele

Terra, a feminine noun in Latin, refers to "earth; land, ground, soil; country; region" (Morwood 2012). It is used in English frequently in science fiction to designate planet earth, and appears in colloquial language mainly in composites, such as *terra firma*, *terra nullius* or *terra incognita*, and then usually in figurative speech. *Terra incognita*, as perhaps the most prominent example, has become the figurative expression for an unknown or unexplored region. In a similar vein, Sigmund Freud **metaphorically** referred to female sexuality as a "'dark continent' for psychology" (1959, 211). Both *terra incognita* and *dark continent* designate metaphorically the unknown. Yet, underneath their "mere" metaphoricity, the literal reference to geographical regions of the earth that are uncharted by Western explorers – that is: the terms' colonial heritage – is audible in both cases. Freud's implicit reference to a continent that Joseph Conrad had figured two and a half decades before as the *Heart of Darkness* (a novel in turn written in the wake of the Berlin Conference in 1884 and the ensuing European "scramble for Africa"); and – somewhat less immediately perceptible and temporally more remote – Captain John Smith's introduction of the term *terra incognita* into the English language in his *A Description of New England* (1616). A soldier and explorer for the English crown, Smith endorsed the Virginia Company's promotion of the colonization of New England and was famously involved with the founding of Jamestown, one of the first European settlements in the New World. His *Description* encouraged the founding of colonies by the British, since there were "such large Regions ... yet vnknowne, as well in *America*, as in *Affrica*, and *Asia*, and *Terra Incognita*" ([1616] 2006, 45), the latter referring to territories occupied by Spain, but in a way a synecdoche for all of these "large regions yet unknown." Since the vast, uncharted geographical expanses promised profits, the British should do as the Portuguese in Africa, for "had not the industrious Portugales ranged her vnknowne parts, who would haue sought for wealth among those fryed Regions of blacke brutish Negers" (21).

In her work on rewriting knowledges, the Jamaican philosopher Sylvia Wynter has powerfully traced the discursive and political shifts that different figurations of the earth have effected – shifts that were informed by empirical experiences of travel and trade, as well as bound up with changing cosmologies. The truth an epoch or a culture holds about the earth is of fundamental significance to that epoch's, that culture's, and that earth's onto-epistemological, symbolical, economical and political make up. In her article "1492," Wynter notes – much like Smith, but with reversed value – the unsettling effects that the Portuguese voyages to Africa had in this regard. The Portuguese rounded the "hitherto nonnavigable Cape Bojador on the bulge of West Africa" (1995, 9) in 1441 and established a trading fort at Elmina (present-day Ghana, a fort which Columbus was to visit) in about 1482. This circumnavigation and the subsequent existence of the fort called into question the feudal, Christian, medieval geographic imagination of the earth as divided into inhabitable and uninhabitable zones. As Wynter explains, Cape Bojador "had been projected, in the accounts of the earth's geography given by medieval Christian geographers, as being the *nec plus ultra* line and boundary marker between the habitable temperate zone of Europe and the inhabitable [*sic*] torrid zones" (9). Such a projection was congruent with the cosmology of

Latin-Christian Europe, Wynter argues, and its "feudal image of a nonhomogenous earth" (25). The medieval Christian cosmology structured itself around a master code of "Spirit/Flesh" (see also Le Goff 1985) – a "represented nonhomogeneity of substance between the spiritual perfection of the heavens ... as opposed to the sublunar realm of the Earth ... as the abode of a post-Adamic fallen mankind" (Wynter 2003, 278) – a master code which was equally projected onto the geography of the earth. In similar spirit/flesh (or life/death, elevated/fallen) terms, the earth was

> divided up between, on the one hand, its temperate regions centered on Jerusalem – regions that, because held up above the element of water by God's Providential Grace, were inhabitable – and, on the other, those realms that, because outside this Grace, had to be uninhabitable. (278–279)

This imagination of an "uninhabitable torrid zone" (Wynter 1995, 22) south of Cape Bojador was ruined and slowly eroded as a result of the Portuguese landfall south of the line after 1441 (and a complementary set of onto-epistemological shifts including the emergent humanism), and once the Portuguese had rounded the cape and had – as Smith notes applaudingly – "ranged ... [Africa's] vnknowne parts." Now, America had become possible, and what had been torrid zones, uninhabitable, became "large regions yet unknown" of a *terra incognita*: unknown, yet inhabitable and therefore exploitable.

In her work, Wynter traces these cosmological-geographical **transformations**, and with and through them the seismic philosophical, symbolical, and political transformations with which they are **entangled**. Wynter does so especially in view of the dominant notion of what it means to be human. For the notion of *terra* that is central here, and its critical purchase, the relevance of Wynter's analysis is clear: Our cosmologies have geographical, spiritual, philosophical, political, epistemological, ontological, and ethical implications; they inform and delimit our conceptions of the earth and vice versa. As a consequence, then, the imagination and empirical experience "we" have of the earth – and it would be crucial to consider the plurality and differentiation of that "we" to which Jacques Derrida gestures at the end of his essay "The Ends of Man" by asking "But who, we?" (1982, 136; see also Wynter 2015, 23) – can be read as one symptom of the *critical* conditions of our times. Understanding in its entangled complexity how "we" imagine the earth is a step toward understanding the current order of things. It is part of a **symptomatology** of the present.

Today, the **experience** of the earth as divided into inhabitable and uninhabitable regions has lost traction – even as a vast expanse of lands that are unknown and out there to be explored and exploited, although the spirit of the latter still lives on in current practices of deep sea oil drilling, Antarctica mining projects, fracking and the like. Despite these very real **specters** of the earth as mere resource, "we" *experience terra* increasingly – and more or less globally (a more or less that is crucial to take into account as it signals fault lines of exclusion, **responsibility**, and **power**) – as a closely interwoven ecosystem, a finite planet whose climate is changing and whose natural resources have been nearly exhausted by the dominant habits of Western man. There are no longer any *terras incognitas* (beyond the merely economic fantasies of subterranean chemical fossils), but there is a *terra critica*: one earth in critical economic, ecological, symbolic, socio-political, intra-species condition. As Félix Guattari puts this in *The Three Ecologies*, "[t]he Earth is undergoing a period of intense techno-scientific transformations. If no remedy is found, the ecological disequilibrium this has generated will ultimately threaten the continuation of life on the planet's surface" (2000, 19).

However, the critical purchase of *terra*, as the term is proposed here, lies slightly elsewhere than in the eco-critical investigations of climate change or what has become known as "the Anthropocene" (e.g. Chakrabarty 2009; Cohen, Colebrook, and Miller 2016; Stengers 2015). Here, *terra* – unlike globe or planet or even its English **translation** as earth – does not so much designate the geological body and ecosystem we inhabit, whose climate change and human grooving need to be examined. Rather, as exhibited here by tracing the historical shifts that Wynter points out and that Smith served to exemplify, *terra* (in its Latin garment) designates the *imagination* of the earth; the way "we" figure and narrate the earth, a figuration that is always crucially interwoven with empirical experiences of it. Since airplanes reach the other side of the globe within the maximum of a day, families span distant geographical locations and virtual spaces enable us to connect across continents, these historical experiences give rise to imaginations that are quite different from feudal Christian Europe or the colonial period. As Édouard Glissant argues in *Poetics of Relation (1997)*, five centuries of colonial domination, migration, deportation and slavery, cultural contact, and genocide were not only nourished by the imagination of *terra(s) incognita(s)*, but *at the same time* also made the imagination and praxis of "Relation" possible, and made it apparent as the (post)colonial condition of earthly existence. The plantation system, Glissant suggests,

> is one of the focal points for the development of present-day modes of Relation. Within this universe of domination and oppression, of silent and professed dehumanization, forms of humanity persisted. (1997, 65)

Its "always multilingual and frequently multiracial tangle" (71) counteracts the clear, linear, appropriative order of Western thought and narrative. What Glissant calls *Tout-Monde* (one world in relation) became possible through this; and what had been "large regions yet unknown" of a *terra incognita* are slowly becoming apparent as a *terra critica*. Acknowledging and keeping in mind the violence, exploitation, and asymmetry that are primary here, this critical condition of *terra* might be a locus from where to give rise to other imaginations of the earth.

Thus, for us, *terra* does not designate the geological object of investigation, but a **perspective**: it calls for the examination of these imaginations, their transformations and for the critical **creation** of new ones for a co-habitable – not merely inhabitable – earth. If after Elmina America became possible, what will have been possible after the Middle Passage, after Fukushima? New archipelagos of oppression or a drift to earthly gentleness?

References

Chakrabarty, Dipesh. 2009. "The Climate of History: Four Theses." *Critical Inquiry* 35 (2): 197–222.

Cohen, Tom, Claire Colebrook, and J. Hillis Miller. 2016. *Twilight of the Anthropocene Idols*. London: Open Humanities Press.

Conrad, Joseph. (1902) 2007. *Heart of Darkness*. London: Penguin Classics.

Derrida, Jacques. 1982. "The Ends of Man." In *Margins of Philosophy*, 109–136. Chicago: University of Chicago Press.

Freud, Sigmund. 1959. "The Question of Lay Analysis," translated by James Strachey. In *The Standard Edition of the Complete Psychological Works of Sigmund Freud*. Vol. XX (1925–1926), edited by James Strachey, 177–258. London: The Hogarth Press.

Guattari, Félix. 2000. *The Three Ecologies*. London: Continuum.

Le Goff, Jacques. 1985. *The Medieval Imagination*. Chicago: Chicago University Press.

Glissant, Édouard. 1997. *Poetics of Relation*. Ann Arbor: University of Michigan Press.

Pocket Oxford Latin Dictionary 2005: Latin–English, 3rd ed. Edited by James Morwood. Oxford: Oxford University Press.

Smith, John. 2006. "A Description of New England (1616): An Online Electronic Text Edition." *Electronic Texts in American Studies*, Paper 4. Accessed April 9, 2016. http://digitalcommons.unl.edu/etas/4/.

Stengers, Isabelle. 2015. *In Catastrophic Times: Resisting the Coming Barbarism*. London: Open Humanities Press; Lüneburg: meson press.

Wynter, Sylvia. 1995. "1492: A New World View." In *Race, Discourse, and the Origin of the Americas: A New World View*, edited by Vera Lawrence Hyatt and Rex Nettleford, 5–57. Washington and London: Smithsonian.

Wynter, Sylvia. 2003. "Unsettling the Coloniality of Being/Power/Truth/Freedom: Towards the Human, After Man, Its Overrepresentation – An Argument." *The New Centennial Review* 3 (3): 257–337.

Wynter, Sylvia. 2015. "Unparalleled Catastrophe for Our Species? Or, to Give Humanness a Different Future: Conversations." In *On Being Human as Praxis*, edited by Katherine McKittrick, 9–89. Durham: Duke University Press.

Terror

Jacques Lezra

Terror, from the Old French *terreur,* and conjecturally, through
the Latin *terrere,* to an archaic Indo-European verb "to tremble."
The concept of terror stands today where any number of paths
cross (Lezra 2010, also Derrida 2003, Redfield 2009). It stands
between our everyday experience (who has not been terrified by
one or another event?); the field of aesthetics (fear, horror, terror
– all of these have a long history in the philosophy of art, from
Aristotle to Jacques Rancière, passing through Immanuel Kant
and Edmund Burke); and the practices and philosophy of politics
(from Maximilien Robespierre's coupling of *virtue* and *terror* in
Revolutionary times to today's so-called "war on terror," various
forms of separatist and fundamentalist violence, state terror).
Terror's sense in each of these domains seems uncontroversial:
every society and every language furnish us with terror. To be
terrified, to experience terror, seem to be experiences as universal as the events or circumstances that are said to cause them:
we all will tremble at a sudden loss, at the unexpected, with pain
or at the fear of pain, from the fear of death and dying. The value
attached publicly to the concept is almost without exception negative. (The global film industry has a special relation to terror: it
is the domain in which the experience is an explicitly *commercial*
token.) The purpose of societies, it seems clear, should be to

reduce as much as possible an individual's exposure to threat, violence, abjection – to terror.

Indeed the first usage of *terreur* that the 1873–74 French *Littré* dictionary records, from Pierre Bercheure's ca. 1350 translation of Livy, concerns "la chose publique," the *res-publica,* the commonwealth: *"Que il voulsissent de celles terreurs delivrer la chose publique. –* That they should want to rid the commonwealth of these terrors" (Livius 1514; also Littré 1873–1874). Terror in this definition becomes "the essence of totalitarian domination," as Hannah Arendt (1948, 464) and Adriana Cavarero (following her) put it, the "realization" and the "execution" of what Arendt calls the "law of movement" (464) – a tendency of thought expressed in fact in the bloody days of the Terror in revolutionary France (between ca. 1792 and August 1794), but characteristic of the great ideologies of the mid-nineteenth century, and consisting in "the refusal to view or accept anything 'as it is' and in the consistent interpretation of everything as being only a stage of some future development" (598; see also Cavarero 2009).

Today, however, these terms and these definitions will no longer serve – not the sense of "society" or "politics" (summoning up the ghosts of *polis* and *politeia* will not exorcise other specters: other cities, other formations of the *agora,* other ways of construing the relation between representation and political value) and not the sense of the word the Arendtian tradition makes out to be their limit: the word terror. To the contrary, today terror must work as a founding, defective concept for political philosophy. Rather than seek to "rid the commonwealth" of terrors, modern political association depends upon producing forms of living and forms of governance or institutions that harbor and protect terror.

This is a deeply counterintuitive claim. Consider *terrorism* rather than *terror.* A terrorist strikes close to home. We know, or imagine, the neighborhoods where the attack occurred; we are familiar with the social and political situation that lead to it; can identify with the victims, who remind us of ourselves or of our

families; we may even on occasion have feelings of sympathy
with the groups carrying out the attack (against, for instance, a
state whose repression we deplore), but also a great distrust for
immediate violent action of the sort represented by the attack. All
of these are rather primitive, even adolescent feelings. Suppose
we try to take account, in the first place, of the strange economy
of the terrorist act: How is the value of the target calculated?
Agreed upon? Understood? By whom? What *is* the target of a
"terrorist" attack or act? The terrible consequences of the attacks
lived since September 11, 2001, from New York to Syria to Paris –
both the lives lost, and the resulting consolidation of a militarist
and xenophobic ideology – make such questions pressing. We
will want to take account, too, in the second place, of the strange
identification that many intellectuals feel with the figure of the
terrorist – one who can and does act directly, whose politics lie
at the other extreme of the highly intellectualized world of the
professional academic. The temptation of heroic immediacy –
of the heroic immediacy of the pure act – should strike us as a
residual romanticism that bears examining, historically as well as
philosophically. Although the terrorist act is not in itself – for this
second reason – a device on which one can establish any kind of
politics suitable to the increasingly differentiated social demands
of the twenty-first century, the *first* observation, the strange
economy or an-economy, of terrorist acts, might provide a clue.

Moving (back) from *terrorism* to *terror*, we strike away from
home. With terror, we enter a *political*, rather than a *domestic*,
economy; we assume the uncanny force of the truly other's
claims. For "terrorism" is not terror, though what are vulgarly
called "acts of terror" or "terrorism" can produce terror in the
sense I intend it. Terror names the experience fundamental to
democratic association in radically differentiated social spheres:
the experience of facing another whose interests and whose
claims cannot be defined in my language; who faces me in a
way I cannot imagine or figure; whose being-other present itself
to him or her in a way that may be entirely other to the way in

which our being-other presents itself to me; an-other who does not recognize my home as such, or as mine. Terror registers any person's incapacity to supply a concept, and indeed to supply a satisfactory concept *of* concept, that will bind his or her interests to another person's. From this failure derives a class of unsatis-factory, defective concepts that can be supplied in place of the classical concepts of political philosophy ("autonomy," "freedom," "individualism," "citizenship") – and these defective concepts and the ephemeral, transparent, and reversible institutions that they make possible can be arranged more or less systematically in a weak relation under the heading of what can be called the "modern republic," *la chose publique.*

What, then, *is* this critical experience of terror? Step away from the dominant, Latinate tradition in which the word registers, from Pierre Bercheure to Robespierre to Jean Paulhan. Recall the dissonant chord that Sigmund Freud plays at the beginning of his 1920 work *Beyond the Pleasure Principle.* The context is a discus-sion of the relation between the neuroses that attend "severe mechanical concussions," including war traumas – "shell-shock," or what today we would call post-traumatic stress disorders provoked by accidents, the shock of war, sudden emergencies – and what Freud helpfully calls the "traumatic neuroses of peace" (Freud 1955, 12). The latter are characterized by their suddenness and by the surprise, fright, or terror (*Schreck*) that attend them. He continues:

> Fright [*Schreck*], fear [*Furcht*] and anxiety [*Angst*] are improperly used as synonymous expressions; they are in fact capable of clear distinction in their relation to danger [*Gefahr*]. "Anxiety" describes a particular state of expecting the danger or preparing for it, even though it may be an unknown one. "Fear" requires a definite object of which to be afraid. "Fright" (or terror), however, is the name we give to the state a person gets into when he has run into danger without being prepared for it; it emphasizes the factor of sur-prise [*betont das Moment der Überraschung*]. (12–13)

The term *Schreck* covers a range of senses, which run in English from horror to pleasant surprise. What most importantly distinguishes "fear" and "anxiety" from "fright" or "terror," though, is the status of the object or circumstance that causes the affect. Fear is a state of mind caused by distinct objects; anxiety is caused by the apprehension of a particular temporal relation to a state of affairs. Finally, *Schreck*, "fright" or "terror," is attached neither to a distinct object, nor to a particular state of affairs, nor to a particular apprehension of time. Freud's terror attaches instead to the disconcerting encounter with something for which one was not prepared, whose "object-ness" or "state-of-affairs-ness" is not given, defined, or established. Terror: I have suddenly encountered something – I don't know what it is, and I don't know what my encountering it means, and as a result I don't know what this encounter then may signify for every other encounter I can imagine, which is to say that this surprise encounter may not be a surprising moment at all but may extend to all the other moments that make up what I remember and to all those that make up what I foresee for myself. In the absence of an object or an event that provokes terror, no provision can be made against it (since it's caused by an encounter that's unforeseeable), and in the immediate instance no therapeutic means of overcoming terror present themselves. Terror's effects cannot be assessed against my past or against the future outcome of my actions; the possibility of terror is itself, one might say, a source of anxiety. Once my fright is over in this or that instance, the terrifying circumstances interpreted, assimilated to a state of affairs, *objectified*, then I may say in retrospect that I feared this or that object or circumstance. But to be terrified is to lack both fear and anxiety: to be in terror is to be without an object one can reckon with and without a time one can assess. The terror of the encounter extends beyond the encounter; indeed, it threatens to become not an anomalous species of but the norm for every encounter, another name for the *event*.

Terror works otherwise than as a classic concept of association, and must be thought otherwise. It is not, as it is for Arendt or Cavarero, "the essence of totalitarian domination," "the refusal to view or accept anything 'as it is' and in the consistent interpretation of everything as being only a stage of some future development" (Arendt 1948, 464). For me to link myself to another today or to find myself bound to another person requires that I distribute **responsibility** for the survival of ethico-political life and that I attend to and guard the occurring of that distribution. Both of these are ethico-political tasks, roughly of a public and a private sort respectively; each is both a positive as well as a negative task, entered into both **affirmatively** and passively. The public task involves devising formal regimes that both recognize and distribute the exceptional positions of subject and sovereign across citizenship, that design and shelter a wounded and divided sovereignty. The private task entails a different sort of **work** – hermeneutic, destructive, or rather, deconstructive, dispositional. Not *cura sui*, as Foucault would have it, but rather the cultivation of *insecuritas sui*.

References

Arendt, Hannah. (1948) 2004. *The Origins of Totalitarianism*. New York: Schocken Books.

Cavarero, Adriana. 2009. *Horrorism: Naming Contemporary Violence*. Translated by William McCuaig. New York: Columbia University Press.

Derrida, Jacques. 2003. "Autoimmunity: Real and Symbolic Suicides – A Dialogue with Derrida, Jacques." In *Philosophy in a Time of Terror: Dialogues with Jürgen Habermas and Jacques Derrida*, edited by Giovanna Borradori, 85–136. Chicago: University of Chicago Press.

Freud, Sigmund. 1955. "Beyond the Pleasure Principle." In *The Standard Edition of the Complete Psychological Words*, edited and translated by James Strachey. London: The Hogarth Press.

Lezra, Jacques. 2010. *Wild Materialism: The Ethic of Terror and the Modern Republic*. New York: Fordham University Press.

Littré, Émile. 1873–1874. *Dictionnaire de la langue française*. Electronic version created by François Gannaz. Paris: L. Hachette. Accessed May 4, 2016. http://www.littre.org.

Livius, Titus. 1514. *Les grandes Décades de Titus Livius, translatées de Latin en Francoys*. Translated by Pierre Berchoire. Paris.

Redfield, Marc. 2009. *The Rhetoric of Terror: Reflections on 9/11 and the War on Terror.* **217**
New York: Fordham University Press.

Transformation

Sybrandt van Keulen

To get a grip on what is at stake concerning transformation, let us linger a few moments over the specific way in which Foucault recoins this concept in his essay *What is Enlightenment?* (Foucault 1984a). Foucault turns away from quasi-universalistic, global scenarios such as passages from one period of history to another (for example, from the Middle Ages to the Renaissance) or projects that claim to be global or radical (such as the French Revolution), and he focuses on "**work** carried out by ourselves upon ourselves as free beings" (47, bold added), as "a patient labor giving form to our impatience for liberty" (50). It is likely that Foucault did not have one clearly defined practice in mind referring to 'work' and 'labor'; he even suggests rather strongly that it concerns "undefined work" (46). Yet Foucault also explicitly states: "But that does not mean that no work can be done except in disorder and contingency" (47). This ambivalence seems to stand or fall with the fact that Foucault talks about a *split* practice "that simultaneously respects [modern] reality and violates it" (41).

Foucault defines transformative work as a task and an obligation to effectuate something, that is, "a change that he ['man'] himself will bring about in himself" (35). In this respect Foucault gives Immanuel Kant full credit for having invented an "attitude of modernity" (38). Yet after having paid his tribute, Foucault's text reads like instances of rephrasing this attitude. To be more precise, the afore-mentioned split affirms partly Kant's progressive ethos – and thus Foucault's respect for modern reality – yet he ventures to problematize Kant's claim to universality. With the help of Charles Baudelaire's *oeuvre* the limitations of Enlightenment's ethos should be made discernable, and in particular the Kantian version of it, stipulated in formulations such as "determinations of my identical self" (Kant 2007, A 129).

A clear definition of the praxis of Baudelaire's painter of modern life – that is, Baudelaire's alter ego Constantin Guys – and of course also of the said work carried out upon ourselves, starts at the moment Foucault uses instead of "change" the word "transfiguration":

> … just when the whole world is falling asleep, he begins to work, and he transfigures that world. His *transfiguration* does not entail an annulling of reality, but a difficult interplay between the truth of what is real and the exercise of freedom. (Foucault 1984a, 41, emphasis added)

This is Foucault's first rephrasing of the modern attitude, that is as a "difficult interplay" and an "exercise," which can be understood as the counterpart or double of the Kantian "determinations of my identical self." The Baudelairean notion of freedom is not exercised by "the truth of what is real" nor as an alternative truth (an escape) but as a doubling of "the real" and a confrontation with it – which all in all seems to imply that at least *two* realities are involved, entangled in that difficult interplay. With regard to this transfigurative force (to which Baudelaire also refers as convalescence), the Baudelairean exercise of freedom seems to work *critically on* the Kantian identical self, powered by "a desperate eagerness to imagine" the "indissociable" Kantian self otherwise than it is (41). Baudelaire captured that eagerness in the following formula: "an 'I' with an insatiable appetite for the 'non-I'" (Baudelaire 2001, 10). Presumably this appetite leaves the "I" not unaffected. The provisional conclusion would then be: The

effect of transformation – as conceived by Foucault – is exercised
by our Baudelairean work on our Kantian limits.

At this point Foucault is able to rephrase the modern attitude
as a "limit-attitude" (Foucault 1984a, 45), and subsequently
the act of transforming (a form) into transgressing (a limit).
Foucault's voicing of the specific critical **power** that is at stake in
his philosophical ethos gradually becomes louder and also more
demanding, or even slightly compulsory: "we have to be at the
frontiers" (45). Why should we?

Certainly, along with the transfiguration – transvaluation or
recoining (*Umwertung*) in the Nietzschean sense – of the modern
attitude into a limit-attitude, Foucault proclaims an *adieu* to the
Kantian command (which demanded an identical self) and, at
the same time – which seems part and parcel of the practice of
difference – this limit-attitude enables to reinvent our selves
while transgressing frontiers (or the other way around). But what
else than transgressing frontiers, boundaries, or indeed limits,
did Foucault have in mind?

Foucault did not refer to particular passages of the *Critique of
pure Reason*, but he certainly must have had in mind at least
this Kantian sentence about "the land of truth": "This domain,
however, is an island and enclosed by nature itself within limits
that can never be altered" (Kant 2007, 251, B 294). Such "natural"
limits Foucault very likely refers to when he calls for the transformation of "the critique conducted in the form of necessary
limitation" (Foucault 1984a, 45). The power of the limit-attitude
does not abolish or erase that limitation, it does not even need to
transform limitation's very shape; that attitude just happens to
change the rigid modality of its own nature: a desire to transform
a historically determined form of respect (for certain limits) into
very own possibilities of transgression. Hence the next step to
finalize his ethos into "a practical critique that takes the form of
a possible transgression" (45). Foucault did not just change the
Kantian limit-concept (*Grenzbegriff*; Kant 2007, B 310–311) into a

limit-attitude, he installed an inventive self with a transgressive desire "to imagine it otherwise than it is" (Foucault 1984a, 41), swerving into "work done at the limits of ourselves" (46).

Perhaps Foucault did nothing more and nothing less than folding back Kant's own insight of the third *Critique* into the epistemological and ethical realms of the first and second *Critiques*, not with the aim to destroy the Kantian definition of nature but to set our very own nature (of our self) free from the Kantian, logocentric imperatives. Indeed, Kant underestimated more or less the impact of his own thought that the "imagination (as a productive cognitive faculty) is ... very powerful in **creating**, as it were, another nature" (*Critique of the Power of Judgment*, 2000, §49, bold added). This second nature – and, in the Kantian phrasing, the second freedom – as Foucault, and also Deleuze knew, appears to be more important, maybe even more essential than the first: "In the ideal of beginning anew there is something that precedes the beginning itself, that takes it up to deepen it and delay it in the passage of time" (Deleuze 2004, 14).

To recapitulate in a few words Foucault's *tour de force* of envisioning a critical ontology, one can say that the concept of transformation turns out to mark an inventive split practice of *giving form* and *transgressing limits*, alternately or simultaneously. Distancing himself from Kant, Foucault emphasized the importance of historical (genealogical, archeological) inquiries "oriented toward the contemporary limits of the necessary, that is, toward what is not or is no longer indispensable for the constitution of ourselves as autonomous subjects" (Foucault 1984a, 43). Yet those inquiries are not goals in themselves; their purpose and drive ("desperate eagerness") is to invent the critical figures and orientations other than the ones that rule "naturally." Indeed, the Foucauldian imperative is to perform historico-practical tests "of the limits that we may go beyond" (47; *que nous pouvons franchir* [Foucault 1984b, 575]). *Franchir*, here translated as "going beyond," should be understood as transgressing a reality with the emphasis on, and steered by, the determined activity

of "producing" not some meta-physical afterworld as a purely
negative realm of redemption but rather different assemblages,
in the sense of different styles and **affective** ways of relating to
each other (other than hegemonic relations). Practices that allow
breaking the dominant everyday systemic veil that controls our
"natural" selves.

Thus form changes into a limit, along with the strong suggestion
that no limit should be treated as a thing in itself (Kant's *Ding an
sich*). Nonetheless, it is likely that *a* limit can be a hidden part of a
bigger, encompassing form or frame with a machinic unconscious
status, such as the formative entity of the nation-state. We don't
know where the borders of the nation-state within ourselves
start or end. In everyday life some parts, particular disciplinary
practices, of this so-called sovereign power (sovereign in the
Hobbesian sense) can just happen to be felt as restrictive. This
might be the reason why Foucault also speaks of "partial transformations" (Foucault 1984a, 47). Hence our work should consist at
least in investigating the legitimacy of the institutional dominance
of *some* limits and rules. Still this work cannot be done without
resistance and inventive transgressive practices attired with the
critical power to reveal that some rules are the remainders of
temporary necessity, and that they can *become* a possibility again,
or an arbitrary accessory, and even redundant.

However, Derrida's adage *il n'y a pas de hors-texte* does indeed
imply that a simple outside or, for that matter, a sheer inside-
the-frame, is not any longer a truth in and for itself, and perhaps
has never been, which indeed does also imply that the analysis
of resistances and the critique of frames, that is, the very ethos
of inventing new conditions and possibilities, and splitting an old
frame in two (three, etc.), entails translative acts between frames,
emerging from what might be called a life in-between-frames – a
singular way of living that has become perhaps even more urgent
than ever.

References

Baudelaire, Charles. 2001. "The Painter of Modern Life." In *The Painter of Modern Life and other Essays*, translated and edited by Jonathan Mayne, 1–41. London: Phaidon Press Limited.

Deleuze, Gilles. 2004. "Desert Islands." In *Desert Islands and other texts (1957–1974)*, translated by Michael Taormina, 9–14. Los Angeles: Semiotext(e).

Foucault, Michel. 1984a. "What is Enlightenment?" In *The Foucault Reader*, edited by Paul Rabinow, 32–50. New York: Pantheon Books.

Foucault, Michel. 1984b. "Qu'est-ce que les Lumières?" In *Dits et Ecrits, tome IV*, 562–578. Paris: Gallimard.

Kant, Immanuel. 2000. *Critique of the Power of Judgment*. Translated by Paul Guyer and Eric Matthews. Cambridge: Cambridge University Press.

Kant, Immanuel. 2007. *Critique of Pure Reason*. Translated by Marcus Weigelt, based on the translation by Max Müller, London: Penguin Classics.

Translation

Jacques Lezra

In the age of its global reproducibility, the university becomes a conforming, converting, *translating* machine: a differentiated, rhizomatic, industry of industry-relevant forms of legitimation and recognition helping to unify the global information economy, forms of legitimation translatable universally and universally consumable. The age of the global reproducibility of the university is the age in which the conception of "universality" tied to the ancient humanistic notion of the "university" has become primarily expressible in the lexicon of (economic and technological) "globality" (Lezra 2013).

To propose that "translation" should, under a renewed definition of the term, stand at the heart of another university and another sense of the humanities is not to assume a reactionary position, to restore an "auratic" experience of the university, or of the humanities, nor to return to the pristine and enlightened days of humanist universalism – days which were not "pristine," "universal," "Enlightened," or particularly "humanistic," since they turned on principles of national, racial, economic, and religious exclusion. To the contrary. A refigured "translation" allows us to envision a *version* of "universalism" and the "university," a *version* of translation and translatability, and a *version* of humanism and of the humanities. It is "translation's" *violence* – which is conceptually of an order quite different from the sorts of violences that did indeed characterize the old myth of humanist universalism – that I'd like to enroll for thought, against and within the "global" university and against global university systems.

The coupling of "humanities" and "translation" echoes arcane debates regarding the differences between world literature, comparative literature, and literature taught in translation (Apter 2013; Casanova 2015; Damrosch 2009 and 2014; Thomsen, D'Haen, and Domínguez 2013). The question of how humanists make the case for the value of their disciplines to others – legislators, the great public, friends, and so on – is a matter of translation. Those things that the humanities take to be their concerns, their objects of study, protocols, ends – all need translating into the technical-commercial language ascendant in the era of austerity, economic competitiveness, and systematic and ideologically driven defunding of non-STEM disciplines.

"Translation" is a term nested *within* the humanities also serving as a gatekeeper *for* the humanities. As to the first, the function of "translation" within the humanistic disciplines, we're divided. Yes, absent some universal standard (the "human" as universal bearer of sense and value; as bearer of "universalism") the question is open whether a work, an Edgar Degas nude, say, or a concept like political autonomy, will be understood and valued, to what degree, how, and to what end, in different moments and societies. Recall the Terentian doctrine that what is "human" about the human animal is its universality. *Nil a me alienum puto*, the human is human inasmuch as it contains multitudes, inasmuch as it is the summation or the *end* of all beings, even (Giovanni Pico della Mirandola's stronger claim, running in the contrary direction) inasmuch as it can *be* any being: I am not untranslatable into anything. Every form of life can be translated into the human and the human animal can, *qua* human, assume the characteristics of any other, translate him or herself into the quality of any other thing. Inasmuch as my *end* is not given, but lies in my potential translatability into any-being, whether animal, angelic, or divine; or in the potential translatability of any-being into me – in this sense it is that I am human.

But on the other hand, we'll want to say something like this: Yes, the quality of general translatability ("nothing is alien to me, I contain multitudes," the shibboleths of humanist universalism) that makes me human cannot reciprocally, mutually, be translated back into every form of life. I share with other human animals, and with them alone, that undisseverable, primary quality: What we call a humanistic discipline is just what resists translation about the object. It's what makes that Degas sketch different from a universally understandable term, or a term in a formal language, or a mechanically-reproduced or – reproducible drawing, that I'll be attending to: the *auratic*, the untranslatable. I'll be inclined to say that I affect to call disciplines humanistic when, and only when, their object of study is to a degree *untranslatable* into other disciplinary frames and into other systems of value. Non-reproducible, because non-mechanical, non-machinic.

And now to the second side of my frame, the side that understands "translation" to serve as a gatekeeper for the "humanities." Here too we're divided. The end of the humanistic disciplines, the neo-liberal economic model teaches us, is to convey cultural value across linguistic, historical, and geographic borders. At the same time, whatever it is that is thus conveyed or translated moves across borders in the way that other products, other commodities, do as well, and is to be understood and valued by analogy to such products. (A cultural commodity is the translation of an economic commodity.) The humanities are thus both instruments of globalization, ancillary to the great value-producing machine of global capitalism; a set of devices and practices for producing and assessing the value of cultural commodities traded on global and local markets; and the product of (one part of) the global economic system. I set the borders and the value of the humanities, and of the objects that the humanistic disciplines produce and affect to study, according to these three, not-quite-coherent, ways of understanding the humanities as translating-machines and translatable-objects or commodities.

What results from the double status and the double value of "translation"? The term is at work *within* the humanistic disciplines and also at work *outside* these disciplines, as a principal device for designating and defining them, for drawing the edges and ends of their concept, for determining its use, for providing the index by means of which the value of the objects designated as "humanistic" are assessed. A peculiarly unstable, even violently unstable, term. Also, however, and in that same degree, an intellectually productive one, since the way in which the two ends of "translation" defeat, limit, and weaken one another will allow us to understand with some clarity what we mean by "value," by the "humanities," and by their relation.

We'll call bare "translation," the gate-keeper internal and external to the humanities and to the human animal, by a new name: "Machine translation."

First let's wrest the term from its old humanist home: just the domain of linguistic transformation, where we move, word-for-word or sense-for-sense, from one natural language to another. Translation, for *zoon logon echon,* will disclose whatever is not accidental (historical, contingent, ephemeral, glottal, merely regional, merely an aspect of this or that human's articulated speech, accentual) about our relation to the word (Heidegger 2000; 1971). We maintain, generally, that this linguistic sense of translation is the philosophically densest and most compelling one, and also that it is (perhaps for that reason) the historical ground on which later declensions of "translation" stand, the literal term to future metaphorical usages, translations of "translation" into other improper or metaphorical domains. There's ample historical precedent for this translation of translation, of course – the term and the practices it designates move around promiscuously in different cultures and at different times, designating transformations of wildly varying sorts, material as well as symbolic. A quick example, taken from Spain: Juan de Junta, an editor in Salamanca in the mid-sixteenth century, publishes eight translations between 1544 and 1549 – from Italian and Latin. What we call "translation" he calls not only "*traducir*," but also "*trasladar*," "*sacar*," "*volver*," and "*romançar*." The earlier word "*trujamanear*," from the Arabic, nestles in the vocabulary of the conquest of America; Covarrubias's 1611 *Tesoro de la lengua castellana o española* refers to "*verter*," to pour. "*Transportar*" is not uncommon. A small controversy haunts even *traducere*, the most common humanist term for translation: Is it first used by Bruni, as Italian scholars maintain, or by Alonso de Cartagena, as some Spanish scholars suggest? A matter of claiming historical precedence for different schools and histories of translation; a matter of national pride (Pöckl 1996–1997).

Everything is staked on the possibility of translating the dispersed and contradictory semantic field that "translation" covers into a systematic and coherent vehicle for the production of subjectivities – subjectivities recognizable amongst themselves, associated on the minimal ground of that recognition, capable of carrying out transactions of an economic, social, and linguistic sort upon that basis. But the term's irreconcilable senses and functions attest not to the systematicity and coherence of the term's senses but to the machinic violence required to imagine that systematicity, and to its fictitious, even *compensatory* quality. Something disturbing but inescapable stands forth in the earliest uses to which "translation" is put, then – in the early modern definitions we have seen, for instance, or in the ways that Thomas Hobbes or Niccolò Machiavelli will construe the granting of "human" rights to sovereign instances and representatives under the aegis of a defective concept of "translation." From the vantage of these sometimes violently antagonistic terms and from the futures into which "translation's" divided semantic field appears to be translated, we knock into something other than the reasonable, contractarian system of mutual recognitions that appear to define the *human* animal in translation. This hard, anti-humanist core renders systematic and properly conceptual the senses of "translation." Machinic, it captures translation's incompatible functions and semantic registers and translates them into a regulated and perspicuous field: a system for assigning (economic and other) values. It makes the transference of rights to others (humans, animals, institutions, positions) and the *recognition* of others as bearers of rights stand upon fictions. We call this hard, anti-humanist core at the heart of the university by the name of "machine translation."

For technical and strategic reasons, it makes sense to turn the humanities toward the figure of translation, and to grant "translation" its patient and appealing sovereignty internally and externally. But this technical and strategic appeal to the human in translation should not keep us from understanding what *may* be the university's genuinely revolutionary task in the age of the global reproducibility of the university-commodity, in the age of the effective transformation of the university into a machine for the production of what Maurizio Lazzarato (2012) calls "the indebted man." That task is to help guard and produce the violence of translation, and on this condition to allow us to imagine, think through, and set in place formal, ephemeral, and reversible regimes of democratic association which are incompatible with the human in translation. It is in this machine inside the machine of the globally reproducible cultural commodity form, in this machinic, anti-humanist core, and on the basis of non-recognition, of the incoherence of the principle of translation, that democratic regimes can and should be imagined – that is, *produced* – today.

References

Apter, Emily. 2013. *Against World Literature: On the Politics of Untranslatability*. New York: Verso.

Casanova, Pascale. 2015. *La Langue Mondiale: Traduction Et Domination*. Paris: Seuil.

D'Haen, Theo, David Damrosch, and Djelal Kadir, eds. 2012. *The Routledge Companion to World Literature*. Oxford: Routledge.

Damrosch, David, ed. 2014. *World Literature in Theory*. Chichester, UK: Wiley-Blackwell.

Damrosch, David. 2009. *How to Read World Literature*. Chichester, UK: Wiley-Blackwell.

Heidegger, Martin. 2000. *Introduction to Metaphysics*. Translated by Gregory Fried and Richard Polt. New Haven: Yale University Press.

Heidegger, Martin. 1971. *On the Way to Language*. Translated by Peter D. Hertz. New York: Harper and Row.

Lazzarato, Maurizio. 2012. *The Making of the Indebted Man: An Essay on the Neoliberal Condition*. Translated by Joshua David Jordan. Los Angeles: Semiotext(e).

Lezra, Jacques. 2013. "Translation," In *Political Concepts: A Critical Lexicon*. New School for Social Research, v.2. Accessed May 3, 2016 http://www.politicalconcepts.org/.

Pöckl, Wolfgang. 1996-1997. "Apuntes para la historia de *traducere*, I: 'Traducir.'" *Hieronymus Complutensis* 4/5. Accessed May 3, 2016. http://cvc.cervantes.es/lengua/hieronymus/pdf/04_05/04_05_009.pdf.

Thomsen, Mads Rosendahl, Theo D' Haen, and César Domínguez, eds. 2013. *World Literature: A Reader*. London: Routledge.

Utopia

Jennifer A. Wagner-Lawlor

For much of the twentieth century, looking back on failures of visionary political revolutions and regime building, utopia was discredited. As long as social harmony is construed as sameness, and perfection defined in terms of an achieved teleology, utopian experiments in the world, and in the worlds of literature and art, will tend toward the disciplining of difference. Utopia's final solution is dissolution of difference. Exclusion rather than inclusion is the ideological motive: "Utopias are designed to keep people out" (Farnsworth, 1998) is what Toni Morrison reminded us of with her novel, *Paradise* (1997). As that narrative shows us, a social body that becomes hardened, inhospitable, and intolerant is a dying body. Without a theory of difference, can utopia be anything but dystopia?

Yet, Oscar Wilde, who knew about the ways in which power disciplines and punishes otherness, will always remind us that a map without utopia on it is not worth looking at. Utopia's reha-bilitation – or, more positively, its conceptual resiliency – lies in its essential radicality. What is the nature of that radicality? Darko Suvin's notion in the 1970s of the *novum* as the radical momentum of the utopian imaginary (Suvin 1979) is fallen out of use. It should be revived and refreshed, because it illuminates the importance of understanding utopia not as a political pursuit for that final solution, or perfect static state, but as a politically radical

process of ongoing critique. The function of the *novum* might be compared to the function of the immature stem cell in a living body: It does not contain but is itself the capacity to take on the form and function of any one of the many specialized cells that self-organize into living being. The virtue of the stem cell is its **plasticity**, containing, as it were, the potentiality for generating, repairing, and regenerating the body.

Like all metaphors, the comparison of *novum* and stem cell eventually falls short, at which point the difference between them is exposed. In this case, the difference lies in the distinction between replication and (re)generation or (re)production. The regenerative function of the *novum* goes beyond simply repairing a political or social "body" and bringing it back to its putatively whole or healthy form; this is replication of a particular ideologic formation. This is status quo. But the *novum* does not close off the possibility of alterity, but introduces it continuously. Therein lies the capacity for critique that defines utopia's political and formal energies. If there can be such a thing as a stem cell for alterity, then it is, in that sense alone, that the *novum* is a conceptual stem cell. The *novum* is the paradoxical point in Catherine Malabou's description, in *What Should We Do with Our Brain?* (2008), of plasticity's contradictory nature at which "possibility, the wholly other version" is held off by "the expectation of the arrival of another way of being," or "a possibility of waiting" (87). Possibility awaits then, now, then again.

For this reason the notion of utopia as representing a "blueprint for the future" is rejected by recent theorists. A static-state utopia is relevant only to an "end-stop" world, as contemporary fiction-writer Jeanette Winterson puts it in *Art Objects* (1997); without the possibility of difference and change, utopia tends toward the fascistic or the dictatorial. A process utopia requires possibility, awaiting. To quote Winterson's entire sentence:

> Process, the energy in being, the refusal of finality, which is not the same thing as the refusal of completeness, sets art,

all art, apart from the end-stop world that is always calling
"Time Please!" (1997, 19)

That refusal of finality (the blueprint model) marks the radical correspondence of process-utopia to critique. What sets utopia apart is its pro-visionality, its looking forward toward a horizon (landmark or boundary) that constantly recedes as any traveler, especially a utopian traveler, will experience. Thus the brilliance of Wilde's epigraph to *The Soul of Man Under Socialism*:

> A map of the world that does not include Utopia is not worth even glancing at, for it leaves out the one country at which Humanity is always landing. And when Humanity lands there, it looks out, and, seeing a better country, sets sail. Progress is the realisation of Utopias. (2001, 139)

Utopia is a state of deferral *and* difference, as the identical etymology of both words indicates.

The real state of utopia is a form of virtual reality, in the several senses of the word *virtual*. Toni Morrison knows and shows us this. The town of Ruby, Oklahoma, is the paradise lost in *Paradise*. Founded during the post-Reconstruction emigration of freed slaves from the U.S. South, Ruby is not a light on the hill but a purposely hidden jewel, one place on the American map where former slaves can thrive free of bigotry, cruelty, and disenfranchisement. Over one hundred years on, however, the utopian town has bred its own forms of intolerance and hatred. Ruby's fatal flaw is its almost absolute intolerance of *any* form of difference, much less anything so challenging as critique. So much the worse for the newly generated community of women at a former convent, where a diverse set of strangers find themselves at home for the time: at home with, in and through their own differences. Their community is open, generous, hospitable—the opposite of what Ruby has become under the leadership of its male leadership: insular, suspicious, inflexible, and gracelessly narcissistic. And so again: without a theory of difference, can utopia be anything but dystopia?

By 1976, when the novel is set, this insular town is at a historical dead end, quite literally: its babies cannot seem to stay alive, either in the womb or outside it; its young people either leave, or stay only to fester in its toxic spiritual environment. The culmination of this toxicity is the July 4th mass homicide that opens the novel. Explained retrospectively over the next several hundred pages is the etiology of the dis-ease that expresses itself in the armed midnight attack on the Convent women. But from that horrific event emerges a certain clarity: that "pre-lapsarian" Ruby is a simulacrum of the town's imagined mythic past. Now, the town appears as it really is, eaten by a cancer in part of its own making, and in full collapse. To this present reality, however, is offered a possibility other than death, thanks to Rev. Misner and his partner Anna, both outsiders, who witness the town's social pathology and remain after the crime as the only possible guides beyond it:

> It was when he [Rev. Misner] returned ... that they saw it. Or sensed it, rather, for there was nothing to see. A door, she said later. "No, a window," he said ... What did a door mean? what a window? ... Whether through a door needing to be opened or a beckoning window already raised, what would happen if you entered? What would be on the other side? What on earth would it be? What on earth? (Morrison 1998, 305).

What on earth, indeed? Misner's return, which comes only after the community expresses its wish for him to stay, is the turning point toward that future. In doing so, they acknowledge that Ruby is no utopia; what Ruby-ites do not know yet is that they have not even set out for utopia. For the moment, no horizon is visible, as they cannot see past themselves. But Misner is reminded just here that his decision to return is the arrival that generates both "the sign" and "the event" of future possibility.

As Misner buries the dead, with a sermon that begins the critical process of examining individual and communal histories, he receives a second affirmation. Even as he closes a coffin, a window appears in the nearby garden, "beckon[ing] toward another place – neither life nor death – but there, just yonder, *shaping thoughts he did not know he had*" (307, emphasis added). This is a brilliant description of what utopia does to us and for us. Utopia makes possible the shaping, the realizing of what was not "known" in any objective sense, but that was there already as potentiality. This process informs philosopher Catherine Malabou's notion of the "possibility of waiting," (2004, xxxii) an achievement in itself: The waiting enacts the process of imagining possibility, the shaping of thoughts we do not know we have, new thoughts, different framings and representations, that take shape as we think and expect other-wise. This plastic process of shaping constitutes the virtual reality that is utopia, as we stand expectant, waiting, worlding. Finally, utopian process effectively performs "the principle of Hope" (Bloch 1995). These performances are forms of *transitive* imagining, and not immobile ideologic constructions. Utopia is plastic, mobile, performative, and inviting: it invites us always *to wonder*, the most reliable and objective sign of hope.

References

Bloch, Ernst. 1995. *The Principle of Hope*. Cambridge, MA: MIT Press.

Farnsworth, Elizabeth. 1998. "Toni Morrison: Interview." *PBS.org*. Accessed May 4, 2016. http://www.pbs.org/newshour/bb entertainment-jan-june98-morrison_3-9/.

Malabou, Catherine. 2004. *The Future of Hegel: Plasticity, Temporality, and Dialectic*. Translated by Lisabeth During. Oxfordshire: Routledge.

Malabou, Catherine. 2008. *What Should We Do With Our Brain?* Translated by Sebastian Rand and Marc Jeannerod. New York: Fordham University Press.

Morrison, Toni. 1998. *Paradise*. New York: Vintage.

Suvin, Darko. 1979. *Metamorphoses of Science Fiction: On the Poetics and History of a Literary Genre*. New Haven: Yale University Press.

Wilde, Oscar, and Linda Dowling, eds. 2001. *The Soul of Man Under Socialism and Selected Critical Prose*. London: Penguin Classics.

Winterson, Jeanette. 1997. *Art Objects: Essays on Ecstasy and Effrontery*. New York: Vintage.

Vision

Jennifer A. Wagner-Lawlor

"Visibility is a trap." This famous Foucauldian statement
is a springboard for the last thirty-plus years of feminist
visual studies. *Visibility* would seem to be, overall, a positive
achievement: "being able to be seen" suggests presence, recognition. Feminist art theory, following Foucault, tells another
story. The passive register of the word is critical: "visibility" is
not simply a matter of physical vision but a matter of visuality: a
matter, in other words, of power. In Western art, women, slaves,
the working class, children – any not-quite-human being (from
the superior perspective of the dominant class) – are "able to be
visible," if at all, through a mediating male gaze. Woman herself is
a cypher, as Mary Wollstonecraft puts it in *Vindication of the Rights
of Woman* (1792) that gains significance only insofar as the male
viewer confers it. Laura Mulvey's theory of visual pleasure and
the gaze, appearing in 1975, illuminates the obscured workings
of the Foucauldian visibility trap. The "hinge" to the trap is
revealed as the very "event" of vis-(a)bility itself, a pleasurable
event because the image of woman is a narcissistic formation.
What is "able to be seen" is not a singular woman but a projection
of a singular male's desire – itself a reflection of (unable to be
seen) ideological figurings of gender and sexuality. Mulvey's
intricate reading suggests that the event of a woman's (be)

coming-into-being-seen is at the fold of the visible and the invisible, and the self-reflection of the viewer.

The poet Christina Rossetti understood these dynamics implicitly. Observing the art practices of brother Dante Gabriel Rossetti and other Pre-Raphaelite colleagues (e.g., William Morris, John Waterhouse, John Everett Millais), Rossetti describes the "visibility trap" quite precisely, well over one hundred years before Mulvey's psychoanalytic account, in a succinct fourteen-line sonnet she wrote in 1856:

> One face looks out from all his canvasses,
>   One selfsame figure sits or walks or leans;
>   We found her hidden just behind those screens,
> That mirror gave back all her loveliness.
> A queen in opal or in ruby dress,
>   A nameless girl in freshest summer greens,
>   A saint, an angel; every canvass means
> The same one meaning, neither more nor less.
> He feeds upon her face by day and night,
>   And she with true kind eyes looks back on him
> Fair as the moon and joyful as the light;
>   Not wan with waiting, not with sorrow dim; ·
> Not as she is, but was when hope shone bright;
>   Not as she is, but as she fills his dream.

> – *"In An Artist's Studio"* (*Complete Poems*, 796)

The nature of the trap is very clear. Furthermore, we might read from this poem a modification of Foucault's statement: "*Vision* is a trap." This recalls Susan Sontag's early notion regarding vision and photography in *On Photography* (1977, 3): vision fetishizes the seen as the known; the reality of what is seen is presumed; the abstract becomes the concrete. Vision as fetish and as capture are antithetical to feminist ontology and feminist epistemology, equally.

Contemporary theories of *visuality* make possible, at least, a rescue from vision's "usage" as an (false) agent of truth and reality. Nicholas Mirzoeff's genealogy of the term traces a distinction between *visuality* and *vision* to a profoundly ideological debate, between social philosopher Thomas Carlyle on the one hand and artist J. M. W. Turner on the other regarding the authority of vision and visuality, respectively. Turner's progressive modernity meant a "refusal to adjudicate between what is seen, what is visible, what is in shade and what is imagined" (Mirzoeff 2006, 64). Turner thus anticipates our own contemporary focus on relations of power that inhere in the notion of visuality, which Mirzoeff describes as a "doubled interaction" (66), or even as "collision, intersection and interaction" (66).

"Collision, intersection, interaction": these are actually excellent descriptors of Turner's boldest work, those magnificent sea- and landscapes in which the viewer – as well as any hapless human figure within the painting – is hardly, if at all, able to discriminate one element from another. Turner's willingness to dwell in ontological and epistemological uncertainties represents a radical aesthetic standpoint remarkable for his time and place. These modes (of collision, intersection, interaction), Mirzoeff adds, "operate in deconstruction, as a relation of difference that is always deferred" (66), and thus beyond ideologic capture. This deferral of difference grounds a complex relational notion of vision and visuality that might usefully be considered, for the moment, as a Baradian **entanglement**. There is no easy separation of the seen from the being-seen; the co-constitution of the one mode and the other, adds Mirzoeff, creates a "space or area, … not bounded by constant time but rather '*time as lived*, not synchronically or diachronically, but in its multiplicities and simultaneities, its presences and absences'" (quoting Achille Mbembe, 76). This pregnant space opens to a simultaneous "sharing and dividing that is political and aesthetic at once" (76), he concludes, with a nod to Jacques Rancière. The multiple entanglements give this space its dimensionality and texture.

Laura U. Marks's elaboration of a *haptic visuality* attempts a further step away from the ongoing "suspicion of vision" and "critique of instrumental vision" (2002, 4), toward a theory of embodied perception. But her work hardly approaches the unique robustness of Karen Barad's work on entanglement *and/ as touching*, offering a theory of relationality complex enough to account for the "working" of difference, without working through or out of it; indeed, such a working through or out is antithetical to "the really hard **work**" (2012, 215) of investigating "the infinity of constitutive inclusions – the in/determinacy, the virtuality that is a constitutive part of all finitude" (215–216). "On Touching," Barad's introduction to a 2012 special issue of *differences*, refers to *visual hapticity*, a reversal of Marks's formulation that signals Barad's prioritization of touch – not as *the* dominant faculty of sense but rather as the "primary concern of physics" (208), since touch is "enacted" from the quantum level upward. In physics, she notes, touch is explored for "its physicality, its virtuality, its **affectivity**, its e-motion-ality, whereby all pretense of being able to sep-arate out the affective from the scientific dimensions of touching falls away" (209). The pretensions of Donna Haraway's "perfect knower" are, quite simply, scientifically and ethically unsound.

Barad's neo-Levinasian proposal that we face "the inhuman – the indeterminate non/being non/becoming of mattering and not mattering" (216) might also direct contemporary clarifications of an *ethics* of vision. The concept of entanglement could ground such an ethics. Barad proposes the "irreducible" binding of self and other, "otherness" being *"an entangled relation of difference* (différance). *Ethicality entails noncoincidence with oneself"* (217), seeing oneself, perhaps, as a stranger at least momentarily. Ethi-cality, she implies, asks us to see pro-visionally and relationally, in recognition of the "noncoincidence with oneself." This kind of vision is self-reflexive but not in the narcissistic sense. To see both oneself and others differently requires, in other words, a **speculative** and *critical* practice. We must no longer see what is known to us, but see other-wise. Turner's critical art practice does just this, challenging us to search for what appears invisible or obscured, but which is able-to-be-seen through the "really hard work" of confronting what is unknown or strange.

Vision cannot simply be conceived as a transaction that begins and ends with ourselves, any more than we can say that insofar as we see reality, we "make" it. Seeing speculatively, and critically, means recognizing that reality makes us, "[s]ee[ing] into the life of things," as William Wordsworth puts it in a poem which is all about vision, in both its physical and abstract dimensions ("Tintern Abbey" 1798, lines 47–49). To envision is to **regard** the lives of things, of self, of others "in [their] multiplicity and simultaneities, [their] presence and absences" (Mbembe 2001, 1), and to identify the complicities of our own gaze. This is the "really hard work" Barad urges upon us: this is critique, which refuses the fetishizing of vision, and makes possible the envisioning of others-as-ourselves, and vice versa. These are more generous visions of worlds to come.

References

Barad, Karen. 2012. "On Touching – The Inhuman That Therefore I Am." *Differences* 23 (3): 206–223.

Haraway, Donna Jeanne. 1991. *Simians, Cyborgs and Women: The Reinvention of Nature*. London: Free Association.

Marks, Laura U. 2002. *Touch: Sensuous Theory and Multisensory Media*. Minneapolis: University of Minnesota Press.

Mbembe, Achille. 2001. *On the Postcolony*. Oakland: University of California Press.

Mirzoeff, Nicholas. 2006. "On Visuality." *Journal of Visual Culture* 5 (1): 53–79.

Rossetti, Christina G. 2001. *The Complete Poems (Penguin Classics),* edited by R. W. Crump and Betty S. Flowers. London: Penguin Classics.

Sontag, Susan. 1997. *On Photography*. London: Picador.

Wagner-Lawlor, Jennifer. 2013. *Postmodern Utopias and Feminist Fictions*. Cambridge: Cambridge University Press.

Wollstonecraft, Mary. 1792. *Vindication of the Rights of Woman*. London: Penguin Classics.

Wordsworth, William. 1798. "Tintern Abbey." *Poetryfoundation.org*. Accessed July 3, 2015. http://www.poetryfoundation.org/poem/174796.

Work

Mercedes Bunz

Critique is work – working with a given situation to **transform** it. It is work that is productive. But what makes critique work? Where does the productivity of this work, or of work in general, come from? And how can "work" at present be critical? In order to find out, this entry seeks inspiration from Karl Marx's text "Estranged Labour" (1844) to transform today's destructive conditions of flexible and precarious work into something more productive.

Working with Marx, one quickly notices the following: Despite the fact that in the twenty-first century work has started to follow us home on our smartphones to stay annoyingly around on the weekend like an uninvited guest, the concept of work has not significantly changed since 1844. Back then, when Marx was writing about "Estranged Labour," he made an observation still relevant today. The following activities are still part of many actual weekend plans: "eating, drinking, procreating," "dwelling, and … dressing-up" (Marx 1844, 275). Back then as much as today, we feel ourselves more freely active in our "animal functions" (275) than at work. Back then as much as today, work is productive and leaves us estranged. Work appears "only as a *means to life*" instead of being "a conscious life activity" (276). Yet work has also changed. As Hannah Arendt (1958) has pointed out, in the Western world "labor" has been replaced with "work," and this means that instead of our bodies acting out physical labor, today only our hands are moving (always typing). Labor is taking place in our minds. We are gathering, penetrating, summarizing, and re-packing information. We are creating connections where there was nothing before. Communication has become hard work, and concentration is immaterial labor. It is exhausting. What did we expect? Most certainly, living kills us. But death has always been a good reason to dance, and Marx wrote texts that are excellent to swing around – when criticizing work, changing **perspective** is necessary.

These days we often find ourselves in work situations which keep us – because they are so fulfilling – precariously overworked or underemployed. Work fulfillment has been turned against us. Helpful when analyzing this ambiguous fulfillment is Marx's manuscript "Estranged Labour," a work unfinished to this day. The text ends right in the middle of an argument that looks into the social conditions exploiting the workers and leaving them estranged. Marx blames unjust property distribution as a reason for this estranged labor. In twenty-first century capitalism, this uneven distribution is still widespread and growing. So, to still ensure and even maximize our identification with work, the "New Spirit of Capitalism" (Boltanski and Chiapello 2005) tricked us with work autonomy and employee-initiative. The Marxian "estrangement" is gone, with the effect that today we work fulfilled while still being exploited. Thus, it "falls to us now to go on thinking," as Virginia Woolf (2006, 62) once put it.

What if back in Marx's time it was not just the unjust distribution that created the workers' estrangement? What if "estrangement" is overall elementary for work? Or, even further, could it allow for a different take, as some theorists ponder? Inspired by a discussion in *Homo Sacer*, in which Agamben explores the concept of an "empty form of relation" (1998, 38), Eva Geulen (2012) has addressed estrangement as a "non-relation," thereby refuting the understanding of estrangement as a deficient term, that hinders an identification with the world. Taking up her line of thought, "estrangement" could be turned into a productive concept. Consigned to itself and non-relational, estrangement becomes nothing but an empty form thereby opening a zone between work and life that can be inhabited in a different way. This zone proves helpful when working with both, today's concept of work, and its critique. An interesting observation Marx makes earlier in his text also points in this direction. In "Estranged Labour," he describes a particularly human capacity that could be read as a capacity for "estrangement." Humans, he points out, are the only species able of creating an object not merely according to their own standards but according to the standards of others:

> An animal forms only in accordance with the standard and the need of the species to which it belongs, whilst man knows how to produce in accordance with the standard of every species, and knows how to apply everywhere the inherent standard to the object. (1844, 277)

Applying the inherent standard of a species, a situation, or an object is working with an estranged perspective. With this, Marx discusses "estrangement" as a productive part of labor, work, and human life. Being more than just a negative effect of the conditions of labor, estrangement here is a capacity to show empathy and to relate to something other – an animal, another human, or a situation. Read in a non-self-relational way, it appears to become far more than a concept that denotes a failing to identify with oneself. Pushing this line of thought even further, Adorno's famous remark that "there is no right life in the wrong one" (1985, 3) comes to mind. Today we can say: the ability to do our work "estranged" – i.e., living a beautiful, "right" life after our work to pay the rent is done in the "wrong" life – does not seem to be an option anymore. In the era of work autonomy and employee-initiative, work has taken over our lives. There seems to be no outside to capitalism. Resistance, however, is inevitable, and the same applies to critique, which finds in its critical toolbox two new appliances: non-relation and estrangement. With these new tools, it enters the workplace again, this time by sneaking in through the backdoor.

As is well known, Marx's philosophical notion of labor gains its political force from the understanding that there are aspects at work simultaneous to when we are working. For Marx and in his time, the following two were the most important: labor as a process that produces a valuable product, and labor as a process that gives one a place as a "species-being" (1844, 275) – for when humans create objects, they also are "posited by objects" (1844b, 336). What applied in Marx's time still applies today. Capitalism has successfully turned us, the human workers, into our own enterprises. We compete with other professionals on the job market for which we become fit by getting an education. For this, we have forced job seekers to become attractive "offers" and we address students as the university's "clients" – a situation that needs to be abused, and it easily can be: we can fall back on a non-relation, we don't need to relate to this.

Worried by the current work-terror, Stefano Harney and Fred Moten bring up such a strategy in their discussion of the American University as a workplace, pointing out that "competition" and "negligence" (Harney and Moten 2013, 30–31) do not need to be at the heart of professionalization. Work can be different: Work, wherever and whatever it may be, paid or unpaid, has always already enabled different situations. Situations that can be further affirmed. History provides us with examples, with the imaginative praxis of the Paris Commune 1871, for example, when people were "… trying to carve out spaces and ways to live on the edges of various informal economies, testing the pos- sibilities and limitations of living differently now," as described by Kirsten Ross (2015, 12). Living differently and working differently today then means kitchens and freelance hubs can become refugee camps from which a new solidarity seizes the workplace; collective team breakthroughs can be kidnapped thereby giving birth to a community; the pain of working set-backs gets com- forted with a solidarity that knows about the vulnerability of all humans. If we become alert and claim these and other moments, we will find a multiplicity of **processes** open for us to become someone else, or something other than the (mere) capitalist worker. After all, work necessarily involves estrangement. And as such work has a transformative potential as it always also leads "somewhere else." So, dare to follow.

Today as much as in Marx's time, work offers both an irritating and enlivening potential that awaits to be uncovered and strengthened. If – as Marx once said – "nature appears [to the worker] as his work and his reality" (1844, 277), then to work – wherever and whatever this work is – can make a difference. For, as it always was, our realities are and will remain out of control. Today, in as much as in 1844, work is an effective tool within this world. And since this world is your work, may we ask what kind of world you are currently working on?

References

Adorno, Theodor W. 2005. *Reflections on a Damaged Life*. Translated by E. F. N. Jephcott. London: Verso.

Agamben, Giorgio. 1998. *Homo Sacer: Sovereign Power and Bare Life*. Translated by Daniel Heller-Roazen. Stanford: Stanford University Press.

Arendt, Hannah (1958) 2013. *The Human Condition*. Chicago: University of Chicago Press.

Boltanski, Luc, and Eve Chiapello. 2005. *The New Spirit of Capitalism*. Translated by Gregory Elliott. London: Verso.

Geulen, Eva. 2012. *Subjekte: ent(-grenzt, -fremdet, -fesselt, -worfen, -schieden): Probleme und Positionen gegenwärtiger Subjekttheorien*. Lecture at Frankfurter Positionen, Zentralbibliothek, 19.09.

Marx, Karl (1844) 1987. "Estranged Labour," translated by Martin Milligan, revised by Dirk J. Struik. In *Karl Marx and Frederick Engels, Collected Works*. Vol. 3, *Marx and Engels, 1843–1844*, 270–282. London: Lawrence & Wishart.

Marx, Karl (1844b) 1987. "Critique of the Hegelian Dialectic and Philosophy as a Whole," translated by Martin Milligan, revised by Dirk J. Struik. In *Karl Marx and Frederick Engels, Collected Works*. Vol. 3, *Marx and Engels, 1843–1844*, 326–346. London: Lawrence & Wishart.

Moten, Fred, and Stefano Harney. 2013. *The Undercommons: Fugitive Planning and Black Study*. New York: Minor Compositions.

Ross, Kirstin. 2015. *Communal Luxury: The Political Imaginery of the Paris Commune*. London: Verso.

Woolf, Virginia. 2006. *Three Guineas*. Boston: Houghton Mifflin Harcourt.

World

Kári Driscoll

In 1939, Gertrude Stein published a book for children entitled *The World Is Round*, about a girl named, inevitably, Rose, her dog Love, and her cousin Willie, who has a lion. Chapter eight, entitled "Rose Thinking," consists of a single sentence: "If the world is round would a lion fall off" (2013, 25). This enigmatic and seemingly whimsical thought raises many questions, but I will limit myself to the following: First, the absence of a question mark here, as elsewhere in the text, makes it ambiguous how the sentence is to be read, and this ambiguity also begins to trouble the constative nature of the book's title, enabling us to question whether the world is indeed round – whether this is not to conflate it with the planet earth, say. Relatedly, we might also question the use of the definite article; is there such a thing as "*the* world" (and if so, is it round?) and so forth. Second, this growing ambiguity is compounded by the abrupt shift from the indicative ("is") to the subjunctive ("would"). How are we to interpret this? And third, if there is such a thing as *the* world, and if it is in fact round, why would a lion in particular be in danger of falling off?

Let us begin with the lion. The title of the first chapter of *The World Is Round* invokes Stein's most famous phrase, "Rose is a rose is a rose is a rose" from her poem "Sacred Emily" (Stein 1922, 187). Like many poets of her generation, Stein felt that words had become worn out and lost their immediacy, so that now when you read or write a poem about roses, "you know in your bones that the rose is not *there*" (Stein 1947, vi). The formula, which Stein reused time and again, was an attempt to reassert the *thingness* of words, and hence to minimize the difference between word and world. Interestingly, while Rose is declared "a rose" and "would have been Rose" by any other name as well (Stein 2013, 1), her cousin Willie's identity is less secure, seemingly because of the lion. The lion, we read, has "a name as well as a mane and that name is Billie" (27). The similarity of the two names appears to invite confusion, and prompts Rose to wonder: "Is a lion not a lion" (21). If a lion is not a lion, would that mean that the lion is not *there*?

By a curious coincidence, shortly after Stein published her book, Ludwig Wittgenstein was also worrying about the proposition "Lion is a lion" and what it meant for the place of lions in the world. In the *Tractatus Logico-Philosophicus* – also a product of the crisis of language and representation, and published, incidentally, in 1922, the same year as Stein's "Sacred Emily" – he had defined the world as "everything that is the case," but in his notes from the year 1944, Wittgenstein was moved to revise his stance on the limits of the world, seemingly for the sake of the lion. According to the *Tractatus*, a statement could have sense only if it represented a state of affairs, i.e., something which is "the case." Thus any and all statements about fictional lions – the lion in the **fable** tradition, say – would be relegated to the realm of nonsense. The *Tractatus* demands that in order for something to be "the case," and hence "in the world," it must be possible to determine not only that it exists but that it does so in a definite number of instances as well. Consequently, the phrase "Lion is a lion" must be taken to be using the word "lion" in two different ways, namely as a name for an individual and as a species designation. But in fables we encounter *the* lion, not *a* lion, "nor yet a particular lion so-and-so," and thus "it actually is as if the species lion came to be seen as a lion" (Wittgenstein 1967, 182; Blumenberg 2010, 63–69). This leads to a contradiction, because it is impossible to determine whether "the Lion" refers to the species or an individual – or indeed whether it is the same lion each time. The criterion for existence in the world of the *Tractatus* was the avoidance of contradictions: it had to be possible to determine whether something is "the case" or not. Now, two decades later, Wittgenstein is no longer satisfied with such a definition. In reference to the formally nonsensical proposition "the class of lions is not a lion," he now asks, simply: "How do you know?" (1967, 182). Even though it "seems like nonsense," Wittgenstein argues that it can be read as a "proper sentence, if only it is taken right" (182), namely as a language-game involving a different kind of certainty than mathematical certainty (see Wittgenstein 1958, 224). For Wittgenstein, the ultimate aim of these ruminations is thus a reevaluation of the problem of certainty, and the lion's rescue is simply a felicitous by-product – but I would like to take this as an argument for literature as a means of extending "the world" beyond whatever happens or appears to be "the case."

How might we relate this to the questions of critique – especially of terrestrial critique, of the question of the planet, the world, the cosmos, and our place in it? The word "world" and its cognates (*Welt, wereld, veröld*) consists of the Germanic roots "wer" ("man"; as in "werewolf" and "virile") and "ald," and means, literally, "age of man." Thus, in a sense, the concept of the Anthropocene is already implicit in "world" – both in terms of its anthropocentrism and, more interestingly, the fact that it denotes a **temporality** rather than a locality. As critics of the term have pointed out, the term "Anthropocene" is nonsensical, etymologically speaking. Moreover, since "Holocene" means "wholly recent," "the decision to bring this epoch to an end would mark the present as a peculiar time, *after the recent*, a time out of time in more than one sense" (Luciano 2015). Time is not only out of joint; it is running out. The "world" would thus seem to name a series of disjunctures between incompatible conceptions of what is "the case": despite its anthropocentric denomination, this new "age of man" also marks a heightened awareness of our **entanglement** and codependence, of the fact that we share a terrestrial space with other creatures and other forms of life, each of which have their own *Umwelten* and hence their own worlds. "World" is thus both singular and plural: there is only one, and there is an infinite variety, each tied to a different mode of being-in-the-world, which is also simultaneously a form of being-with. Is it not the task of critique to interrogate the interstices of these two senses of "world" – as something that is simply *there* but simultaneously cannot simply be taken for granted, and as something, especially if we want to conceive of it as something we have *in common* with other forms of life on this planet, that we must actively work to produce?

Perhaps this might help us understand the abrupt shift from indicative to subjunctive in Rose's question. In his 1929–30 lectures on *The Fundamental Concepts of Metaphysics*, Martin Heidegger notoriously posited that "the animal is poor in world," in contrast to man, who is "world-forming" (1995, 177). Thus, while man "has world" in the full sense, the animal has world only in a circumscribed capacity – and hence its mode of being-in-the-world is not a being-*there* (*Da-sein*). The difference, for Heidegger, lies in the notion that the animal does not have a relation to the world *as such* – the lion, say, sunning himself on the savannah, does not perceive the warmth of the sun *as such*. To which Wittgenstein might quite reasonably respond: "How do you know?" And, conversely, as Jacques Derrida puts it, how do you know that "man, the human itself, has the 'as such'" (2008, 160)? This apophantic "as"-structure grounds Heidegger's approach to the problem of world. But is there such a thing as "the world *as such*"? In his final seminar, Derrida opposed this indicative "as" with a subjunctive "as if": The unity and community of the world is "nowhere and never given in nature" (Derrida 2011, 9). In fact, "[t]here is no world, there are only islands" (9). And yet, we carry on "*as if* we were inhabiting the same world" (268), and this *as if* is an act of poetic creation. Thus, as Michael Naas summarises, it is "*as if* there were a performative *as if* lodged within all our constative assertions and reassuring statements about the world, a *comme si* at the heart of every claim that the world is *comme ça*" (Naas 2015, 58). In other words, the subjunctive precedes the indicative – the lion's hypothetical fall comes before whatever is "the case" [*der Fall*] – and every "world" is contingent upon the possibility of other worlds, even ones in which a lion would not fall off.

References

Blumenberg, Hans. 2010. *Löwen*. Berlin: Suhrkamp Verlag.

Derrida, Jacques. 2008. *The Animal That Therefore I Am*. Edited by Marie-Louise Mallet. Translated by David Wills. New York: Fordham University Press.

Derrida, Jacques. 2011. *The Beast & the Sovereign*. Vol. II. Edited by Michel Lisse, Marie-Louise Mallet, and Ginette Michaud. Translated by Geoffrey Bennington. Chicago and London: The University of Chicago Press.

Heidegger, Martin. 1995. *The Fundamental Concepts of Metaphysics: World, Finitude, Solitude*. Translated by William McNeill and Nicholas Walker. Bloomington: Indiana University Press.

Luciano, Dana. 2015. "The Inhuman Anthropocene." *Avidly*. Accessed March 22, 2016. http://avidly.lareviewofbooks.org/2015/03/22/the-inhuman-anthropocene/.

Naas, Michael. 2015. *The End of the World and Other Teachable Moments: Jacques Derrida's Final Seminar*. New York: Fordham University Press.

Stein, Gertrude. 1922. "Sacred Emily." In *Geography and Plays*, 178–188. Boston: The Four Seas Press.

Stein, Gertrude. 1947. *Four in America*. Introduction by Thornton Wilder. New Haven: Yale University Press.

Stein, Gertrude. 2013. *The World Is Round*. Illustrated by Clement Hurd. New York: Harper Design.

Wittgenstein, Ludwig. 1922. *Tractatus Logico-Philosophicus*. Translated by C. K. Ogden. Introduction by Bertrand Russell. London: Keegan Paul.

Wittgenstein, Ludwig. 1958. *Philosophical Investigations*. Edited by R. Rhees and G. E. M. Anscombe. Translated by G. E. M. Anscombe. 2nd ed. Oxford: Blackwell.

Wittgenstein, Ludwig. 1967. *Remarks on the Foundations of Mathematics*. Edited by G. H. von Wright, R. Rhees, and G. E. M. Anscombe. Translated by G. E. M. Anscombe. Cambridge, MA: MIT Press.

Diagrams: Visualizing Connections

Although the critical terms in this book are presented in alphabetical order, this does not imply that they are bound to a lexical structure. Instead, with the following diagrams we want to invite the reader to consider the terms of this vocabulary as a dynamic constellation, as terms in relation to each other. Clustering the terms can sharpen our usage of them as well as reinforce their analytic powers. In what follows, we suggest four constellation-diagrams that for us visualize some of those possible connections: How, for example, criticality can be read as a striving for **change**; or how critical practice does not merely witness from a distance but modifies where it intervenes, something clustered here under the caption **writing**. Equally, many terms foreground critical analysis as an entangled practice so that **relating** becomes a foundational aspect of this critical map. And last but not least, **diffraction** is an onto-epistemological starting point for several terms. It transforms the practice of critique itself from a dissective endeavour into creating new patterns.

Each of the suggested diagrams offers a *perspectival* clustering. This is intentional, as we neither aim to present a complete lexicon (that is, other terms could be added to each constellation, from within and without the vocabulary), nor an exclusive map (i.e. many other constellations and perspectives can be distilled from the presented terms). Instead, the suggested constellations hope to provide vistas of possible and provisional assemblages of terms, serving the reader as 'think-maps' to draw out significant dimensions of critique, to navigate the vocabulary when used and to work with its entries in further constellations.

The blank pages at the end of this section leave space for each reader's individual sketches and diagrams. In this way, we hope for the vocabulary to produce further patterns and creative openings, and to trigger the reassessment and sharpening of our critical vocabularies for the issues and challenges of our times. So, revisit, resist and revamp!

Change

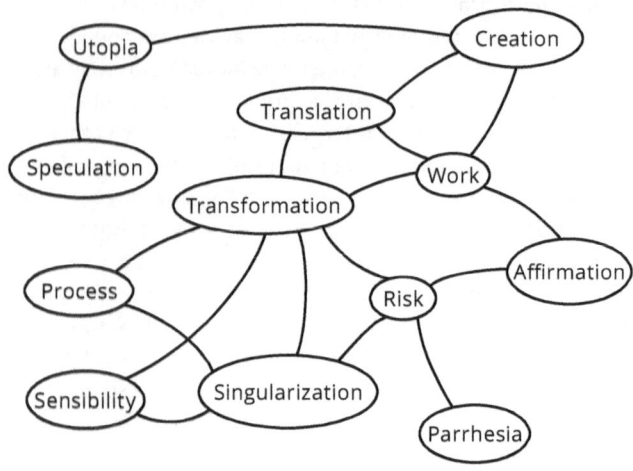

Diffraction

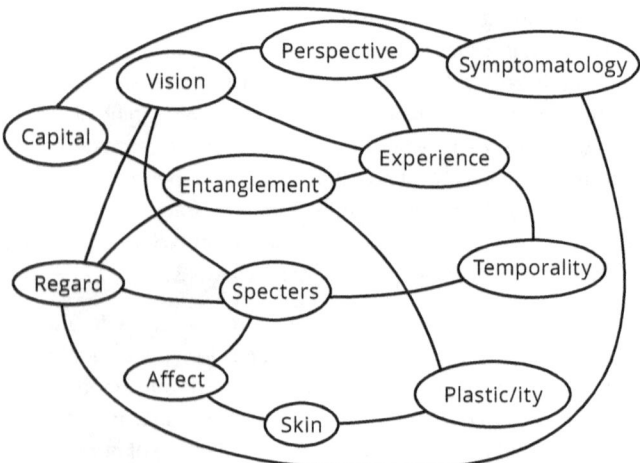

Relating

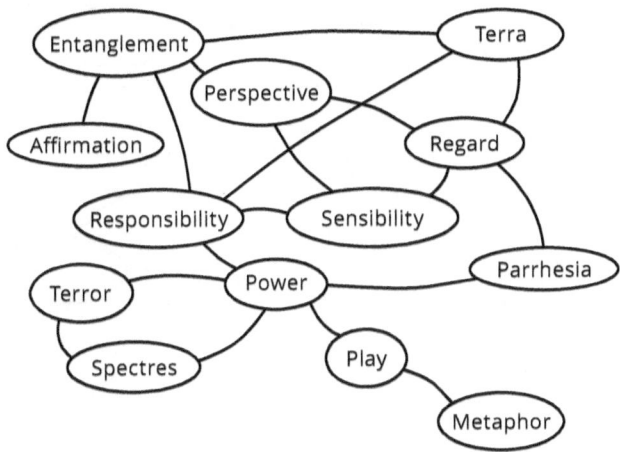

Writing

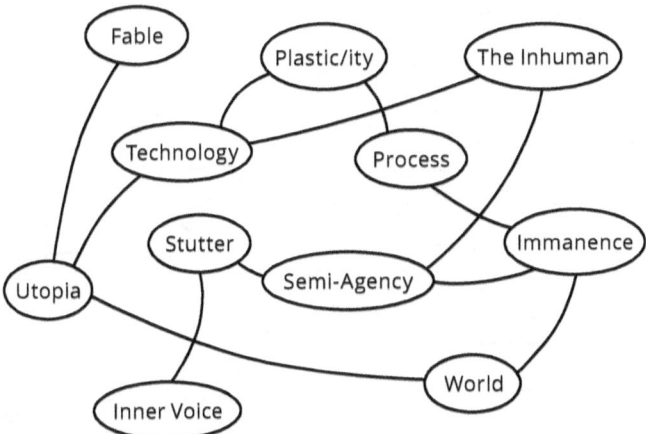

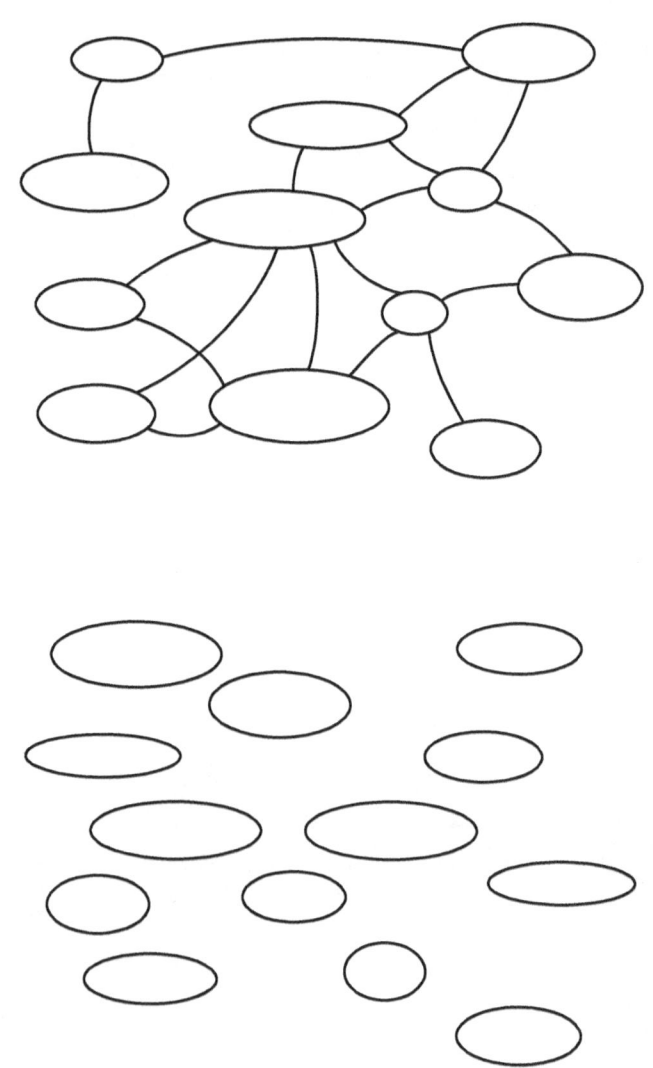

About Terra Critica

Terra Critica is an interdisciplinary research network for the critical humanities, founded as a forum to discuss the task of critical theory and critique today, for the twenty-first century and a globally entangled world. The international network meets regularly for intensive workshops and other activities to exchange ideas across disciplines; a group of core members as well as a wider circle of local participants contribute to these activities. Initiated by Birgit Mara Kaiser and Kathrin Thiele, *Terra Critica* started its work in 2012, with a workshop entitled "Terra Critica: Re-visioning the Critical Task of the Humanities in a Globalized World" held at Utrecht University. Informed by their background in comparative literature, feminist philosophy, and critical theory, both initiators felt that a differentiated response to the neoliberal pressure put on the humanities was urgent. Kaiser and Thiele coordinate the network since its inception in 2012.

The discussion of the initial workshop continued a year later in 2013 with another meeting at Utrecht University, for which two texts served as joint basis: Virginia Woolf's *Three Guineas* (1938) and Félix Guattari's *The Three Ecologies* (1989). These texts gave the second workshop its title: "From Three Critiques to Three Guineas and Three Ecologies: Grappling with critique beyond negativity and judgment." Its focus lay on the challenges that immanence – speaking of an entangled and co-emerging universe as multiplicity or manifold – poses to critique, and on what critique beyond its classical meaning – negation and judgment – might imply. Instead of paper presentations, both workshops invited short position papers from each of the participants, which were shared with everyone beforehand for preparation. The discussions were clustered around focal points distilled from the position papers (now online http://terracritica.net/publications/); a set-up that was chosen in order to experiment with more conversational modes of engagement and exchange. This practice did succeed in shifting the traditional academic gesture – to stake one's own claims – to a more affirmative encounter with the questions posed, also allowing the network to start thinking through contemporary problems *with* each other.

The third meeting took place within the framework of the 2014 annual conference of the American Comparative Literature Association (ACLA), which was held at New York University in March 2014 and was devoted to "Capitals." The *Terra Critica* ACLA seminar "Capital(s) of Critique" invited papers to reengage with *Three Guineas* and/or *The Three Ecologies* methodologically (how do they practice critique?), theoretically (how are they pushing critique beyond judgment?), and thematically (how do they engage with capitalism?). An edited volume collecting all papers presented at this meeting is in preparation, to be published in the *New Critical Humanities* book series with Rowman & Littlefield International.

The present book, on the other hand, is the outcome of the May 2015 meeting "Terra Critica: Symptoms of our Planetary Condition" at Leuphana University Lüneburg (Germany). At the center of the two-day workshop were the short texts that make up this vocabulary. Instead of delivering a neutral overview over the most important theoretical catchwords, each participant was asked to select a term they viewed as key to contemporary practices of critique and reflect on this term against the background of their own theoretical perspectives and (inter)disciplinary practices. The meeting took place at the *Hybrid Publishing Lab* of Leuphana University and drew also on the lab's expertise with experimental and collaborative peer reviewing. After the successful workshop experience, more authors were invited still to propose terms; all of them had previously participated in the 2012–2014 *Terra Critica* events. The introduction to this book has been authored collectively.

"Transactions" was the focus of the most recent meeting to date, in December 2015, at the conference "Critical Transactions: Engaging the Humanities East & West" organized by the School

of Humanities at Hong Kong University and *Terra Critica*. Held in
Hong Kong, this meeting examined the kinds of transactions and
knowledge transfers that are currently under way between "East
& West" and how they might contribute to a reevaluation of the
conventional matrix that sees "North & South" or "East & West"
as markers of dis/privilege or non/hegemony. Which transactions
occur between (and beyond) the traditional humanities disciplines, but also between spaces, regions, and social contexts,
between the academy and the societies of which it is a part?
Terra Critica will further explore the relation between ethics and
critique implied in such questions in the next intensive workshop
at Penn State University in May 2017.

As a local initiative in Utrecht, *Terra Critica* has also established a
series of meetings entitled "ReadingRoom" in collaboration with
Casco – Office for Art, Design and Theory, which are open to all.
ReadingRoom is a space for careful and generous conversations
in the humanities, arts, and beyond. A first series (December
2014 – June 2015) discussed "speculation & fabulation – critique in
the SF mode," a second series (September 2015 – February 2016)
looked into "relationality – envisioning new wor(l)dings" with a
focus on Caribbean poetics and philosophy. A third series on "Politics and Poetics in the Affirmative" is running from September
2016 – May 2017.

Terra Critica has been kindly supported by several academic
institutions, including Utrecht University, New York University,
Leuphana University Lüneburg, University of Westminster,
Hong Kong University and Penn State University. In addition,
the network's projects have been made possible by the
generous support of the Institute for Cultural Inquiry (ICON),
Utrecht University; the former Research Focus Area Cultures &
Identities, Utrecht University; The Netherlands Research School
for Gender Studies (NOG); The Netherlands Research School
for Literary Studies (OSL); the Netherlands Institute for Cultural Analysis (NICA); the Amsterdam Center for Globalization
Studies (ACGS); Radboud University Nijmegen; Vrije Universiteit

266 Amsterdam; the Kattendijke Drucker Stichting; the NWO-Project "Back to the Book"; as well as by the Strategic Research Theme in China-West Studies at Hong Kong University and the Louis Cha Fund.

Authors

Kiene Brillenburg Wurth is Professor of Literature and Comparative Media at Utrecht University. Kiene works on literature and (new) media, music, aesthetic theory. She is author of *Musically Sublime* (2007) and *Literature and the Future of Writing* (forthcoming), editor of *Between and Screen* (2009), *Book Presence* (forthcoming) and *Literature and the Material Turn*, a special issue of *Comparative Literature* (forthcoming).

Rosemarie Buikema is Professor of Art, Culture and Diversity at Utrecht University. She chairs the UU Graduate Gender-programme and is scientific director of the Netherlands Research School of Genderstudies (NOG). In that capacity she also co-ordinates the UU share in the Erasmus Mundus Master in Genderstudies GEMMA, the Horizon 2020 ITN Cultures of Equality (GRACE) and the annual international Summerschool in Gender-studies (NOISE). She has widely published in the field of feminist and postcolonial theory. Her latest publications are *Doing Gender in Media Art and Culture* (2017, ed. with L. Plate and K. Thiele) and *Theories and Methodologies in Feminist Research* (2011, ed. with G. Griffin and N. Lykke). Her forthcoming monograph *Revolutions in Cultural Critique* (2017) concerns the role of the arts in processes of political transitions.

Mercedes Bunz is Senior Lecturer at the University of Westminster, London where she teaches media studies and journalism. Her work combines technology and digital media, philosophy, and publishing. Her most recent book is *The Silent Revolution: How Digitalization Transforms Knowledge, Work, Journalism and Politics without Making Too Much Noise* (2014). She is co-founder of the open access publishing house meson press. From 2009–2010 she was the technology reporter of *The Guardian*.

Kári Driscoll is a Lecturer in Comparative Literature at Utrecht University. He holds a PhD in German Language and Literature from Columbia University. His research focuses on the poetics of animality (zoopoetics). He is author of *Book Presence in a Digital Age* (2017; ed. with K. Brillenburg-Wurth and J. Pressman), and of *Memory after Humanism*, a special issue of *Parallax* (2017, ed. with S. C. Knittel).

Yvonne Förster is Professor for Philosophy of Culture and Art at Leuphana University Lüneburg (Germany). Her research and publications focus on theories of embodiment, phenomenology, philosophical foundations of posthumanism, aesthetics and fashion theory. She published *Experience and Ontology of Time. Perspectives of Modern Philosophy of Time* (2012) and is currently working on the impact of neuroscience and technology as narratives of the post-postmodern era.

Annemie Halsema is Assistant Professor at the Department of Philosophy of Vrije Universiteit Amsterdam. Her research interests are in the field of phenomenology, hermeneutics and feminist philosophy. She published two books on Luce Irigaray (*Dialectiek van de seksuele differentie* [1998]; *Luce Irigaray and Horizontal Transcendence* [2010]); a volume on Paul Ricoeur (*Feminist Explorations of Paul Ricoeur's Philosophy* [2016, ed. with F. Henriques], and a volume in Dutch on Judith Butler (*Genderturbulentie* [2000]).

Birgit Mara Kaiser is Associate Professor of Comparative Literature and Transcultural Aesthetics at Utrecht University. Her research interests are aesthetics and affect, Deleuzian and (new) materialist literary criticism, postcolonial and transnational literature. Recent publications include *Figures of Simplicity. Sensation and Thinking in Kleist and Melville* (2011), *Postcolonial Literatures and Deleuze* (2012, ed. with L. Burns), "Diffracted Worlds – Diffractive Readings: Onto-Epistemologies and the Critical Humanities" *Parallax* (2014, ed. with K. Thiele), *Singularity and Transnational Poetics* (2015, ed.). She currently works on a book project on Cixous, Guattari and the production of subjectivity. With K. Thiele, she is founder and coordinator of *Terra Critica*.

Leonard Lawlor is Edwin Erle Sparks Professor of Philosophy at Penn State University, where he continues to teach and serve as Director of Graduate Studies in Philosophy. He is the author of seven books, among which are: *This is not Sufficient: An Essay on Animality in Derrida* (2007), and *Derrida and Husserl: The Basic Problem of Phenomenology* (2002). His most recent book is called *From Violence to Speaking out* (2016), published with Edinburgh University Press.

Jacques Lezra is Professor of Spanish and Comparative Literature at New York University, and Professor of Hispanic Studies at the University of California – Riverside. His work straddles the fields of political philosophy and early modern literary studies. Lezra's most recent books are *Contra los fueros de la muerte: El suceso cervantino* (2016), *Lucretius and Modernity* (2016), and *Wild Materialism: The Ethic of Terror and the Modern Republic* (2010). He is the co-translator into Spanish of Paul de Man's *Blindness and Insight,* and the co-editor of *Dictionary of Untranslatables* (2014) and of Sebastián de Covarrubias's ca. 1613 *Suplemento al 'Tesoro de la lengua ...'* (2001).

Sam McAuliffe is a Lecturer in the Department of Visual Cultures at Goldsmiths, University of London. His teaching and research is chiefly devoted to modern European philosophy, in particular its intersection with modern and contemporary art and aesthetics. He has published articles on Adorno and Deleuze, and is currently working on his first monograph, a reading of Blanchot's thesis: "speaking is not seeing."

Timothy O'Leary is Professor of Philosophy and Head of the School of Humanities at the University of Hong Kong. He has published extensively on the work of Michel Foucault, in particular in relation to ethics and literature. He has also edited several volumes and journal special issues on topics including Foucault, classical Chinese ethics, happiness, and Hong Kong's Umbrella Movement.

270 **Bettina Papenburg** is Assistant Professor at the Institute of Media and Cultural Studies at Heinrich-Heine-University Düsseldorf, Germany. She teaches, researches and publishes on topics at the intersections of affect theory, theories of the body, feminist theory, science and technology studies, visual culture, and the grotesque. She was Marie Curie Postdoctoral Research Fellow (2009–2011) and Assistant Professor of Gender Studies (2011–2013) at the Department of Media and Culture Studies at Utrecht University, the Netherlands.

Esther Peeren is Associate Professor of Literary and Cultural Analysis at the University of Amsterdam, Vice-Director of the Amsterdam School for Cultural Analysis (ASCA) and Vice-Director of the Amsterdam Center for Globalization Studies (ACGS). She is the author of *The Spectral Metaphor: Living Ghosts and the Agency of Invisibility* (2014) and *Intersubjectivities and Popular Culture: Bakhtin and Beyond* (2008), as well as the co-editor of *Popular Ghosts: The Haunted Spaces of Everyday Culture* (2010), *The Spectralities Reader* (2013) and *Peripheral Visions in the Globalizing Present* (2016).

Asja Szafraniec teaches at Amsterdam University College. She is the author of *Beckett, Derrida and the Event of Literature* (2007) and *Words. Religious Language Matters* (2016, ed. with E. van den Hemel). Her research focuses on the relation between various strands of contemporary philosophy and a range of cultural phenomena.

Melanie Sehgal is holding a PhD in philosophy and is currently Professor of Literature, Science and Media Studies at European University Viadrina, Frankfurt (Oder). She is the author of *Eine situierte Metaphysik. Empirismus und Spekulation bei William James und Alfred North Whitehead* (2016). Together with artist Alex Martinis Roe she is leading the transdisciplinary and experimental working group *FORMATIONS*, exploring ways of knowing beyond modern habits of thought.

Kathrin Thiele is Associate Professor in Gender Studies and Critical Theory at Utrecht University. Her research expertise lies in feminist and continental philosophies, theories of difference(s), and posthuman(ist) studies. Most recently she edited "Diffracted Worlds – Diffractive Readings: Onto-Epistemologies and the Critical Humanities" *Parallax* (2014, ed. with B. M. Kaiser), *Doing Gender in Medien-, Kunst- und Kulturwissenschaften: Eine Einführung* (2016, ed. with R. Buikema) and *Doing Gender in Media, Art and Culture: A Comprehensive Guide to Gender Studies* (2017, ed. with R. Buikema and L. Plate). With B. M. Kaiser, she is founder and coordinator of *Terra Critica*.

Sybrandt van Keulen is philosopher, editor and independent researcher. He lectured at several Dutch institutes including the University of Amsterdam, the Jan van Eyck Academy (Maastricht), Frank Mohr Institute (Groningen), PhdArts (The Hague). His most recent publication is *How Art and Philosophy work* (Hoe kunst en filosofie werken [2014]). His PhD thesis appeared in 2005 entitled *Kosmopolitieken* (*Cosmopolitics*, according to Kant, Levi-Strauss and Derrida).

Veronica Vasterling is Associate Professor Gender & Philosophy at Radboud University, Nijmegen, the Netherlands. She has published widely on the work of Judith Butler and Hannah Arendt. She co-edited books on female philosophers from Antiquity to the present time (*Vrouwelijke filosofen: Een historisch overzicht* [2014]), on interdisciplinarity (*Practising Interdisciplinarity in Gender Studies* [2006]), and on feminist philosophy (*Feministische Phänomenologie und Hermeneutik* [2005]).

Jennifer A. Wagner-Lawlor is Associate Professor in Women's, Gender, and Sexuality Studies and English at The Pennsylvania State University. Her most recent book is *Postmodern Utopias and Feminist Fictions* (2013), and her many essays range in topic from utopian literature and feminist aesthetics to environmental art and literature, focusing on the ecological impacts of plastic waste. Wagner-Lawlor currently serves as president of the international Society for Utopian Studies.